RTI in Practice

A Practical Guide to Implementing Effective
Evidence-Based Interventions in Your School

James L. McDougal
Suzanne Bamonto Graney
James A. Wright
Scott P. Ardoin

WILEY

John Wiley & Sons, Inc.

Library of Congress Cataloging-in-Publication Data:

RTI in practice: a practical guide to implementing effective evidence-based interventions in your school / James L. McDougal . . . [et al.].
    p. cm.
  Includes bibliographical references and index.
  ISBN 978-0-470-17073-1 (paper/cd-rom)
  1. Remedial teaching.   2. Slow learning children—Education. I. McDougal, James L.
  LB1029.R4R75 2010
  371.9′043—dc22

                                                     2009031718

Printed in the United States of America

10 9 8 7 6 5 4 3 2 1

Contents

Preface v

PART I INTRODUCTION 1

1 History of Learning Disabilities and Emergence
of a New Model 3

PART II TIER I: EFFECTIVE GENERAL EDUCATION
AND UNIVERSAL SCREENING/PROGRESS
MONITORING 23

2 Effective Academic Programs for All Students 25

3 School-Wide Data Collection for Screening
and Outcome Decisions 53

4 Using Data to Make Decisions in
General Education 75

PART III TIER 2: TARGETED INTERVENTIONS
AND PROBLEM SOLVING FOR STUDENTS
AT RISK FOR FAILURE 95

5 Developing Interventions 97

6 Setting Goals, Monitoring Progress,
and Graphing Intervention Outcomes 127

7 Making Decisions After Intervening 153

PART IV TIER 3: INTENSIVE INTERVENTIONS/
INDIVIDUAL EDUCATION PLAN
CONSIDERATION AND DEVELOPMENT 179

8 Moving to Tier 3: Eligibility Determination 181

9   IEP Goal Development   197

10 Considering Reintegration and Special
    Education Exit Decisions within an RTI
    Service Delivery Model   221
    Kelly A. Powell-Smith

PART V ORGANIZATIONAL CONSIDERATIONS
        AND CONCLUSIONS   253

11 RTI and Systems Change   255

12 Conclusions   277

    References   287

    Author Index   307

    Subject Index   311

    About the CD-ROM   321

Preface

My experience in the schools began in 1990. I received my first fulltime position as a school psychologist in a diverse urban elementary school. The majority of the students were on free/reduced lunch and many came to school lacking basic developmental skills like language concepts and exposure to written text. At that time we had many models of reading instruction—some that emphasized phonics and others that focused on reading in story books. The assessments used were inconsistent, varied by the classroom, and were of varying technical quality. While many students learned to read, many also struggled and languished in school, receiving one literacy program or another but not one tailored to their specific needs. My role as the school psychologist was that of gatekeeper to special education. That was incredibly troubling to me as I was responding to students' needs too late to make a real difference and my assessments were usually diagnostic and not intervention oriented.

Based on the work of some innovative educators from our district (including Jim Wright) and a neighboring university, I worked closely with a first-grade teacher to design a reading intervention program for our students. With her master's degree in reading and my increasing skills in Curriculum Based Measurement (CBM), we trained para-professionals (i.e., teacher assistants) to implement supplemental instruction and progress monitoring assessments with struggling primary grade students. Meeting weekly with these para-professionals, we significantly improved the reading of most of our intervention students and substantially reduced the rates of initial evaluations for special education. I quickly became convinced that this was the way to do business in the schools. At the same time, I became increasingly frustrated.

I had to beg and borrow to get $500 for a set of leveled reading books for our intervention project. Meanwhile, the system had no problems handing down numerous student retentions—estimated at $8,500 per student—an expensive "intervention" without empirical support and one linked to increased dropout rates and other deleterious outcomes.

This frustration, coupled with support from my family and my administrative supervisors (Dr. Denise Johnson and "Special" Ed Erwin), led to my return to school for doctoral training. There, under the tutelage of Drs. Joel Meyer and Bonnie Nastasi, I received solid training in consultation, prevention, and educational intervention. I became increasingly convinced that responding to one academic (usually literacy) crisis after another was not the way to educate children. I wanted to participate in an educational model that ensured that all students were developing basic academic and behavioral skills (especially those related to literacy), one that was systematic and schoolwide, and one that responded to a student's need early in their school careers.

Just prior to working on this preface I had the good fortune to attend a presentation from John Corcoran sponsored by the School of Education at SUNY Oswego. John is the author of *The Teacher Who Couldn't Read*, which chronicles his life as an illiterate child, adolescent, and adult who eventually cracked the code to literacy at the age of 48. I was taken with the emotion in John's presentation, which for the audience was quite moving. John spoke of his first years in school, entering at the age of six filled with an eagerness to please, with enthusiasm, and innocence. John labeled this time and this portion of his personality as "Johnny the innocent." He described how he persisted in his eagerness to learn even after being put in the "dumb row" in class. By third grade, John knew he was in trouble and that he couldn't read. He prayed for help so that he would wake up being able to read like the other children in his class. Falling further behind and still unable to read or to complete the required schoolwork in middle school, John became the "Native Alien," the outsider who peered in at the literate world without access to it. At school he was angry, frustrated, and a behavior problem who would rather fight, spit, and turn desks over than allow the literate society to harm and embarrass him further, requiring tasks from him for which he did not have the tools. In high school, John described "going underground"—hiding his illiteracy and creatively using his athletic and social skills and his intelligence to survive. He chronicled his elaborate schemes for getting test answers, having friends sneak him exam booklets for essays, and passing courses without literacy. These strategies were successful enough for him to obtain a college degree and secure a job as a teacher, even though he could not read or write a simple sentence.

As John described his shame as a member of the illiterate society, I felt the powerful and raw emotion of my own shame. This shame was rooted in my participation in the bureaucratic educational machine that produced plenty of John Corcorans, many of whom lacked the social skills, creativity, and athletic ability to negotiate the tremendous barrier of illiteracy. I participated in meeting after meeting that responded to academic causalities much too late, with too little, and without seriously focusing on the obvious goal of teaching the student to read. I wasted hours doing irrelevant assessments (some even involving puzzles and blocks) so that I could tell teachers what they already knew—that Johnny couldn't read. We would give students time to see if they would eventually get it and argue over which largely ineffective intervention to apply—retention or social promotion. My guts would churn at having to play by the rules, which meant that you didn't criticize literacy instruction even if it lacked a direct and explicit focus on important early skills such as phonemic awareness and phonics. It meant I had to try to manufacture a discrepancy between an IQ score and an achievement score to get a student the needed reading services. I am guilty of administering additional tests to a student because I did not obtain the desired severe discrepancy required by my district in order to label a student as learning disabled. I would explain my additional testing in professional meetings as my search for the student's true potential and level of functioning, all the while fully knowing that additional scores add error to the discrepancy formula and make it more likely that I could eventually call the student "disabled." I had to play by rules that required me to sit on my hands and observe struggling students until the standardized tests I used could measure the extent of their academic failure. My only option for many students was special education; it was given only to "eligible" students and it was designed largely to reduce expectations for these students and "modify" or slow down the curriculum for them.

In special education, students were often served too late (after third grade) and the monitoring of their academic progress was even worse than in regular education. I once read an Individualized Educational Plan (IEP), which is required for all special education students. The goal for a second-grade student with a severe learning disability in reading read as follows: "Michael will decode unknown sight words with 80% accuracy by June 15th." The progress monitoring was done quarterly and included a rating scale from NP (no progress) to P (progress). So although Michael was challenged by a significant barrier to literacy, he received no direct or focused instruction for it, nor did his goal contain any specific elements that were directly measured. Further, his IEP for the year indicated that he had made SP—some progress. My assessments of Michael indicated that while he was in third grade, he lacked the phonemic awareness and decoding skills of an average first-grade student. After multiple meetings with the school and a tremendous effort on the part of his mother, Michael was given targeted literacy instruction and his IEP goals were changed to reflect specific growth levels in phonemic awareness and decoding tasks. Now in middle school, Michael is still behind his peers, yet he has broken the code of literacy. Without a tremendous amount of advocacy for Michael over the course of several years, he would have continued to be a non-reader, another Johnny Corcoran.

Today there is little debate over what constitutes explicit and systematic early literacy instruction that is required to assist nearly all children to learn to read. In essence, the reading wars are over. We also have well researched progress monitoring techniques, especially in literacy, which can be used to screen all children for skill deficits and to monitor their progress toward grade-appropriate functioning. These tools are available for use by educators and in many instances they are available online and free of charge. Yet the troubling fact remains that these tools have yet to become the standard in the industry. Many districts and even some states have been slow to adopt RTI procedures and continue to use the failed practices of the past. We have the tools to eradicate almost all illiteracy in our nation and we are not consistently using them. This is tremendously troubling to me and a major impetus for coordinating the writing of this book.

With that as my segue, I would like to introduce my coauthors and then give a brief summary of the book. I have known Jim Wright since I went to pursue a master's degree in School Psychology. We both went through the same program, we were both employed in the same district for a dozen or so years, and we both sought to change the status quo. Jim has doctoral-level training in school psychology, and training and certification in both school psychology and school administration. For many years, Jim has devoted much of his time to what I believe is the finest educational web-based resource available today, Interventioncentral.org. Jim and I have worked together for many years and it has always been to my benefit when our paths have crossed. Suzanne Graney and I first met when I was applying for a position at a neighboring college. While I did not obtain that particular position, I did meet a wonderful colleague with extraordinary training in RTI and progress monitoring. She has university training as well as experience and skill working with educators in the real world of the public schools. Scott Ardoin and I first met when he was a doctoral student and I was his supervisor for a field experience in consultation. As is often the case, the supervisor learned as much as the student. Scott has been a friend ever since; he makes a wonderful gumbo, and has done some pivotal research advancing our understanding of student progress monitoring. Lastly, Kelly Powell Smith was asked to join us to discuss the reintegration of students from special education into the typical classroom. We are thankful to Kelly for taking the time work with us.

In the preparation of the book we wanted to develop one comprehensive guide to implementing RTI in the school setting. We wanted to strike a balance of presenting background, conceptual information, and relevant research with hands-on forms for implementation, recommendations for educators, and case examples. We have organized the book into five sections. The first section provides an introduction that includes some history of both learning disabilities as well as emerging models of RTI. The next three sections cover assessment, instructional considerations, and decision making across the three tiers of RTI. The last section addresses the numerous organizational considerations in implementing a far-reaching schoolwide model for improving instruction and accommodating students' learning concerns. In addition to the text, we have also created a companion CD that contains forms and resources for educators implementing RTI procedures.

While we acknowledge the shortcomings and unknowns in implementing comprehensive models of RTI, we are also convinced that these comprehensive and innovative strategies constitute a better way of conducting the business of education. Universal student screenings, evaluation of core instruction, early and responsive intervention for struggling students, and informed instructional decisions based on concrete data are the educational practices that will ensure that the next Johnny Corcoran will break the code to literacy in the primary grades and not middle adulthood. Having participated in the traditional educational model that responded to academic failure with retention, social promotion, and referral to special education, we are now at a time where the science and educational best practices dictate that we prevent academic failure and respond to delay with timely interventions that are sufficiently intense to be effective. These practices constitute a major evolution and will take considerable time and effort to be fully embraced by our educational system, but we feel that this will be time and effort well spent. We are hopeful that this text can be a support for this educational evolution and that it can be useful for guiding and training the educators of the present as well as those to be recruited for the future.

Jim McDougal
State University of New York
Oswego, NY
October, 2009

INTRODUCTION

I

History of Learning Disabilities and Emergence of a New Model

1

LEARNING DISABILITIES: DEFINITION AND BACKGROUND

The concept of learning disabilities dates back to the early 1960s. In 1968 the label of "specific learning disability" was added as a federally designated category of handicapping conditions (Hallahan, Kauffman, & Lloyd, 1999). One of the first to address the definition of learning disabilities was Samuel Kirk. In 1962 Kirk wrote:

> A learning disability refers to a retardation, disorder, or delayed development in one or more of the processes of speech, language, reading, writing arithmetic, or other school subject resulting from a psychological handicap caused by a possible cerebral dysfunction and/or emotional or behavioral disturbances. It is not the result of mental retardation, sensory deprivation, or cultural and instructional factors (Kirk, 1962, p. 263).

In Kirk's description can be seen many components of the modern definition including a conceptualization that LD (1) is a deficit in processing (2) that results in reduced academic performance in one or more areas, (3) is possibly related to a cerebral (pertaining to the central nervous system) dysfunction, and (4) is not the result of other handicapping conditions. Later in 1965, Barbara Bateman proposed a modified definition of learning disabilities that removed emotional factors as causal in LD and more significantly suggested that it could be identified by an "educationally significant discrepancy" between estimates of intellectual potential and actual-performance level (for discussion, see Hallahan, Kauffman, &

Lloyd, 1999; Smith, 1998). This discrepancy notion was further supported by the epidemiological work of Rutter and Yule in the early to mid-1970s. By studying the IQ predicted reading achievement of children ages 9 to 13 on the Isle of Wright they concluded that there was an abnormal distribution of reading performance scores suggesting that (1) reading underachievement occurred at a higher than expected rate and (2) that different patterns of sex distribution and of neurological deficit and development were observed in the "under achievement" group (Rutter & Yule, 1975). Thus support for the first severe discrepancy provisions for learning disabilities emerged.

THE HISTORY OF LD

Arguably the most important landmark legislation providing rights and educational privilege to students with disabilities was PL 94–142 enacted by Congress in 1975. Prior to 1975 approximately 200,000 individuals with significant disabilities were institutionalized in state-run settings and generally provided minimal standards of care (Ed.gov. 5/21/2007). Further, in 1970 only one in five children with disabilities was educated in public schools. Perhaps one of the most debated classification categories in the PL 94–142 regulations was with respect to learning disabilities.

While crafting a definition of LD in 1976 for the PL 94–142 regulations, the United States Department of Education (USDOE) considered the addition of a severe discrepancy formula (e.g., achievement falling 50 percent or more below the child's expected achievement level) within the LD definition. While these efforts were offset by a number of objections from national experts of the time offering an array of conceptual and statistical difficulties with this procedure, the notion of seemingly objective discrepancy criteria was not entirely abandoned. The final definition for learning disabilities in PL 94–142 was as follows:

> The term "specific learning disability" means a disorder in one or more of the basic psychological processes involved in understanding or using language, spoken or written, which may manifest itself in an imperfect ability to listen, speak, read, write, spell, or to do mathematical calculations. The

term includes such conditions as perceptual handicaps, brain injury, minimal brain dysfunction, dysfunction, dyslexia, and developmental aphasia. The term does not include children who have learning disabilities which are primarily the result of visual, hearing, or motor handicaps, or mental retardation, or emotional disturbance, or of environmental, cultural, or economic disadvantage. (U.S. Office of Education, 1977, p. 65083)

While the actual definition in the pivotal regulations did not include a severe discrepancy formula, the section of the law that identified criteria for identifying students with learning disabilities stipulated that:

a. A team may determine that a child has a specific learning disability if:
   1. The child does not achieve commensurate with his or her age and ability levels in one or more of the areas listed in paragraph (a) (2) of this section, when provided with learning experiences appropriate with the child's age and ability levels; and
   2. The team finds that a child has a severe discrepancy between achievement and intellectual ability in one or more of the following areas:
      i. Oral expression;
      ii. Listening comprehension;
      iii. Written expression;
      iv. Basic reading skill;
      v. Reading comprehension;
      vi. Mathematics calculation; or
      vii. Mathematics reasoning
b. The team may not identify a child as having a specific learning disability if the severe discrepancy between ability and achievement is primarily the result of:
   1. A visual, hearing, or motor handicap;
   2. Mental retardation;
   3. Emotional disturbance; or
   4. Environmental, cultural, or economic disadvantage. (Federal Register, Dec. 29, 1977, p. 65083)

Therefore, while the severe discrepancy language did not make it into the formal LD definition, the inclusion of the preceding language essentially added these procedures to the classification. Following the publication of PL 94–142 most states adopted severe discrepancy provisions in their identification procedures for learning disabilities (e.g., Frankenberger & Franzalglio, 1991). However states varied in terms of the tests used to ascertain a discrepancy, the formulas used to compute the discrepancy, and the magnitude required for identification purposes (for discussion, see Fuchs, Mock, Morgan, & Young, 2003).

CRITICISMS OF DISCREPANCY-BASED MODELS

Criticisms of discrepancy-based models for understanding and identifying learning disabilities are numerous and have a long history. Essentially these criticisms can be conceptualized along two domains: problems with the reliability of a discrepancy-based approach for identifying students with disabilities and problems with the discrepancy-based model for conceptualizing and treating students with learning disabilities. Therefore, basic criticisms of the discrepancy-based model are that this method for understanding and identifying learning disabilities lacks adequate reliability and validity. In terms of reliability, the 300 percent increase noted in the population of students identified with learning disabilities over the last 30 years suggests a lack of stringent criteria for making the diagnosis (President's Commission on Excellence in Special Education, 2002).

PROBLEMS WITH RELIABILITY

One specific difficulty hampering reliable diagnosis is that there are four major methods for determining the presence of a severe discrepancy and each uses different criteria. The methods include assessing the discrepancy in terms of (1) deviation from grade level, (2) Standard deviation from the mean, (3) Standard Score comparison, and (4) Standard Regression analysis. The first, *deviation from grade level,* suggests that if Kate is in the fourth grade yet reads at a second-grade level then she may be seen as having a severe discrepancy in her reading achievement. In this method

Kate's academic performance is compared to her peers. The second method, *standard deviation from the mean*, might assess Kate on an individually administered achievement test. Given that her score overall or in a specific academic area was at least a standard deviation below the norm she may be perceived as evidencing a severe discrepancy commensurate with an LD diagnosis. This method would compare Kate's achievement with that of a standardized sample of same-age students from across the country. In the third method, *Standard Score comparison*, Kate's performance on an individually administered intelligence test would be compared to her performance on an individually administered achievement test. If she achieved an IQ score of 100 (average score) and an achievement score one or more standard deviations below the mean, she may be seen as evidencing a severe discrepancy commensurate with an LD diagnosis. With this method Kate's academic performance is compared to her performance on an intellectual assessment. Given that the comparison groups for Kate's academic performance differ across these three methods (e.g., compared to peers, a national sample, and to her own IQ score), it is not hard to imagine why the result would be different for students diagnosed as learning disabled depending on the discrepancy method utilized. In essence, different methods of calculating a discrepancy will result in different students being classified. The fourth method, *Standard Regression analysis*, utilizes the Standard Score comparison technique and additionally employs a regression formula as an attempt to statistically account for the measurement error associated with the tests, the reliability of them, and the correlations between them. While this is perhaps the most psychometrically sound method for assessing IQ/achievement discrepancies, it is not without additional inherent difficulties.

In a replication of an earlier study Mercer, Jordan, Allsopp, and Mercer (1996) surveyed all state education departments in the United States and found that 98 percent of them included a discrepancy in their definition of and identification criteria for learning disabilities. As indicated in the 1997 NYS Part 200 Regulations of the Commission of Education, "a student who exhibits a discrepancy of 50% or more between expected achievement and actual achievement determined on an individual basis shall be deemed to have a learning disability." This determination in contemporary assessment was often completed using an intelligence test as the measure of *expected achievement* and a norm-referenced, standardized, academic test as a measure of *actual achievement*. The difference between the two scores is used to assess the discrepancy.

This brings us to the second major difficulty significantly hampering the reliability of LD diagnoses made with discrepancy based methods: The norm-referenced, standardized measures commonly employed in this assessment process are inadequate for measuring both *expected achievement* and *actual achievement*. In terms of expected achievement, while IQ tests are good general predictors of educational attainment they are inadequate for assigning an expected achievement outcome for individual students for several reasons. First, IQ test components most linked with reading performance are often verbally mediated and are somewhat dependent on reading. Therefore poor readers may have lower verbal IQ test scores and therefore be denied special education services due to a lack of assessed discrepancy (see Siegel, 1989; Stanovich, 1989). Secondly, this approach assumes that IQ can accurately predict academic performance. To explore this further we can look at the correlations between IQ and achievement reported on the most recent version of a popular standardized achievement measure, the Wechsler Individual Achievement Test-Second Edition (WIAT-II, 2002). The examiner's manual of the WIAT-II reports that the correlations between full-scale ability (assessed by the WISC-III) and achievement (assessed by the WIAT-II) range from .3 to .78. To understand how well the WISC-III predicts achievement we can square these correlations to determine the amount of shared variance between these scores. The result suggests that the WISC-III accounts for 9 to 61 percent of the variance in a given student's achievement test score. This also suggests that from 39 to 91 percent of the student's achievement score is not accounted for by the IQ test. This lends considerable doubt to the notion that an IQ test can accurately assign an expected level of achievement, at least at the level of the individual student. Second, with respect to *actual achievement*, the concept that a student's actual academic performance can best be assessed with a norm-referenced test administered at a single point in time has received considerable criticism as well. Among these criticisms are that nationally normed standardized achievement assessments often do not reflect the skills in a given local curriculum, they suffer from regression to the mean effect, and the fact that all psychometric tests include measurement errors that vary across students and across characteristics of the student (see Francis, Fletcher, & Morris, 2003). In single point assessments measurement error creates fluctuations in test scores that vary by test, age, ability level, and ethnicity. Applying cut-off scores to these types of score distributions is problematic since there is generally little or no actual difference between children at or around that cut-off regardless of their assigned status. Score fluctuations (above or below assigned cut-off scores) have been assessed in both real and simulated data sets suggesting that up to 35 percent of cases change status based on measurement error when single tests were used. Similarly, with respect to discrepancy scores, actual data from the Connecticut Longitudinal Study, analyzed by Francis et al. 2005, found that approximately 20 percent to 30 percent of students studied change disability status from third to fifth grade based on discrepancy scores.

Given the cited limitations with the discrepancy model it is easy to see how it lacks reliability in diagnosis. The fact that different criterion are used across different states significantly impairs consistency in identification. In addition, the limited ability of IQ tests to predict the achievement of an individual measurement error, and the difficulties associated with assigning cut-offs in either single test or discrepancies between tests significantly limit the reliability of this approach. In sum the use of discrepancy-based psychometrically oriented models for diagnosis are unreliable and insufficient to accurately designate individuals with learning disabilities (Francis, et al., 2005; Fletcher et al., 2005).

PROBLEMS WITH VALIDITY

In addition to reliability concerns, discrepancy-based models also have been heavily criticized with respect to validity. Since the validity of a construct relies on its uniqueness and utility, the validity of the discrepancy-based model assumes that IQ-achievement discrepant students are qualitatively different from "regular" (non-discrepant) low achievers. If this model were valid, these two groups of students would differ in terms of their prognosis (development of reading ability), response to intervention (discrepant and non-discrepant groups should show differential response to reading intervention), and with respect to the cognitive profiles thought to underlie reading abilities (e.g., Francis et al., 1995).

The literature in this area has been generally unsupportive of the discrepancy-based model for LD classification. Studies by Stanovich and Seigel (1994) and by Fletcher et al. (1994) suggest that IQ discrepant and non-discrepant low-achieving groups did not differ on measures of independent reading ability. The two groups were also found to have no significant differences with respect to cognitive abilities believed to underlie reading development. Both of these independent studies found that language-based measures were better predictors of early reading ability than performance on IQ tests. In addition several meta-analyses have found little difference in the cognitive process of IQ discrepant and non-discrepant low-achieving groups and further that these groups did not differ with respect to reading development (e.g., Hoskyn & Swanson, 2000; Stuebing et al., 2002).

With respect to Response to Intervention (RTI), a series of studies conducted by Vellutino and colleagues at the University of Albany provided longitudinal data on students' reading development. In one study incorporating an intense reading remediation component, Vellutino, Scanlon, and Lyon (2000) followed 118 impaired readers and 65 control students from kindergarten through third grade. Their findings suggested that IQ scores could not distinguish between impaired and normal readers, nor were IQ scores helpful in predicting impaired readers who were difficult to remediate versus impaired readers who were readily remediated. Further, they found that in normally developing students IQ did not predict reading achievement nor was it correlated highly with measures of reading ability (e.g., word identification, phonological decoding). The conclusion of this study was that "when intense remediation resources are made available to impaired readers representing a broad range on the intellectual continuum, response to remediation is not associated with measured intelligence" (p. 237).

In sum the literature investigating the validity of discrepancy models has generally been unsupportive. Findings suggest that IQ discrepant and IQ non-discrepant groups of students do not differ in terms of their cognitive profiles, their prognosis in reading, or in their RTI. Included in the President's Commission on Excellence in Special Education Report (USDOE, 2002) are two poignant quotes included here, the first from Dr. Sharon Vaughn and the second from Commissioner Wade Horn.

> *"There is no compelling reason to use IQ tests in the identification of learning disabilities. And, if we eliminated IQ tests from the identification of individuals with learning disabilities, we could shift our focus on making sure that individuals are getting the services that they need and away from the energy that's going into eligibility determination." (p. 22)*
>
> *"I would like to encourage this Commission to drive a stake through the heart of this over reliance on the discrepancy model for determining the kinds of children that need services. It doesn't make any sense to me. I've wondered for 25 years why it is that we continue to use it and over rely on it as a way of determining what children are eligible for services in special education." (p. 25)*

A PLACE FOR INTELLIGENCE TESTING IN LD DIAGNOSIS?

Criticisms aside, there are reasonable proponents for the continued use of intelligence testing in the assessment process for learning disabilities. Fuchs, Mock, Morgan, and Young (2003) aptly point out that the empirical support for the relationship between IQ and school achievement has a history spanning more than 50 years. Further they illustrate the practical pedagogical implications associated with instruction provided to all children ranging in IQ from 70 to 155. The authors contend that IQ testing may help to preserve our historical conceptions of LD as a distinct diagnostic category understood as children failing to learn with average or above-average intelligence and adequate participation in the general curriculum. In their emerging model for LD assessment the authors suggest that children not responding to an effective general education curriculum, and demonstrating a lack of response to a more intense level of instructional intervention, would then be administered "valid cognitive assessments" to "facilitate identification of students with LD in historical terms." There does seem to be some utility in administering cognitive assessments to students demonstrating a failure to progress despite increasingly intense instructional interventions shown to be effective for others. This utility may be ruling out cognitive delays as potentially impairing academic functioning and in providing additional information relevant to the diagnosis. Based on the literature previously provided however, it would appear that the routine use of IQ tests to ascertain an aptitude-achievement discrepancy with a single point-in-time assessment may not be warranted.

EMERGENCE OF CONTEMPORARY MODELS OF LD

HISTORY

The period from the late 1970s to the mid 1990s evidenced a substantial increase in the numbers of students identified with specific learning disabilities (SLD). Summaries of prevalence data over this timeframe suggest that SLD rates have risen by as much as 300 percent, that roughly 80 percent of these SLD students evidenced unaddressed deficits in reading, and that as many as 40 percent to 50 percent of all children served in special education had not been adequately instructed in reading (i.e., President's Commission on Excellence in Special Education, 2002; U.S. Office of Special Education, NJCLD, 2002).

In response to the apparent overidentification of students as learning disabled, prereferral intervention and the use of prereferral intervention teams became popular by the mid to late 1980s. These teams typically provided for collaborative consultation to teachers toward instructional modifications or accommodations to increase student performance prior to or without special education referral. Perhaps the earliest widespread teaming initiative was the Teacher Assistance Teams reported on by Chalfant, Pysh, and Moultrie (1979). These teams were formed to provide an avenue for teachers to assist other teachers in intervening with and accommodating for students seen as difficult-to-teach. While some data was reported in terms of large-scale implementations of these teams, by in large they were not well studied nor were data on student progress or the integrity of the team process typically provided (e.g., Fuchs, Mock, Morgan, & Young, 2003).

As prereferral intervention teams evolved, many adopted components of behavioral consultation that structured the problem-solving process and relied on student monitoring data to inform intervention design and revision. A major facilitator to this evolution was the emerging literature supporting the use of Curriculum-Based Measurement (CBM) procedures and behavioral observation methods to monitor student's academic and behavioral progress in the schools. Research has generally indicated that team consultation procedures and quality prereferral interventions can lead to increased student performance and decreases in special education (Graden, Casey, & Bonstrom, 1985; Flugum & Reschly, 1994; Rosenfield, 1992).

Perhaps the most comprehensive evaluation of prereferral intervention teams was conducted by Doug and Lynn Fuchs and colleagues. These researchers, supported by the Office of Special Education Programs, developed and evaluated a Mainstream Assistance Team (MAT) model implemented in the Metro-Nashville school district in the mid to late 1980s. The Fuchs utilized graduate students, a scripted behavioral consultation process, and prescriptive interventions to address teacher concerns of referred students. Over the three-year project the Fuchs demonstrated that these procedures lead to a significant decrease in special education referrals, 75 percent or more of referred students meeting teacher generated goals, and high teacher perception of effectiveness. While effective, the MAT project did not sustain much past the life of the grant funding (Fuchs et al., 1996), due perhaps to the prescriptive nature of the program or the artificial/external development and infusion of the project into the host site.

Based on the work of the Fuchs the School Based Intervention Team (SBIT) model was developed and implemented in a large urban district in Central New York (McDougal, Clonan, & Martens, 2000). This team-based prereferral intervention model was similar to MAT's in that it followed the behavioral consultation process but was developed and implemented largely by in-district personnel. The authors' contention was that by creating an "in-house" model and by attending to principles of organizational change an effective and sustained project would result. A two-year evaluation of four SBIT teams indicated that they were successful in decreasing special education referrals by 40 percent compared to similar non-SBIT schools and that referred students overall evidenced significant increases in academic and/or behavioral performance (McDougal et al., 2000). In terms of sustainability, while SBITs still function in the host district after the initial report, the functioning and effectiveness of these teams has not since been reported.

Although considerable research has documented the effectiveness of high-quality prereferral intervention, the process has some inherent structural limitations. Prereferral intervention teams generally provide intervention services toward individual students referred by the classroom teacher. This requires (1) that the student's level of functioning is poor enough to generate considerable teacher concern, (2) that the classroom teacher is willing to take the time required to complete the referral and intervention team process, and (3) that the team itself has adequate time to devote to the referral. In essence, even good models for prereferral intervention suffer some of the inherent limitations found in traditional approaches for special education identification, including an approach that waits for students to evidence failure; idiosyncratic student identification based on teacher referral; a focus on individual students rather than whole classrooms, grade levels, or schools; and the development of individualized interventions as opposed to systemic development of increasingly intense resources based on student need.

RTI: A General Definition

Given the preceding concerns more systemic large scale implementations of Response-to-Intervention models have been initiated in the schools. In reviewing the literature, Fuchs et al. (2003) identified critical components of RTI implementation. In general Fuchs et al. suggest that:

"In broad terms RTI may be described as follows:

1. Students are provided with generally effective instruction by their classroom teacher;

2. Their progress is monitored;

3. Those who do not respond get something else, or something more from their teacher or someone else;

4. Again their progress is monitored; and

5. Those who still do not respond either qualify for special education or for special education evaluation" (p. 159).

Based on this general description four large-scale implementations have been identified and reported in the literature. Two large-scale implementations of RTI include Ohio's Intervention Based Assessment (IBA) and Pennsylvania's Instructional Support Teams (ISTs). These implementations focused on the provision of prereferral intervention services prior to the referral to special education. The other two models of implementation, Heartland Agency (Iowa) and Minneapolis Public School's Problem-Solving Model (MPSM) actually utilize student progress monitoring data to designate eligibility for a "non-categorical" designation into special education. Each of these large-scale RTI implementations has their roots in the team-based prereferral intervention model incorporating a collaborative team approach following a behavioral consultation model. Each model is briefly described below.

THE FIRST LARGE-SCALE IMPLEMENTATIONS OF RTI

The Ohio IBA and the Pennsylvania IST models were similar in that they were both large-scale implementations of structured prereferral intervention team initiatives. The IBA started in 1992–93 as a volunteer initiative supported by a special education waiver from the Ohio State Department of Education. In the beginning 35 schools from across the state were recruited to provide school-based intervention services to struggling students. They followed a behavioral problem-solving process including problem definition, collection of baseline data, setting specific goals, hypothesizing a reason for the student difficulty, developing an intervention and monitoring plan, and evaluating the intervention via student progress data compared to baseline levels (e.g., Telzrow, McNamara, & Hollinger, 2000). An evaluation of IBAs reported by Telzrow in 2000 indicated that by 1997, 329 school teams were running though only 227 were included in the study. In reviewing "best case" documentation from participating teams, Telzrow and colleagues found that most teams were not applying the problem-solving model with integrity especially as related to documenting that the developed student interventions had been implemented as designed (for discussion see Fuchs, Mock, Morgan, & Young, 2003).

The Pennsylvania IST model was also supported by the respective State Department of Education. In addition to the collaborative and behavioral problem-solving process, the IST model utilized a full-time support teacher responsible for assisting the classroom teacher to implement student interventions developed by the team. This student-directed support is monitored continuously with CBM and/or behavioral assessment and periodically evaluated to refine intervention procedures. The IST support is limited to 50 school days when the team meets to decide if further evaluation is warranted. Evaluations of the IST model suggest that teams successfully follow the prescribed model, that ISTs lead to decreases in special education referrals and placements, reductions in the use of grade retentions, and increases in general measures of student behavior and academic performance (e.g., Hartman & Fay, 1996; Kovaleski, Gickling, Morrow, & Swank, 1999). Overall while these results seem promising the IST evaluations have been criticized for a lack of direct measures both of team functioning and student outcomes, a lack of inter-rater reliability data, and a lack of specific descriptions of the interventions utilized (Fuchs et al., 2003).

Perhaps the pioneer in using RTI procedures for eligibility determinations is Heartland, Iowa's largest educational agency providing technical assistance and training to 350 schools across 56 districts. Heartland's reform dates back to the mid 1980s when state support for noncategorical models of special education and direct assessments of student performance emerged. The Heartland model utilized a four-level (tier) model for intervention and assessment. The levels include (1) collaboration between the teacher and the parent, (2) referral to the Building Intervention Team, (3) referral to district staff (e.g., school psychologists and special educators), and (4) considerations of special education. In the Heartland model student academic level and learning rate are compared to local classroom or grade-level norms to ascertain the need for increasing levels of support. This model is noncategorical in that low-performing students are not ultimately labeled as LD, MR, and so on, but rather as students eligible for special education services. Again, evaluations of the Heartland model suggested generally positive results in terms of reductions in special education referrals and placements and with regard to student performance, though these studies too were critiqued for a lack of empirical rigor (i.e., Ikeda, & Gustafson, 2002; Fuchs et al., 2003).

The Minneapolis Public School's Problem-Solving Model (MPSM) was developed in the early 1990s as an assessment and intervention model to in part reduce the overrepresentation of minorities in special education and also to create a focus on instruction and student performance. Similar to the Heartland model, MPSM began as a four-tier behavioral problem-solving process. As with the Heartland model, student academic level and rate of progress as compared to local norms is used to assign the need for increasingly more intense levels of service. In addition, MPSM too uses lack of student progress to decide eligibility for special education placement and also employs a noncategorical approach to identification. Published evaluations of MPSM have suggested more proportionate representation of minorities in special education, a stable overall identification rate of approximately 7 percent, and increases in referred students' academic performance especially in the area of reading (Marston, Muyskens, Lau, & Canter, 2003). These studies too were critiqued with respect to the empirical rigor of the employed measures and design (Fuchs et al., 2003).

SUMMARY

In reviewing the major field-based implementations of RTI, all utilized a collaborative team-based approach and followed a behavioral model of consultation to format the problem-solving process. The IBA and IST initiatives were large-scale, state-supported models for providing prereferral interventions to students prior to (or instead of) referral for special education eligibility determination. The Heartland and MPSM projects were implemented in large district (or "agency") settings, and while similar to IBA and ISTs, these two models utilized student progress data compared to class or grade level norms to ascertain eligibility for special education. In addition both Heartland and MPSM employed a noncategorical approach to special education, not requiring school professionals to conduct further diagnostic assessment to assign the student to a diagnostic category. In general, data from these implementations are promising though far from complete. While reductions in special education referrals and placements are noted along with increases in students' academic and behavioral performance, most of these studies suffer methodological difficulties inherent in field-based evaluations. These difficulties include reporting on incomplete and restricted samples, lack of direct performance or integrity measures, lack of detailed intervention protocols, use of "convenience" data sets, and a lack of consistency in measures/outcomes employed across studies. Further, while not discussed here, prior reports of these implementations also include considerable concerns with the amount of professional development required for implementation and the difficulty maintaining consistency in model implementation both across time and school setting.

RESEARCH-BASED RTI MODELS

In addition to field implementations several research-based RTI models have been implemented. These research models typically employ a standard protocol approach to intervention as opposed to a problem-solving approach. This standard protocol approach offers the same empirically based treatment to all children identified with low skills. The advantages to a standard protocol procedure is that it is easier to validate, train practitioners, and measure the integrity of one intervention being implemented as opposed to many possibilities derived from the problem-solving models (e.g., Fuchs et al., 2003).

Research-based models have generally been implemented in the primary grades with struggling readers. Vellutino et al. (1996) tracked the literacy development of a significant sample (n = 1407) of children from kindergarten through fourth grade. In the study intense reading intervention was provided to low readers from the middle of first grade to the middle of second grade (depending on student progress). Interventions were daily 30-minute tutoring sessions focusing on phonemic awareness, decoding, sight words, comprehension, and text reading. Students were provided 70–80 sessions over the course of a semester. Based on this work Vellutino found that two-thirds of tutored readers demonstrated "good" or "very good" rates of progress. Further, based on normative measures, they had reduced the percentage of children classified as disabled readers to 3 percent by the spring of second grade (see Vellutino, Scanlon, Small, & Fanuele, 2003). While employing a rigorous methodology, the study's results have been critiqued as Vellutino excluded students with IQ scores below 90 and due to concerns that schools would not have the resources to replicate these results by providing struggling readers with 70 to 80 one-on-one tutoring sessions with highly trained educators (e.g., Fuchs et al., 2003).

An additional study employing standard protocol procedures focused on second-grade students at risk for learning disabilities. Vaughn, Linan-Thompson, and Hickman (2003) provided three tiers of reading interventions delivered sequentially based on student progress. Low-performing students were initially provided 10 weeks of empirically based supplemental small-group instruction. Based on predefined criteria students were either dismissed from supplemental services based on their progress or grouped for another 10 weeks of instruction (either at the same level of service or a more intense level). After 30 weeks 75 percent of students had been returned to general education and 25 percent referred for special education consideration. Thus they provided an empirical illustration of a preventative three-tier model for RTI: "with primary intervention consisting of the general education program, secondary intervention involving the fixed duration, intensive, standard protocol trial (with the goal of remediating the academic deficit rather than enhancing general education), and tertiary intervention synonymous with special education" (Vaughn & Fuchs, 2003, p. 139). While the results achieved by Vaugh et al. are quite promising, follow-up of discontinued students suggested that a subgroup did not continue to thrive in general education and could have benefited from continued delivery of supplemental services.

SUMMARY

Research-based models of RTI have been successfully implemented in the schools. These models have focused on the use of scientifically based standard protocol interventions provided in the area of literacy to struggling primary grade students. In general these models have demonstrated significant efficacy and the promise to effectively intervene with the majority of referred students without necessitating the need for special education referral. Serious questions remain, however, in terms of the feasibility of these practices for widespread use in the schools based on the training and resources required to implement them. In addition, as the study conducted by Vaughn et al. points out, at least some of these remediated students may require ongoing support in order to progress in general education.

OUR PERSPECTIVE: WHERE ARE WE NOW?

Currently we are at a crossroads in the identification of children with learning disabilities. The traditional road traveled has been soundly criticized for employing identification techniques lacking in reliability and validity and assessment procedures lacking in instructional utility and fraught with cultural bias (e.g., Gresham, 2002). Further, traditional practices employ a "wait to fail" procedure relying on teachers to recognize that a student demonstrates severe learning problems prior to referring them for support services. This imprecise screening practice has lead to students with instructional delays referred to special education, those with learning disabilities not referred, and in general all services being provided too late to remediate children such that they can respond to the general education curriculum (Bradley, Danielson, & Doolittle, 2005; Vaughn & Fuchs, 2003). In response, legislative initiatives and professional groups have advocated the charting of a new course, that of Response-to-Intervention. This model holds the promise of early identification and effective treatment, more comprehensive and non-biased identification practices, increases in student performance and accountability, and decreases in the numbers of students referred for special education.

The road toward RTI is still under construction with in-complete results obtained from both research-based models and field-based implementations. Further, RTI implementations have employed a variety of techniques with problem-solving or stan-dard protocol procedures. In general, however, core features of RTI have been identified and include "(a) high quality, research-based classroom instruction, (b) universal screening, (c) continu-ous progress monitoring, (d) research-based secondary or tertiary interventions, (e) progress monitoring during interventions, and (f) fidelity measures. Decisions about needed services are based on the quality of student responses to research-based interventions (Bradley, Danielson, & Doolittle, 2005, p. 486)."

Based on these features the remainder of the book offers school-based practitioners and those professions in training a potential map for a road that is currently under construction. Based on our review of the literature, our combined research, and our ongoing experience assisting school settings to implement these procedures, we offer this not as a complete work but rather one that reflects what we know at this time. Our model for RTI employs three tiers of intervention and monitoring of increasing intensity as required to produce student progress. We also address eventual considerations for special education eligibility based on the model developed in Iowa combined with the work of the National Research Center on Learning Disabilities. This eligibility model is articulated in Chapter 8 and includes assess-ments of discrepancies in student performance and rate of progress as well as the demonstration of instructional need. Further, we make a recommendation for a comprehensive eval-uation, including cognitive assessment for students suspected of possessing an educational disability. In addition, we address the considerable task of organizational change that is required from schools and districts attempting to implement and sustain RTI initiatives. In conclusion, we hope to summarize the promise of this approach, the current limitations and unknowns, and what we consider next steps in the development of this model for not only the identification of students with learning disabil-ities but also for the more successful and effective education of all children.

CASE EXAMPLE: MOVING FROM A TRADITIONAL TO AN RTI MODEL: TBD

Located in the Northeastern United States, Baylor Schools is a suburban school district with a student population of about 6,000 students. The district has literacy and mathematics test scores that are about average when compared with districts throughout the state that have resources and student populations similar to Baylor's. The district has five elementary schools (grades K–4), a middle school (grades 5–6), a junior high school (grades 7–8), and one high school.

While Baylor's overall scores on the state accountability tests were generally average, the percent of students in special education programming was 17 percent, which was higher than the state average of 12 percent. Further, relatively few students transitioned out of special education programming once they entered. A district-level task force studied the problem and found that the largest segment of students in special education were those designated with learning disabilities, most generally involving reading. Many of these students had evidenced academic delays in the primary grades and many had received one or more grade retentions prior to classification. The task force also reported that the five elementary schools implemented different core curriculums in literacy and math and had no consistent measures for monitoring students' progress in basic skills other than the state-mandated assessments.

When the task force issued its report the school superintendent, Ann Douglas, had served in her current position for three years. She was knowledgeable about RTI and wanted to establish as a priority the goal of instituting an RTI process in her school district. Referencing the report of the district-level task force, she made a presentation to the school board regarding RTI, highlighting the strengths of this preventative approach in terms of consistent assessment and instruction, screening and progress monitoring, and efficacy in early intervention. Based on this presentation, the Board of Education at Baylor convened a study group to more thoroughly investigate RTI and, if it appeared promising, to make recommendations for the district to move forward with implementation.

TIER I: EFFECTIVE GENERAL EDUCATION AND UNIVERSAL SCREENING/PROGRESS MONITORING

II

Effective Academic Programs for All Students

F EW WILL DISPUTE that general education classrooms in America are increasing in student diversity. Increases in child poverty (e.g., Fass & Cauthen, 2007), cultural and linguistic diversity (e.g., Trent, Kea, & Oh, 2008), inclusion of students with disabilities (Florian, 1998), and changes in family structure (Amato, 2001) all increase the range of student preparedness to benefit from instruction within general education classrooms. Many students, often referred to as "diverse learners," have responded poorly to instruction typically provided in general education classrooms. Although recent reports indicate the gaps in achievement are narrowing, certain groups of students (e.g., English Language Learners, students with disabilities, those eligible for free or reduced lunch, and children from most major cultural minority groups) consistently are less successful on national assessments of reading (Lee, Grigg, & Donahue, 2007), writing (Salahu-Din, Persky, & Miller, 2008), and mathematics (Lee, Grigg, & Dion, 2007) than their average-achieving peers. To meet the needs of a wider range of students in their classrooms, it is critical that general education teachers are able to diversify their instruction to increase the success of all students in their classrooms.

The foundation of any RTI model is the universal provision of effective classroom instruction in all academic areas and at every grade level. When this foundation is not firmly established, providing effective interventions for students who need more support will be particularly challenging. The support system in place for these students will likely be burdened with referrals, taxing district resources and decreasing the probability of intervention success. Services for students are likely to be fragmented and lack a connection

2

Chapter

to the general education curriculum. Although making changes to the general education programming may seem like a daunting task, it is a critical component of a successful RTI implementation. Educators with a working understanding of effective instruction can be more successful at advocating for students' instructional needs and supporting classroom teachers in meeting those needs. The purpose of this chapter is to address the following questions:

1. What general elements of effective instruction should I be seeing in classrooms at my school?
2. What are the important components of literacy and mathematics instruction?
3. How do I know if my school is implementing effective Tier 1 instruction?
4. What can I do to influence change in my school if I see inadequacies in the Tier 1 instruction provided?

GENERAL ELEMENTS OF EFFECTIVE INSTRUCTION

When discussing Tier 1 programs, a common question is "what *is* research-based instruction?" It is well understood that different learners have different curricular and instructional needs, and that no single approach is effective with all students. However, decades of research on effective teaching points to particular strategies that tend to work well with most students in general (e.g., Ellis, Worthington, & Larkin, 1994; Marzano, Pickering, & Pollock, 2001) and diverse learners in particular (e.g., Carnine, 1994). Therefore, in making decisions about curriculum and instruction we need to consider the variability in student response to particular teaching strategies while drawing on the extensive literature base regarding which strategies tend to be most effective overall.

Learning is produced by a complex interaction between student characteristics, the curriculum, the instruction, and the student's classroom and home environment (Kame'enui & Simmons, 1990). An important distinction must be made between curriculum and instruction, and each needs to be considered in choosing, developing, and implementing a program. Curriculum refers to the learning objectives, the content, the "what to teach." For example, "all students will master phonemic awareness by the end of kindergarten" is a curricular objective. Determining specific sub-skills of phonemic awareness to be taught on the way to achieving that goal (e.g., rhyming, syllable counting, segmentation, blending, deletion) and the sequence in which these skills will be covered also are curricular issues.

Instruction refers to the way in which the curricular content will be delivered (Howell & Nolet, 2000). It is the interaction between student and teacher, student and peer, and student and medium, aimed at increasing student knowledge and/or skills. Instructional approaches range from highly teacher-directed to highly student-generated. Instructional considerations include materials, time, teaching strategies, group size, and motivational strategies. Independent seatwork and collaborative group work also are instructional strategies.

Selecting particular instructional techniques depends on the student, the content, and the desired outcome. Some types of learning goals lend themselves well to student-directed or collaborative work, while others might require more teacher modeling and student practice. When material is fairly straightforward, such as the attraction properties of magnets, a student-generated approach might be more engaging and effective than a direct instruction approach. For this content, the teacher can provide students with magnets and guide them as they learn how magnets are attracted to each other and to other types of objects (i.e., metals). Students can learn about the polar charges by attempting to stick two magnets together in various ways, learning how they cling to each other when their opposite poles are matched, and feeling the force keeping the magnets from touching when attempting to match like poles. This knowledge can be useful and interesting for students even without knowing why magnets work in this way, and this activity may spark curiosity in some students leading them to seek to learn more. However, when the task involves learning a number of new concepts and subsequently incorporating them into performing a higher-level skill, students often need more direct teaching of the basic content and higher-level strategies. For example, to complete applied math problems, students must have learned a variety of basic calculation skills as well as various strategies for solving the problem. They are not able to solve the problem without these prerequisite skills and strategies in the same way they were able to describe the properties of magnets without understanding their underlying properties. For many students, direct teaching and practice will be needed before they are able to perform these types of tasks accurately and efficiently.

The effectiveness of the instructional approach also is influenced by student characteristics, especially the student's existing knowledge and motivation to learn the content (Howell & Nolet, 2000). In general, the more knowledgeable and skilled, and the more motivated students are to learn the particular content, the more likely they are to benefit from student-generated approaches such as independent and collaborative work. When students lack requisite skills, knowledge, or motivation to learn the task, a more explicit instructional approach often results in greater learning than a student-generated one. An effective teacher is adept at matching instructional approach to student attributes and learning objectives.

Although student-generated approaches often are popular among educators, a robust body of evidence indicates that teacher-guided approaches consistently result in greater student learning (Kirschner, Sweller, & Clark, 2006). In particular, students who are at risk for learning or behavioral problems often require instruction that is teacher-directed, explicit, and systematic (e.g., Carnine, 1994; Foorman & Torgesen, 2001). These students often need direct explanation of concepts and skills, modeling by the teacher, guided practice and immediate feedback. If given a complex task with minimal direction and the intent of having students construct their own meaning, many diverse learners may not understand the task or what they were meant to learn from it. Further, that particular task will not result in increased understanding or skill, even if the student-generated approach is more effective for some of the student's peers. For example, if a student with poor literacy skills—laborious decoding, limited vocabulary and comprehension strategies, and weak writing skills—is asked to read a passage independently and write an essay incorporating the main points of the text, he or she is likely to find the task extremely difficult and require a great deal of assistance in completing it. The student may not learn much from the activity except perhaps that he or she needs help completing tasks most other students in the class seem to perform with ease. On the other hand, if the teacher selects a passage carefully based on the student's ability to decode the words and its connection to recent decoding lessons, preteaches vocabulary that might be unfamiliar to the child, reads the passage aloud with the student, gives the student immediate feedback on his or her decoding accuracy, and teaches or reinforces explicit strategies the student can use in comprehending the main points of the passage and writing his or her response, the student is more likely to perform the task successfully and benefit from the assignment. In short, this student requires more complete instruction than would be required of a student who already possesses the decoding, vocabulary, comprehension, and writing skills needed to perform this task successfully.

Providing complete instruction, as illustrated above, requires a great deal more teacher planning than simply giving an assignment for students to complete independently, even after a period of large-group instruction aimed at explaining the task. It also requires more understanding of students' skill levels and instructional needs, and continual evaluation of tasks and student skills. Teachers need to know which skills are important to teach in every subject, and a sequence in which diverse learners can acquire and integrate these skills. Unfortunately most teachers are not sufficiently prepared by their preservice education programs to engage in this level of planning (Trent et al., 2008). In addition, many prevailing educational tools do not facilitate adequate instruction for meeting the needs of diverse learners (Carnine, 1994).

WHAT ARE THE FEATURES OF EFFECTIVE INSTRUCTION FOR DIVERSE LEARNERS?

The research literature on teaching diverse learners consistently reveals a common set of curricular and instructional features that lead to higher achievement for these students. Although terminology and emphasis on particular features varies across reports, the following are consistently identified as important features of effective instruction for students at risk for academic difficulties.

Most of these strategies are aimed at increasing academic learning time (ALT), an important concept in the literature on effective teaching. ALT is defined as the time a student spends meaningfully engaged in appropriate instructional activities with a high degree of successful responding (Fisher & Berliner, 1985). It is one of the strongest predictors of student learning.

1. *Explicit teaching.* Explicit instruction is a teacher-directed approach involving teacher modeling and explanation of concepts and strategies followed by student practice to mastery. Explicit instruction is consistently related to greater learning, especially for diverse learners (Kirschner, Sweller, & Clark, 2006). Teachers using an explicit approach begin a lesson by orienting students to the task, and continue to explain the skill to the students, model the skill so students can see it performed, and provide students multiple opportunities to practice the skill. For example, when teaching students to identify equilateral triangles, the teacher can begin by telling the students they will be learning to identify equilateral triangles. The teacher then explains the properties of an equilateral triangle in simple, consistent language (e.g., "all sides on an equilateral triangle are the same length"). The teacher proceeds by showing a range of examples of triangles, equilateral and non-equilateral, saying "this is an equilateral triangle, all sides are the same length" or "this is not an equilateral triangle, all sides are not the same length" accordingly. After showing a range of examples, the teacher presents examples (some previous and some new) and asks the students to identify each as equilateral or not equilateral. If students make errors, the teacher will correct the error immediately, again using wording consistent with the initial explanation ("this triangle is not equilateral because not all sides are the same length" or "this is an equilateral triangle because all its sides are the same length"). Instruction continues in this way until students can identify equilateral triangles with perfect or near-perfect accuracy.

2. *Scaffolding.* The term "scaffolding" is borrowed from a construction analogy, where a scaffold is built to support a new building structure before the framework is in place allowing the structure to stand on its own. Similarly, scaffolding instruction refers to providing students with more support as they are in the

initial stages of acquiring a skill, then gradually reducing that support as the child gains independence and confidence with the skill. For example, reading instruction typically begins with teachers reading aloud to students so they are able to understand how text is related to meaning and enjoyment, and to develop a purpose for learning to read. As students begin to learn to read text themselves, teachers may listen to them and provide prompts and corrections as needed. After continued practice, students are able to read independently and silently, and teachers can simply ask questions after students are finished reading a passage or book. A "model-lead-test" instructional format is an effective way of scaffolding instruction within a lesson (Simmons & Kame'enui, 1990). First, the teacher models the skill or content he or she wants the student to learn. Second, the teacher asks the student to complete the task with the teacher. Finally, the teacher asks the student to complete the task independently. Scaffolding involves not only providing support, but gradually removing that support as students gain skills and confidence.

3. *Opportunities to respond*. Student responding is a key factor in learning. Active engagement is more effective than passive listening, even when the students are attending to a lecture. Responding can be oral, written, or performance-oriented. Students can respond orally to teacher questioning. Response rates are increased during group instruction when teachers ask students to respond chorally rather than asking questions and calling on individual students to answer. Although choral responses may be perceived negatively by some educators, they increase the opportunities for each student to respond and are effective in keeping students engaged. Use of hand signals increases the effectiveness of choral responding by decreasing the likelihood that students will take their cues from peers rather than respond on their own.

Written responses also can be effective, assuming the task is not too difficult for the student to complete independently, either because the student has sufficient writing skills to perform the task or that support is provided to the student in completing the written task. In addition, students can respond by building or making something, such as completing a puzzle, painting a picture, or playing a musical instrument, if these activities are aligned with the purpose of the lesson.

4. *Systematic instruction.* "Systematic" is often used in conjunction with the word "explicit" to describe a structured, teacher-directed instructional program. Where explicit refers to direct teaching of concepts and strategies, systematic refers to purposeful sequencing and ample review of content so that learners are able to master new concepts and integrate them into higher-level skills. An illustration of systematic instruction is considering a sequence for teaching letter-sound correspondences in beginning reading. Rather than beginning with A and ending with Z, a systematic program would begin instructing students on content that is (1) easiest to learn and (2) most useful for higher-level skills. For example, the letter "m" is associated with a continuous sound,/m/, which is often easier for young children to isolate and pronounce than stop sounds, such as/b/ or/k/. The letter "m" is also found in many words, so it has high utility. Teaching/m/early in the sequence would facilitate early success and opportunities to integrate skills. Within a lesson or two, students can be taught/m/,/s/, and/a/and be able to make a few words (am, as, Sam, ma). As letter sounds are added to the sequence, additional considerations would include separating highly similar letters to minimize confusion before a letter sound is mastered (e.g., "p," and "b," and "d"). When content is reasoned through logically and introduced and reviewed in a systematic way, students will have an easier time learning and retaining the content as well as integrating it into more complex tasks.

These five concepts represent a sampling of the prominent features of effective programming that can benefit a range of students, particularly those at risk for academic difficulty. The list is not exhaustive, but provides some key indicators in examining an existing instructional program, or selecting/developing new curricula and instructional practices. These concepts can be applied across a range of subject areas and grade levels. Specific application of these concepts to the instruction of basic skills, such as reading, writing, and mathematics, will be discussed below in more detail.

IMPORTANT COMPONENTS OF LITERACY AND MATHEMATICS PROGRAMS

The basic skills of reading, writing, and basic mathematics have been the foundation of American education since it first became compulsory in the mid- to late nineteenth century. These skills are essential to future learning and overall life success. Because they are so central to an individual's functioning in society, these basic skills are referred to as "cultural imperatives" (Reynolds & Birch, 1977). The students who experience the most difficulty in school often are those who have not mastered these skills by the time they are required to use them. Although effective instruction is vital at all levels and for all subjects, a necessary first step in facilitating wide-ranging academic success involves teaching these basic skills so that all students will master them.

READING/LITERACY

Literacy is fundamental to academic success. Without adequate skills to read complex text effortlessly and with understanding, students have trouble learning the content required for success in late elementary through post-secondary education. Reading also is essential for success in life, even when advanced education is not pursued. Citizens need reading and writing skills to participate meaningfully in society—to complete an employment application, to assemble and/or operate a small household appliance, to read a voters' guide in determining which candidate for office will best represent one's interests, and so on. Lack of adequate reading skills diminishes the quality of life for many people. The impact of reading and writing ability on overall life success in modern society underscores the urgency in meeting student needs, especially considering that approximately 80 percent of academic referrals are due to reading difficulties (President's Commission on Excellence in Special Education, 2002).

To become successful readers, all learners must master a number of essential literacy skills, including phonemic awareness, alphabetic principle, reading fluency, vocabulary recognition, use, and development, and meaning construction (NRP, 2000). When students have difficulty reading, usually they have failed to master one or more of these essential skills. Most often, the reading problem is due to difficulties in efficient word recognition. In a few cases, word recognition is not an issue but the student has trouble constructing meaning. Many reading difficulties can be prevented when effective classroom instruction is in place. Students who do not learn to read by mere exposure require explicit instruction and practice in the key areas leading to reading success. When the Tier I instruction is delivered with attention to these components, the need for additional support is reduced, freeing up resources to provide more support to students who need it.

Phonemic Awareness   One of the more important breakthroughs in the science of reading instruction has been the discovery that many reading problems can be prevented by ensuring all students have adequate understanding of the sound structure of the English language (Adams, 1990). This understanding, known as phonemic awareness, is the understanding that whole words are comprised of individual sounds, or phonemes. A phoneme is the smallest speech unit in spoken language. The English language contains approximately 44 phonemes, although this number varies somewhat across linguistic experts. Phonemic awareness is defined as "the ability to hear, think about, and manipulate individual sounds in words" (Torgesen, 1998). A child navigating the initial stages of language development does not differentiate the sounds within a meaning unit. For example, when hearing the word "cat," she will process it as a single sound and (assuming the child has prior experience with the word) immediately associate that sound with the word's meaning. If asked to produce the sounds in the word "cat," this child may respond with "meow." This is because she has not yet learned to abstract the concept of "word" from the meaning of each word in her developing vocabulary. This abstraction is the first step in learning phonemic awareness.

Beginning with an ability to think abstractly about words, phonemic awareness involves skills such as sound isolation (e.g., hearing initial, medial, and final sounds in words), segmentation (breaking a word into its component phonemes), blending (putting phonemes together to make a word), deletion (identifying the new word when a phoneme is deleted), and manipulation (changing phonemes in words to make new words). Without explicit teaching in phonemic awareness, approximately 30 to 60 percent of students will not acquire these skills by first grade (Torgesen 1998). However, this percentage is decreased dramatically when kindergarten teachers employ an instructional focus on phonemic awareness. This is often accomplished through carefully sequenced yet fun, developmentally appropriate "word game" activities allowing students ample opportunity to play with the sounds. Teaching phonemic awareness within the classroom does not require a great deal of time. Many students can learn these skills within approximately half of the kindergarten year, given up to 20 minutes of instruction three days per week. When included as an instructional focus in kindergarten and explicitly taught via classroom instruction, a large proportion of students will master the skill by the end of their kindergarten year.

A smaller percentage of students do not acquire phonemic awareness even when it is purposefully addressed in the classroom. These students require more explicit delivery with more opportunities to practice than what is afforded through high-quality classroom instruction. Daily small-group or one-to-one instruction with frequent progress monitoring is often provided to these students. This additional support would represent a higher tier of the RTI model (e.g., Tier 2). However, ensuring all children acquire these skills prior to receiving word identification instruction increases the likelihood that more students benefit from high-quality Tier 1 instruction in first grade and beyond.

Phonics/Alphabetic Principle   It has been estimated that children will need to learn more than 80,000 words, which includes recognizing them in print and knowing their meanings, by the end of third grade (Adams, 1990). This development of word vocabulary continues throughout a child's education. It is impossible to directly teach students all the words they will need to know to be successful readers and learners. Students need to learn effective strategies for identifying the unknown words they inevitably will encounter in text. In an alphabetic system, these strategies involve understanding the relationships between letters and sounds and how words are commonly structured, and the ability to apply that understanding to identifying an unknown word in text. In short, students must learn the alphabetic principle and be able to apply it in identifying previously unknown words when encountering them in print.

The development of word recognition skills is likely the most hotly debated aspect of beginning reading instruction. Most educators agree these skills are important but disagree over how best to teach them. Some believe that children will develop these skills on their own with exposure to print and practice reading authentic texts. Others believe students require direct, explicit instruction in phonics rules to develop these skills effectively. This issue has been researched extensively and the evidence supports explicit, systematic teaching of phonemic awareness and phonics for beginning readers, regardless of ability or experiential background (Torgesen & Foorman, 2001). However, this research has not been universally embraced, and several beginning reading programs claiming to address phonemic awareness and phonics do not include sufficient attention to these skills to be effective in supporting the reading development of diverse learners (Moats, 2006). Practitioners need to be aware of this debate and be sufficiently informed to distinguish research-validated practices and direct, systematic instruction in phonics from instruction that claims to teach these skills but does so inadequately or not at all.

To know simply whether a curriculum or teacher addresses phonics in a reading program may not be sufficient for determining whether these skills are taught adequately, especially for diverse learners. Teachers use various approaches to teaching phonics, some of which are more explicit and systematic than others. The most explicit approach is often referred to as "synthetic phonics." The word "synthetic" refers to the teaching of letter sounds and combinations and blending those sounds and combinations into whole words (as opposed to "fake," which often is implied by opponents of this approach who emphasize "real reading"). Well-structured reading programs utilizing synthetic phonics follow teaching of sounds with reading practice in decodable connected text—that is, text containing words and spelling patterns students have already been taught. On the other end of the spectrum of approaches is the implicit approach, which emphasizes the use of strategies other than alphabetic decoding to identify an unknown word encountered in connected text. Teachers using a more implicit approach tend to embed phonics instruction within more global reading and writing tasks. Instead of focusing on alphabetic skills, the focus in these lessons tends to be on comprehension and interacting with the text at a conceptual level. Therefore, texts tend to be thematically based and selected according to meaning rather than to alphabetic decoding requirements. Phonics instruction occurs as students encounter difficulty in decoding the text, and therefore is more incidental than planned and explicit. Students are often taught to use multiple strategies in decoding words, such as guessing from context, identifying familiar spelling patterns, using picture cues, and rereading the sentence to determine if the guessed word seems to fit. Implicit approaches tend to be popular with teachers because they tend to be more fun and meaningful to them and to their average and high-performing readers. Their low-performing readers also can engage in discussions of the text meaning as long as they are given adequate support in decoding the text, or if the text is read to them. However, this approach does not help diverse learners achieve the fluency in decoding required to perform higher-level comprehension tasks independently (Foorman et al., 1998).

Fluency The acquisition of print skills culminates in automatic, effortless identification of words in connected text. This facility with print is referred to as reading fluency. Definitions of reading fluency range from a simple formulaic representation (i.e., accuracy plus speed) to a global judgment of the smoothness and flow of a student's oral reading ability. Measurement of oral reading fluency mimics these definitions. Precise measures of fluency involve listening to a child read and recording the rate per minute of words read correctly (e.g., Fuchs, Fuchs, Hosp, & Jenkins, 2001). However, several diagnostic reading assessments used by teachers and reading specialists involve a global rating of the student's fluency, based not only on accurate and efficient word identification but on other factors such as appropriate voice inflection, responding to punctuation marks, and translating the text into speech in a smooth manner (Schreiber, 1991).

The NRP recognized the importance of fluency and identified it as an essential area for reading instruction. Fluent readers are able to focus their attentional resources on comprehending the material being read (LaBerge & Samuels, 1974), and therefore fluency is critical in the ability to construct meaning from text. Particularly in the early elementary grades, measures of oral reading fluency are highly correlated with measures of comprehension (L. Fuchs, Fuchs, & Maxwell, 1988).

Instruction in fluency involves practice with material a student can read with a high degree of accuracy. It can begin with learning to identify isolated letter sounds fluently, then word lists, then connected text. If fluency practice precedes accurate sound or word identification, students may end up practicing ineffective strategies and specific errors and reinforcing these poor habits. Once practiced, errors and use of ineffective strategies become more difficult to unlearn. Because measures of oral reading fluency are often used as indicators of reading development, educators must understand that low scores on fluency measures can be the result of a variety of problems and not jump to implementing a fluency intervention.

Vocabulary   Knowledge of word meanings and the ability to learn new words is a key component in developing as a successful reader. Children who know and use a variety of words are better able to identify words in print and to comprehend written text. The relationship between vocabulary and comprehension is well documented, and often the two skills are discussed together. In fact, the NRP subcommittee on comprehension divided its work into three components: vocabulary instruction, text comprehension instruction, and teacher preparation and comprehension strategies instruction.

Although "vocabulary" in general refers to knowledge and use of words, the term is broad enough to create difficulty in definition and measurement. Vocabulary can be oral or written, receptive or expressive. A child might know a word in speech but not recognize it in print, or vice versa. A student might recognize a word and understand its meaning when used in a particular context but not use the word in writing and/or speech. Further, a child might see a word in print and recognize it automatically (i.e., "sight vocabulary") rather than after a concerted attempt to decode the word. Most attempts at measuring vocabulary focus on one dimension (e.g., expressive oral vocabulary).

Regardless of the way in which vocabulary is operationalized, the English language contains a vast number of words—more than can possibly be taught directly. To increase vocabulary and facilitate reading success, students need to develop strategies for learning new words in addition to being taught new words directly. Although direct instruction on word meanings has been shown to improve a student's vocabulary and comprehension (Stahl and Fairbanks, 1986), an approach to vocabulary development that combines direct instruction with indirect methods is more effective (NRP, 2000). Particular methods with research supporting their effectiveness include semantic mapping (developing categories of new and familiar words and learning their similarities and differences) and engaging students in discussion of word meanings (Carnine, Silbert, & Kame'enui, 1990).

Comprehension   Comprehension is unlike the other four skills in that it is the desired end product of reading, while the others can be thought of as contributing to this end. Comprehension has been described as the "essence of reading" (Durkin, 1993). Obviously, it is the ultimate reason we read.

Comprehension is the result of a complex interaction of factors. Failure to comprehend a text could be the result of inadequate print skills or fluency, limited vocabulary or language comprehension skills, inadequate prior knowledge, or failure to engage in comprehension strategies. Instruction in any of these areas can be considered comprehension instruction, although most often comprehension instruction involves teacher modeling of comprehension strategies (e.g., previewing, questioning, summarizing), engaging students in discussion about specific texts, and creating assignments for students that would draw on their reading comprehension skills. More explicit comprehension instruction is focused on teaching children strategies and having them practice the strategies with feedback, scaffolding, and review.

The National Reading Panel report describes seven instructional strategies for facilitating comprehension development in students. These strategies include comprehension monitoring, cooperative learning, use of graphic and semantic organizers, question answering, question generation, story structure, and summarization. These strategies have research support for their effectiveness, especially when used in combination and with students who do not have reading disabilities. Three of these strategies fall under the general category of "metacomprehension," which refers to students' ability to monitor, evaluate, and adjust their own comprehension as they read (Carnine, Silbert, & Kame'enui, 1990). Metacomprehension strategies can be taught successfully to low-achieving readers and those with learning disabilities using a variety of direct instruction techniques, and this instruction improves reading comprehension (Carnine et al., 1990). As with most academic skills, students with mild disabilities and low-achieving children tend to benefit more from a systematic, direct instructional approach.

Evaluating Reading Programs   After reading the preceding overview of key elements of effective reading instruction, you might be left wondering whether your school's reading program is as complete and effective as it could be. Or your school may be in the process of selecting a new published program to use in teaching beginning reading. As adoption of a new program requires significant monetary and time investment, it is important to evaluate the existing and potential alternative programs against research-based criteria. Publishing companies are in the business of selling their product, and all can deliver a seductive sales pitch, so it is critical to know what is most important in a published program. Fortunately schools now have access to tools for evaluating programs, and even independent expert evaluations of many published programs.

One useful tool for evaluating reading programs is available online at the University of Oregon's Big Ideas in Beginning Reading website (http://reading.uoregon.edu/curricula/con_guide.php). It is called "A Consumer's Guide to Analyzing a Core Reading Program Grades K–3: A Critical Elements Analysis" (Simmons and Kame'enui, 2006). A review using this instrument begins with the most important consideration, that is, whether credible evidence for a program's effectiveness is available.

However, many published programs do not have outcome data, so a more detailed review on the critical elements is required. The Consumer's Guide is a lengthy and comprehensive document, requiring a substantial time investment in using it to evaluate a program. However, the exercise is highly instructive, as personnel involved in conducting the review will gain a thorough understanding of important program components, as well as the strengths and limitations of existing programs. The knowledge and understanding gained in undertaking a review is likely to be considered well worth the effort required in conducting the review.

Another source of information about reading programs available online is the Florida Center for Reading Research website (http://fcrr.org). This website has a section containing reviews of several published reading programs. Each review is approximately two to three pages long, and covers the basic program components, strengths and weaknesses, and an overview of the research evidence available to support the program's effectiveness. At the time of this writing, reviews were available for 10 published core reading programs and scores of supplemental or intervention programs. The FCRR terminated its review of programs in the summer of 2008, citing a restructuring of priorities as Reading First funds diminish.

Finally, the What Works Clearinghouse (http://ies.ed.gov/ncee/wwc/) housed by the Institute for Education Sciences contains reviews of programs according to research evidence. To date most programs mentioned do not have credible research evidence supporting their efficacy, primarily because well-designed and executed studies have not been conducted on these programs. For the programs that do have research available, the studies were reviewed and the results summarized in a user-friendly way. However, the focus of reviews at the WWC tends to be on intervention programs rather than comprehensive reading programs.

MATHEMATICS

Like reading, mathematics proficiency is one of the essential skills comprising the major curricular foci of compulsory education (i.e., the second "r," for "rithmetic"). Facility with numbers and their manipulation is tied to success not only on an individual level, but also a societal one. The United States enjoyed many decades as a leader in math achievement; however, declining achievement in the latter part of the twentieth century became a source of concern among citizens and policymakers. Although the prevalence of reading disabilities far exceeds that of math disabilities, a significant number of students experience difficulty in math that arguably could be prevented through more effective math programming. To address these concerns, the National Mathematics Advisory Panel (NMAP) was commissioned in April 2006 to review the national trends in mathematics achievement and empirical research on effective math instruction and to develop recommendations for teaching math in elementary and secondary schools. The NMAP released its recommendations in a 2008 report.

Curricular Issues   In reviewing the skills most linked to math-related success, the NMAP determined that school algebra represented the most essential achievement in mastery of mathematics. Therefore, a prekindergarten through eighth-grade curriculum that effectively prepares students to learn algebra is key to this success. The NMAP proposed three clusters of skills, referred to as the Critical Foundations of Algebra, which must be addressed thoroughly and effectively if students are to benefit maximally from school algebra instruction. These skills are fluency with whole numbers, fluency with fractions, and particular aspects of geometry and measurement. The Critical Foundations are not meant to comprise an entire preschool-to-algebra curriculum, rather they are intended to represent an essential core of skills that all students must master in order to be successful. The NMAP identified a set of two to six benchmarks for each of the Critical Foundations, to be attained across grades 3–7. See Table 2.1 for a listing of the proposed benchmarks by grade level. The benchmarks are based on expert judgment and to date have not been validated empirically, although this would be an important item for the research agenda on mathematics instruction.

An examination of current practice in elementary mathematics revealed that teachers often attempt to teach too many topics in a given year without devoting enough instructional time to each

Table 2.1 Proposed Benchmarks for Critical Foundations of Algebra, by Grade

End of Grade 3:
  • Proficiency in addition and subtraction of whole numbers (FWN).

End of Grade 4:
  • Identify and represent fractions and decimals, and compare them on a number line or with other common representations of fractions and decimals (FF).

End of Grade 5:
  • Proficiency with multiplication and division of whole numbers (FWN).
  • Proficiency with comparing fractions and decimals and common percent, and with the addition and subtraction of fractions and decimals (FF).
  • Ability to solve problems involving perimeter and area of triangles and all quadrilaterals having at least one pair of parallel sides (i.e., trapezoids) (GM).

End of Grade 6:
  • Proficiency with multiplication and division of fractions and decimals (FF).
  • Proficiency with all operations involving positive and negative integers (FF).
  • Ability to analyze the properties of two-dimensional shapes and solve problems involving perimeter and area, and analyze the properties of three-dimensional shapes and solve problems involving surface area and volume (GM).

End of Grade 7:
  • Proficiency with all operations involving positive and negative fractions (FF).
  • Ability to solve problems involving percent, ratio, and rate and extend this work to proportionality (FF).
  • Familiarity with the relationship between similar triangles and the concept of the slope of a line (GM).

Note: FWN = Fluency with Whole Numbers; FF = Fluency with Fractions; GM = Aspects of Geometry and Measurement.

topic to facilitate mastery before moving on to another topic. By contrast, nations with the highest math achievement tend to teach fewer skills more thoroughly. One possible source of this tendency for curriculum in U.S. schools to "spiral" (i.e., revisit the same topics year after year with insufficient time to facilitate mastery) is the variation among state standards. Textbook publishers, in an attempt to reach the widest possible market for their tools, include lessons and activities to address the state math standards of each state. This often results in textbooks that address too many topics and lack sufficient coherence for students to master and gain fluency with the critical skills. These textbooks often become the guides for teacher planning, therefore resulting in classroom instruction that mirrors the organization of the textbooks.

Instructional Issues   The subject of mathematics has not escaped the ubiquitous debate over whether teacher-directed or student-centered instruction is most beneficial to students. The NMAP found insufficient research support to recommend either approach as a sole method for instructional delivery. However, as with most subjects, students in the early stages of skill acquisition (including most diverse learners and students with disabilities) benefit most from explicit and systematic instruction with ample opportunities for practice, feedback, and review.

Finally, teacher preparation to plan and deliver effective mathematics curriculum and instruction is paramount. Many general teachers, particularly at the elementary level, lack the math proficiency required to teach math effectively. However, teacher content knowledge of mathematics is positively related to student achievement. Unfortunately the literature on math instruction does not sufficiently address questions of preservice education, professional development, or the possibility of using math content specialists to provide instruction to students or coaching to teachers. It is currently unknown exactly what and how much math knowledge a teacher needs to be maximally effective. More research on these questions is needed. In the meantime, schools and districts should explore ways for increasing teacher knowledge and competence for teaching math and evaluate these attempts by continually assessing their effectiveness.

Research on effective math programs lags behind the corresponding literature base for beginning reading programs. Moreover, a "Consumer's Guide" does not exist for elementary mathematics programs. The WWC does contain a section on mathematics programs, but the reviews there are limited due to the paucity of research on the subject. Practitioners wishing to examine the general math programs at their schools might want to begin by reviewing the NMAP report, available online at http://www.ed.gov/about/bdscomm/list/mathpanel/report/final-report.pdf.

EVALUATING YOUR SCHOOL'S TIER 1 INSTRUCTION

Evaluating the academic programs in any district requires a clear articulation of the curricular content and instructional practices currently in place, which can form the basis for comparison to standards for research-based programs. Student outcome data also are important to consider. These data can point to areas in the program that are working well, that is, leading to desired learning outcomes, as well as specific areas that need further attention. A checklist of factors to examine is provided on the Resource CD. Although the factors discussed in this chapter and outlined on the CD checklist are not exhaustive, they provide some direction that could lead to a deeper examination in certain areas. In addition, the CD contains a list of links to more specific checklists and evaluation tools available online.

To evaluate the programs at your school, begin by examining important outcomes. Is there need for change? A few indicators collected in most or all schools can provide answers even if the school is not yet engaged in universal screenings. One source of information readily available in most districts is standardized test results. What proportion of students performs successfully on the test? If that number is less than 90 percent, consider the effectiveness of Tier 1 instruction in the classrooms. This information also can be examined in conjunction with any end-of-the-year assessment conducted within the school to determine whether students have met grade-level standards and are prepared to move to the next grade. A second important piece of information is referral rates. What percentage of students are either identified as needing special education or somewhere in the referral process? What percentage of students receives some kind of additional support beyond the classroom instruction (e.g., extra tutoring, small-group, one-on-one, etc.)? If a large proportion (approximately 80 percent) of students is successful in the curriculum with minimal or no additional support, the programs might be sufficiently meeting student needs.

After reviewing student outcome data, most schools are likely to identify weaknesses in their programs in some areas or at some levels. Perhaps students progress easily through the early grades and begin to struggle after reaching second or third grade, indicating a disconnect between what is taught and mastered in the early grades and what is required for success later on. Perhaps the students are very successful in math but have difficulty in reading, suggesting a more successful program in math than in reading. Examining the outcomes can point to potential areas of strength as well as those needing improvement, which may be very helpful for identifying action steps (i.e., building on the strengths) as well as avoiding unnecessary efforts.

When academic programs are producing less-than-optimal results, an examination of various aspects of the programs is warranted. This examination can occur at both the school-wide level and the classroom level. Some schools might also need to examine district factors, especially when district policies heavily influence the curriculum and instruction, professional development, and/or service delivery within the school.

At the school-wide level, four areas to examine are administrator support and leadership, expectations for student performance, collaboration among teachers and other staff, and a common understanding and articulation of essential content and objectives for instruction. An effective administrator is knowledgeable of effective instruction and can be sure teachers have that knowledge and implement it by having high expectations and supporting teachers in meeting those expectations. For example, an elementary principal asked the teachers to collect and use data on their students' reading performance at various points during the year. At first the teachers were skeptical, but the principal committed to giving them the choice of discontinuing the assessment after one year. During that year, the principal sought out resources for the teachers to help them understand how to use the assessment. The principal met with the grade-level teams once per week, and approximately once per month brought in the district's expert on the assessment for a question-and-answer session. Over the course of the year, the teachers grew to understand and value the assessment. When asked at the end of the year whether they would continue to implement the assessment, the teachers voted unanimously to keep it in place.

Another key indicator is a culture of high expectations for students. Effective teachers are more confident in their ability to help diverse learners succeed, and therefore are more likely to hold high expectations. High expectations are linked to student achievement. Teachers who believe in their students and hold them to high (yet realistic) expectations communicate a positive message to the students, and the students are likely to put forth more effort. Additionally, teachers holding high expectations are more likely to make changes to their instruction when students are not learning, and these changes often result in greater student success.

A common articulation of goals and teacher collaboration are indicators that a school is focused in its mission to educate all students and coordinated in accomplishing that mission. Teacher collaboration in itself does not guarantee that effective instructional practices are followed, but it could involve, or lead to, teachers supporting each other in implementing procedures learned through professional development. Teachers who have a common understanding of *what* they are teaching and regular communication about *how* they are teaching can be more focused and have more opportunities to learn and implement new techniques, and to receive feedback on their teaching.

An evaluation of the Tier 1 instruction would be incomplete without examining what is happening in the classrooms. Although data and school-wide indicators reflect classroom practice, it is important to look at essential instructional factors, as discussed earlier in the chapter. In the classroom, look for clear, focused lessons linked to the articulated curriculum, explicit instructional delivery, high degree of student engagement, and flexible, differentiated instruction according to student skills.

INFLUENCING CHANGE IN TIER 1 PROGRAMS

Many educators, school psychologists, related service personnel, and even special education teachers may feel they have limited influence over large-scale general education programs. Indeed, programs typically are selected by building and/or district administrators, at times in collaboration with classroom teachers. School psychologists and other personnel may not be consulted in making these decisions. However, individual practitioners may be in a position to assist administrators in making these decisions by securing a position on curriculum adoption committees. This is likely to require a proactive approach, as you may not be aware of such committees until they already have formed and begun their work. By speaking with administrators and/or teachers, try to learn whether curricular changes are on the horizon and express an interest in becoming involved. It may not have occurred to those in charge of curriculum adoption that a variety of disciplines might have some knowledge to add in selecting a program, and they may welcome the additional perspectives.

Perhaps an even more valuable opportunity to provide input will be in the use of assessment data collected through the school psychologist's universal screening efforts. School psychologists are more likely to be viewed as having a role in data collection, interpretation, and use, and are often the personnel with the most knowledge of assessment in general. They can assist a building's team in identifying what the school-wide assessment reveals about the effectiveness of the general education programs. School psychologists can organize data to address questions such as "How much progress do students at the various grade levels make overall?" "What proportion of students achieves end-of-the-year standards in each grade level?" and "What proportion of students is identified as needing additional instructional support?" The answers to these questions are likely to prompt further discussion and examination of classroom instructional practices and other factors influencing the effectiveness of Tier I programs.

Professional development is a likely, if not inevitable, component of changes made in general education. Now that research on effective school programs is more widely available, teachers need to learn about the research on effective instruction and how to implement and evaluate that instruction in the classroom. The NRP and NMAP each identified professional development as a critical need and also an area requiring more research. Currently little is known about the best approach to professional development when the desired outcome is more successful students. However, it is clear that one-shot workshops with little coordination or follow-up have little impact on classroom practices. More promising models for professional development include coaching, teacher collaboration, and follow-up meetings (e.g., Bos, Mather, Narr & Babur, 1999). In general, providing teachers with information (the "why"), practical and concrete strategies (the "how"), clear expectations for teachers to try out and practice the new strategies, and follow-up support so teachers can ask questions and deepen their understanding and skills may be the most effective approach to fostering changes in classroom practices. This approach requires a clear focus and strong leadership willing to commit the time and resources to seeing the change through without being distracted by the next hot topic.

The amount and nature of professional development needed to facilitate changes in classroom instruction will vary from school to school. It is best selected after evaluating the strengths and weaknesses of the current program, as well as teachers' interests and dispositions toward change. In general, the more educators understand about effective classroom instruction, the better able they will be to provide support to teachers when dealing with a child's academic problem. You will be able to evaluate the instruction a child receives in the classroom and build upon that knowledge in assisting to develop an intervention. Therefore, having all educators participate in this process is likely to benefit the students served.

Developing Effective School Programs

Lakeside Elementary School is a K–5 building located in the suburbs of a medium-sized city in the Midwest. It is one of nine elementary schools in the Woebegone Central School District, which also includes three middle schools and two high schools. Lakeside educates approximately 600 students, with four to five classrooms per grade level. The school also employs four special education teachers, a literacy specialist, a reading intervention teacher, two speech-and-language pathologists, and a half-time school psychologist. Two of the special education teachers are responsible for self-contained classrooms, and the instructional duties of the other two include a combination of resource room and in-class support.

The Woebegone Central School district allows schools considerable autonomy over their academic programs. Although district personnel may give recommendations for curriculum and instruction, their role is more supportive than directive, and ultimately curricular decisions are within the purview of the school administration. Prior to beginning their RTI initiative, Lakeside Elementary did not have a coordinated reading program. It provided books and materials for teachers and allowed them considerable latitude in deciding what and how to teach reading. However, the principal had an interest in literacy and was beginning to initiate discussions with the teachers about effective reading programs. She was disposed favorably toward using a guided reading approach and was concerned about providing teachers with the knowledge and motivation needed to implement this approach effectively.

(continued)

(continued)

The Woebegone district administrators, particularly the director of special education and assistant superintendent for pupil personnel services, had learned about RTI and were interested in beginning an initiative in their schools. These special education administrators were particularly interested in beginning the data collection and intervention development aspects of the model. They were not particularly concerned about the general education programs and had presumed that most of their efforts would be directed at developing, implementing, and monitoring academic interventions for students who needed additional support and/or who may eventually need special education services.

In collaboration with the elementary principals, the Woebegone special education administrators coordinated a series of workshops for the building personnel to learn how to collect, organize, and use universal screening data (see next chapter). Lakeside Elementary, along with the other elementary schools within the district, sent a team of general and special education teachers, school psychologists, speech and language specialists, and literacy specialists to these trainings. The team learned to administer and score brief screening measures of early literacy and reading development in all grade levels K–5.

After the first round of data collection was completed and the school team examined its report, Lakeside Elementary staff discovered that an unacceptably high percentage of students (37 percent) was identified as needing additional support across the grade levels. This concerned the team and prompted discussions of how to provide supports for the students at risk, as well as how to ensure greater success without needing additional support. Initially the team members were overwhelmed by the multidimensional nature of the task before them, but after a few discussions they decided to proceed by examining their classroom reading instruction and developing a structured, team-based approach to developing and implementing interventions.

Lakeside staff began examining their programs by having all classroom teachers describe their reading instruction. Although the teachers used many of the same materials, there was considerable variability in terms of instructional approach, grouping, supplemental activities, the amount of time spent on reading, and even instructional foci. For example, Ms. White, a second-grade teacher, used a thematic approach to reading. She typically began her lessons by leading the class in a whole-group activity related to the theme, but not necessarily focused on reading skills. This lesson was followed by an assignment for students to complete independently. As the students completed their assignment (again, aligned with the theme and focused more on comprehension than decoding skills), the teacher called small groups of students to sit with her in the back of the room to complete a guided reading lesson. Here the students would take turns reading out of a small book aligned with the current theme, and the teacher gave feedback and asked prompting questions before, during, and after reading. When children struggled to decode a word, the teacher would encourage them to use a set of strategies she had previously taught them in decoding an unknown word. These strategies included looking at the picture, rereading the sentence, covering part of the word to see if they can identify a smaller part, guessing at the word, and, finally, sounding the word out. Groups were selected to be heterogeneous in skills so that lower-performing readers can observe higher-performing students and to avoid stigmatizing students in grouping them by skills. This teacher did not emphasize phonics, as she believed that it was more important to have students engaged in text reading and comprehension activities rather than practicing letter-sound correspondence. She assumed that practice in reading literature was sufficient for students to develop the decoding skills they needed to be successful.

Ms. Parke, another second-grade teacher, took an entirely different approach. Her reading program was structured around decoding skills. She selected texts based on the opportunities they afforded students to practice the skills just taught as well as whether students could read them with a high degree of success. These texts were not selected based on their content or alignment to a theme. Ms. Parke typically began her lesson by reviewing content taught the previous day, and then introducing the next skill in the sequence she used. After a brief whole-group lesson and practice, she too assigned an independent activity for the students and worked with small groups. She arranged her student groupings according to their skills and focused on their most pressing instructional need. Some groups received additional practice on decoding sounds and words, followed by passage reading of highly decodable text. Other groups read more challenging books together and discussed content. This teacher's instruction was heavily focused on word identification skills, because she believed that without adequate skills in reading the words in a text students would not comprehend the material. She felt responsible for teaching the students those skills and believed many students needed more than guided reading practice to be successful and fluent decoders.

Ms. White and Ms. Parke represented the most extreme differences in approach and instructional focus, and most of the other teachers in the building fell somewhere between these two. Particularly at the kindergarten level, variability across classrooms was evident in the universal screening data collected. In some classrooms virtually all students were meeting expectations, while others identified up to 50 percent of their students as needing additional support. Although these patterns concerned the teachers, the school psychologist helped them to understand the variability was not a pure reflection of the effectiveness of their programs, as combinations of individual student characteristics may vary between classrooms. However, many believed they had room to improve, and given the high rate of students identified as needing additional support, they probably were correct.

After discovering this lack of consistency in providing instruction for a skill as important as reading, Lakeside staff decided to have regular grade-level meetings focused on (1) defining a standard set of learning outcomes for each grade, (2) learning what curricular and instructional factors are most effective according to evidence, and (3) learning how to implement those strategies in their classrooms resulting in higher student achievement. They hired a consultant to guide them through the process of strengthening and coordinating their programs. The consultant examined their data and

(continued)

(continued)

addressed their questions, observed in their classrooms, and helped them to identify a common set of objectives for each grade level. Follow-up professional development was provided to assist teachers in learning and implementing effective instructional practices and use of assessment data in teaching.

Lakeside Elementary did not have the time or resources to make all the desired changes at once, so it set priorities and a timeline for implementation. As they learned about the importance of phonemic awareness and a foundation for reading success, the staff decided to set kindergarten as their first priority. Therefore, resources for curriculum, instruction, and professional development were allocated to kindergarten reading instruction first. After one year, the focus shifted to first grade, then second, then third and above. Even though the priority was concentrated on one grade level at a time, all grades did what they could to strengthen their programs each year given the resources available to them.

The results of these efforts began to appear in the data after one year. Kindergarten outcomes improved dramatically after teachers began to address phonemic awareness in their classroom reading programs. In the first year of data collection, only 37 percent of students reached the end-of-the-year benchmark for phonemic awareness in kindergarten, and nearly 30 percent were identified as needing substantial support. At the end of the second year, 85 percent of students met the end-of-the-year benchmark, and only 4 percent required substantial support. Subsequent years' data reflected further improvements at other grade levels. Lakeside did not focus exclusively on Tier 1 for the amount of time it would have required to fully implement the instructional changes needed to ensure maximum effectiveness of the classroom instruction. It prioritized Tier 1 but also made changes to the intervention delivery, identification procedures, and progress monitoring assessment for students receiving additional support and potential special education. However, the staff examined the big picture each year and learned that their efforts were continually resulting in incremental gains in student outcomes.

School-Wide Data Collection for Screening and Outcome Decisions

Chapter

S CHOOL-WIDE DATA COLLECTION is an integral part of RTI. This data collection addresses a few key decisions made in Tier I. First, universal screening provides for frequent checks of student performance so that students who may need additional instructional support can be identified and provided with support as early as possible. Second, these routine checks allow teachers and administrators to make programming decisions leading to increases in student achievement. This information helps teachers obtain an objective picture of their students' overall performance in key academic skills (e.g., reading, math, written expression), and it allows them to make immediate teaching decisions, such as setting up groups for instruction and determining an appropriate starting point. Administrators and school improvement team members can examine the data to determine what, if any, changes are needed to the general education program or additional service options within the school. This information can help administrators make decisions about curriculum and instruction, professional development, service delivery, resource allocation, and so on. In short, school-wide data collection has the potential for facilitating effective instructional programs and services at all three tiers.

Although few would argue against the need for periodic school-wide assessment of student skills, how to accomplish this as effectively and efficiently as possible is much less clear. A multitude of assessment instruments are available, and choosing among them can be a daunting task. This difficulty is compounded when school leaders and teams are not familiar with the salient considerations for making this choice and instead are led by more peripheral factors such as advertising, common sense, or political pressure. This chapter will cover the features of effective screening tools. A checklist, entitled *Evaluating Potential Screening Tools: A Checklist of Essentials*, reflecting the ideas discussed in this chapter can be found on the Resource CD.

CHARACTERISTICS OF SCREENING TOOLS

An evaluation of any assessment tool depends on the purpose for which it will be used. Two basic categories of factors to consider when evaluating a potential screening tool are (1) evidence for the tool's validity for use in screening, and (2) the tool's "ecological palatability" within any given school. The first category includes considerations of traditional reliability and validity with a particular emphasis on the degree to which the results lead to identification of all students who truly need additional services without erroneously identifying students who do not need support. The second category refers primarily to issues of efficiency and cost, so that any screening procedure implemented within a school can be sustained indefinitely. It should yield information of sufficient value to offset the instructional and professional time spent in collecting and analyzing data. This category also refers to issues of buy-in by teachers and staff. Although screening can be implemented without buy-in, the degree to which teachers and staff understand and value the information is likely to impact how effectively these data are used. In short, the two categories refer to considerations of the properties of the tool itself as well as the more ecological issues of implementation, sustainability, and buy-in.

VALIDITY FOR SCREENING PURPOSES

As with any assessment, credible evidence for a specific tool's validity (including reliability) is essential. Any tool lacking in this evidence may lead to spurious decisions about students' education. Children may be over- or underidentified for intervention services. Schools may elect to change effective programs or fail to change ineffective ones. Validity is a singular but multifaceted attribute involving several considerations depending on the intended use of any assessment procedure being evaluated

(Messick, 1995). Most important, does the procedure (or tool) provide information that leads to some improvement in the students' educational program? Does it lead to increased success for some or all students?

Issues of validity include evidence for reliability in scores as well as traditional notions of content, criterion-related, and construct validity (Salvia, Ysseldyke, & Bolt, 2009). Typically this information is found in a particular tool's manual. However, your district may be considering assessments that lack key reliability and validity information, such as a locally created set of procedures or a placement test from a published curriculum. In that case, it is important to weigh this lack of evidence when deciding what to use for screening, and consider undertaking a local reliability and validity study.

RELIABILITY

Evidence for reliability in scores is a fundamental criterion in evaluating the validity of a test or procedure. Without reliability, other questions of validity are rendered moot. Reliability refers to the consistency and stability of a test's scores when basic conditions, such as the time of assessment (test-retest), person scoring and/or administering the assessment (inter-rater/inter-scorer), or specific items (internal consistency, alternate form) vary. Reliability is expressed numerically as a correlation coefficient between scores obtained under these varying conditions, and it has an inverse relationship with the amount of random error present in an assessment procedure. For example, if the reported coefficient is $r = .80$, approximately 80 percent of the variation in scores can be attributed to actual performance on the test (i.e., "true score"), and the remaining 20 percent can be attributed to error. A test's manual or published studies on a procedure should report several correlation coefficients representing the results of various types of reliability evidence at various age or grade levels.

A high degree of evidence for a tool's reliability is essential if scores are to be used in important decision making in schools. If reliability is low, a school would have little confidence in the obtained scores, as they may be attributed largely to random error instead of students' true performance on the assessment.

According to Salvia et al. (2009), coefficients exceeding $r = .80$ indicate adequate reliability for screening decisions. This standard is somewhat lower than the $r = .90$ recommended if a tool is to be used for important individual decisions about students. The lower standard assumes that follow-up evaluation will be conducted and that scores on the screening assessment are not given undue weight in decision making. For example, performance below an established cutoff score on a screening tool would not form the primary basis or justification for a decision to retain a student in a grade or to place that student into a special education program. These decisions would follow a process that may have begun with a low score on the screening assessment but ultimately involved a greater amount of information than is typically gathered by a screening tool.

Establishing the reliability of a tool under consideration is an essential first step in determining the appropriateness of that screening procedure. If reliability is deemed insufficient (i.e., studies have been conducted and results indicate overall reliability below $r = .80$), this particular tool is unlikely to lead to accurate screening decisions. The overall validity of an assessment hinges on reliability; without it, validity is impossible because too much random error is involved in the scores. However, reliability evidence alone is insufficient to judge the overall validity of an assessment. Reliability establishes that scores represent a student's true ability to perform the tasks given on the test; however, the meaning of those scores and whether they reflect the student's performance on the skill of interest is a question of construct validity.

CONSTRUCT VALIDITY

Historically, construct validity involved testing hypotheses to support or fail to support the validity of an assessment procedure. For example, if the assessment is designed to measure a developmental skill, one would expect that, on average, older children would earn higher scores on the measure than younger children. Failure to establish this pattern when testing a sample of students of varying ages might indicate a problem with the instrument's validity. If a tool is to be used in screening, another important hypothesis is that the scores will be reliably different among subgroups of students—that is, low-performing students will earn lower scores than average- or high-performing students. More recent conceptualizations of construct validity include aspects of validity that were previously considered as distinct from construct validity, that is, content validity and the various forms of criterion-related validity. However, these types of evidence also increase one's confidence in the tool's ability to measure the construct of interest. Therefore, they also may be considered evidence for a tool's construct validity (Messick, 1995).

Content validity involves an evaluation of the alignment of a test with the content a student is expected to learn. Evaluation of content includes its appropriateness for the intended grade level(s) and the skill or construct the tool is designed to measure. Generally, teachers and other school personnel are equipped to judge the content validity of a procedure by examining how the materials and tasks align with their curriculum. This can be accomplished by having a small group of faculty examine the materials and determine whether the content is appropriate and provides sufficient coverage of the skill area. Judgments of content validity obtained in this manner need to be considered along with other types of validity evidence and should not be the sole criterion for adopting or rejecting a particular tool, especially when there is reason to believe teachers have limited understanding of the content or ancillary reasons for judging a tool favorably or unfavorably (e.g., apprehension over the time burden imposed by the screening or how scores might lead to judgments of their teaching). However, these evaluations can be helpful in determining strengths and limitations of particular tools under consideration.

Criterion-related validity is a widely used approach to establishing a tool's ability to assess a skill of interest. This type of validity evidence is gathered by examining correlations between scores on the screening tool in question and another test (i.e., the criterion) already judged to be a reliable and valid measure of the skill of interest. Criterion-related validity can be concurrent (i.e., the screening measure and the criterion were administered at or near the same time) or predictive (i.e., the screening measure was administered at some time before the criterion). Validity of the criterion measure is a key consideration when weighing this type of evidence in evaluating a screening tool. Several recent criterion-related validity studies of RTI screening tools have used statewide high-stakes tests as criterion measures (e.g., Crawford, Tindal, & Stieber, 2001). Given the potential impact of statewide test performance on the future of an individual student and/or the school, knowing the relation between a screening tool and the high-stakes test can be very helpful.

Decision-Making Criteria

When using assessment information to identify students for services or determine whether a program results in student success, school personnel need guidelines for interpreting scores. Typically these guidelines are expressed as criterion scores or levels of performance resulting in a dichotomous judgment: likely/unlikely to need additional support, met/did not meet outcome standards. If school-wide data collection is used for both screening and outcome decisions, two types of criteria are used. The first type is a screening cut score, a level of performance at or below which a student is identified for possible intervention. The second type is a goal or benchmark, used as a standard against which student performance (and therefore instructional programming) is evaluated.

The cut score and benchmark may be an identical score on some screening procedures, but often they differ. For example, DIBELS Oral Reading Fluency (DORF) involves a benchmark of 40 correct words per minute by the end of first grade (Good, Simmons, & Kame'enui, 2001). This score is used as a target for judging whether individual students are meeting expectations as well as evaluating the effectiveness of the early reading program as a whole by examining the percentage of students meeting this goal. The cut score for the end of first grade on DORF is 10 words per minute. Students performing at or below this level are likely to require additional instructional support if they are to become successful readers. Students whose performance falls between the cut score and benchmark have unclear predictions based on DORF scores. A way to deal with this uncertainty is to monitor these students' performance more frequently, possibly giving additional support if indicated through the more frequent (strategic) monitoring or other relevant information.

Criterion scores can be based on norms, expert judgment, or empirical linkages to later outcomes. The norm-referenced approach is straightforward; the test developers or school users determine which proportion of students should be classified as at-risk, and select their cut score accordingly. For example, a test manual might specify the 20th percentile (or its corresponding standard score) as the criterion for determining whether a student is at risk. An advantage of this approach is that schools or districts can serve the proportion of lowest-performing students they have adequate resources to accommodate. If a district is able to provide intervention services to 25 percent of its students, it can identify the lowest-performing 25 percent and provide services accordingly. The obvious disadvantage to this approach is that 25 percent might not be the proportion of students actually needing the intervention support. Perhaps only 15 percent need the support, and the provision of services to 25 percent limits the intensity of support provided to the students who struggle most. Conversely, perhaps 35 percent of students need support, but only 25 percent are identified for possible support, resulting in missed opportunities to help children succeed.

The norm-referenced approach is problematic when applied to setting benchmarks. Typically a school would aim to have the vast majority, if not all, of their students attain benchmark performance. This would be impossible using a norm-referenced approach, unless the basis for the benchmark score was a separate norm group (e.g., a national sample or a local sample in a given year). If the school sets the 50th percentile as the benchmark, half of the students will not meet it. The 50th percentile, for example, becomes a moving target as the achievement of a population increases.

Another concern regarding a norm-referenced approach to benchmarks parallels the issue with using it for determining cut scores. The selection of the level of desired achievement might be arbitrary and not related to the achievement a student needs to be successful. Decision-makers can generate educated guesses regarding the level of performance needed to facilitate success, but without a study examining the link between benchmark performance and future outcomes, these guesses might result in benchmarks that are either too high or too low.

A second approach to determining specific criteria is to base them on expert judgment. For example, teachers might examine the items on a particular tool and decide what students at a given grade level should be able to perform. Alternatively, screening tools might have published cut scores based on expert judgment. Informal reading inventories and associated measures (e.g., the Developmental Reading Assessment, Beaver, 2001; Fountas and Pinnell Benchmark Assessment System) often involve interpretation of performance based on expert judgment. For instance, a student is judged "competent" at a given level of the assessment if they read orally with 95 percent accuracy with "adequate" comprehension based on some post-reading activities (e.g., question answering, retell). The selection of the 95 percent accuracy criterion, the grading or leveling of the materials, the selection of post-reading activities, and the development of the rubric or criteria used to judge the comprehension all are based on expert judgment. Occasionally these activities and scores are validated empirically, but often this is not the case.

The third approach to developing cut scores is to use a linkage between the screening instrument and an important outcome, such as performance on state tests. By comparing sets of scores on the screening instrument and the later outcome, cut scores can be established that represent the probability of poor (or successful) outcomes. For example, a third-grade student who reads fewer than 90 words per minute on a grade-level reading passage is unlikely to achieve a passing score on a high-stakes test unless he or she makes substantial progress (ostensibly through effective intervention) during the time between the screening assessment and administration of the outcome measure (Good et al., 2001).

Diagnostic Accuracy   Regardless of how screening criterion scores are established, they also are subject to empirical validation. This validation, referred to as diagnostic accuracy, is similar in concept to a predictive validity approach but takes it a step further. In addition to examining the strength of the relations between students' performance on the screening measure and an outcome measure given later, diagnostic accuracy is an evaluation of whether the screening criterion scores lead to accurate decisions. This evaluation involves a set of relatively simple calculations and can be conducted when both sets of scores (screening and outcome) have been gathered for a sample of students. A few published studies have examined the diagnostic accuracy of curriculum-based reading measures (e.g., Hintze, Ryan, & Stoner, 2003; Hintze & Silberglitt, 2005), but the analysis is simple enough to be conducted on a local level, which would increase confidence in the adequacy (or provide for adjustment) of the cut scores and benchmarks as applied in a given district.

Four possible outcomes of a screening are illustrated in Table 3.1. These include true positives (students at risk who perform below the cut score), false positives (students not at risk who perform below the cut score and therefore are incorrectly identified as at risk), true negatives (students not at risk who perform above the cut score), and false negatives (students at risk who perform above the cut score). Moreover, the four possible outcomes include two categories of correct identification and two error categories. The error categories also are referred to as Type 1 (false positives) and Type 2 (false negatives).

Diagnostic accuracy involves five primary metrics: sensitivity, specificity, positive predictive power, negative predictive power, and correct classifications. The first two calculations refer to the measure's ability to identify those students at risk and those not at risk. *Sensitivity* refers to the proportion of students at risk who are correctly identified by the screening measure. That is, out of all the children at risk, which proportion obtains a score on the screening that falls below the cut score? A measure with low

Table 3.1 Screening Outcomes

	Outcome	
Screening Performance	**At Risk**	**Not At Risk**
Below Cut Score	True Positive	False Positive (Type 1 Error)
Above Cut Score	False Negative (Type 2 Error)	True Negative

sensitivity will fail to identify an unacceptable number of students at risk. *Specificity* is the proportion of students not at risk who are correctly identified as not at risk. In other words, specificity refers to the proportion of students not at risk who perform above the cut score. A measure with low specificity will result in a large number of false positives, possibly taxing district resources by providing support to students not needing it.

The next two calculations refer to the correctness of decisions indicated by the screening criteria. *Positive predictive power* refers to the proportion of students who performed below the cut score who actually were at risk. Like specificity, positive predictive power (PPP) is inversely related to the number of false positives. If PPP falls below .50, the screening cut-off will identify more not-at-risk students than at-risk students as needing support. *Negative predictive power* (NPP) refers to the proportion of students who performed above the cutoff who were not at risk. NPP reflects false negatives—the lower the NPP, the more at-risk students will not be identified by the measure. Therefore, for screening, it is important for NPP to be high.

The final diagnostic accuracy calculation discussed here is *correct classifications* (CC). CC is an index of the students correctly identified either as at-risk or not-at-risk, divided by all students. Higher CC values indicate more accuracy overall in screening decisions, thus limiting both types of screening errors (false positives and false negatives). One might consider this index the primary consideration in selecting or evaluating a cut score. However, sometimes the consequences of one error type are more serious than the other, and therefore trade-offs can be made when selecting a criterion. The CC index reflects both error types and therefore gives limited detail needed to select an optimal cut score or benchmark.

Using Diagnostic Accuracy to Select Criteria   In selecting a screening cut score, it is important to minimize false negatives. False negatives are children who were truly at risk that performed above the screening cut score and therefore were missed by the screening. These students may be overlooked for instructional support they need to be successful. On the other hand, false positives may lead to students unnecessarily being identified as at risk. The consequences of too many false positives include a taxing of resources in providing intervention (or additional assessment) to students who do not need it. In many cases, the consequences of a false negative are more serious than a false positive, especially when additional assessment steps are undertaken to further screen out the false positives. However, if the school uses screening information for high-stakes decisions such as grade retention, one can see how a false positive could have dire consequences for the students. For this reason it is critical to have a highly accurate assessment process to assist with those types of decisions, and schools must not base high-stakes decisions on a single screening score. It is important that even a well-implemented screening process not result in so many false positives as to render the screening useless. One could virtually eliminate false negatives if the cut score is set high enough, but if in doing so we identify every student in the school as at risk, we have defeated the purpose of conducting the screening in the first place.

Benchmark criteria reflect outcome goals. They are meant to represent a level at which the students are highly likely to succeed, so benchmark goals can be used to evaluate instructional programs at all tiers of service delivery. In setting a benchmark goal, even more false positives can be tolerated as long as, again, the school does not base high-stakes decisions on the benchmark. Benchmarks should represent high standards for performance that instill confidence regarding the future performance of students who meet them. The ultimate goal for a school is to have virtually all students meet these benchmarks. Benchmarks should be meaningful enough that students who do meet them have the essential skills they need to continue successful learning as they progress through school. For benchmark criteria, false negatives should be virtually eliminated—as long as doing so does not result in a goal few students can achieve.

Table 3.2 contains sample diagnostic accuracy data from 90 urban third-grade students' spring DORF scores and their performance on the state reading test given in February of that same year. Statistics are calculated for three potential DORF criterion scores for comparison. The first four rows contain actual numbers of students in each category: true positive (scored below the

Table 3.2 Sample Diagnostic Accuracy Statistics

	Potential Criterion Scores		
	80	95	110
True Positives	43	56	63
False Positives	6	15	17
True Negatives	18	9	7
False Negatives	23	10	3
Sensitivity	0.65	0.85	0.95
Specificity	0.75	0.38	0.29
Positive Predictive Power	0.88	0.79	0.79
Negative Predictive Power	0.44	0.47	0.70
Correct Classifications	0.68	0.72	0.78

criterion score and failed the state test), false positive (scored below the criterion score but passed the test), true negative (scored above the criterion and passed the test), and false negative (scored above the criterion but failed the test). Below these actual numbers are the five indices. As the criterion increases, so does sensitivity—at the cost of specificity. In this scenario, correct classification increases as the criterion increases. At some point, however, correct classification will decrease to the base rate (actual failing rate on the exam) because all students will be identified if the criterion exceeds every student's score.

With the exception of specificity and positive predictive power, the diagnostic accuracy data appear to support a cut score of 110. However, it will result in over-identification because only 10 students performed above 110, and 80 performed below it. The 110 might be an ideal benchmark because it resulted in only three false negatives. However, it may identify too many students to be used as a screening cut score. For a cut score, 95 might be more appropriate. It still identifies a large number of students and results in a high number of false positives (15), but it is preferable to a score of 80, which results in even more (23) false negatives. Trade-offs are involved in setting and evaluating criteria, and it is important to understand the various factors involved in screening and the consequences of each type of incorrect decision. Hopefully this discussion also underscores the limitations of screening data so schools are cautious in using these scores for major decisions, and follow-up on any screening score with additional considerations as appropriate.

VALUE OF INFORMATION

Validated screening instruments sometimes yield information that can be used for additional purposes, such as grouping for classroom instruction, planning for individual instruction, and individual progress monitoring. Use of data for additional purposes increases the value of the information collected, thus providing a greater return on the school district's time and monetary investment. However, because an assessment procedure's validity hinges on its intended use, one cannot assume that tools valid for screening also are valid for other uses. It is important to seek evidence that a tool under consideration is valid for uses other than screening. The following discussion will address basic characteristics of an assessment tool used for classroom grouping, instructional planning, and individual progress monitoring.

Classroom Grouping   To increase the effectiveness and efficiency of small-group instruction in the classroom, teachers often group students according to their instructional needs. Many screening tools likely can provide an initial consideration in grouping students, as long as the content is relevant to what students are learning in the classroom. However, grouping decisions often are based on a number of factors not evaluated on the screening, such as behavior concerns, peer relationships, and attendance. In addition, a student's performance on the screening might not accurately reflect what he or she is able to do in the classroom. For example, a student who experiences anxiety over a testing situation might not demonstrate his or her competence on the test, resulting in placement into an instructional group that is not sufficiently challenging. Alternatively, a student who performs poorly in the classroom but does well on the screening because he or she is more engaged in a one-to-one interaction might be placed into a group with a higher expectation for independent work than this particular student is able to sustain without considerable support. Teachers must evaluate screening performance in light of additional assessment information and/or observations of the students during various instructional and social activities in making grouping decisions.

Individual Instructional Planning   An assessment for instructional planning is typically an in-depth analysis of student strengths and weaknesses on specific skills. To determine objectives and a starting point for instruction, teachers need to know what a student can and cannot do, what he or she knows and does not know. Teachers gather this information in a variety of ways, typically through observation and informal assessment or curriculum-linked placement tests. Most screening tools lack the depth required to gather enough information for specific instructional planning. However, screening performance might help focus a teacher's or specialist's investigation into a student's individual instructional needs.

Individual Progress Monitoring   If the screening tool also is appropriate for progress monitoring, it can provide a seamless process from screening to intervention evaluation. In some cases, the screening score can be used as the initial data point in the progress evaluation.

Additionally, recent studies indicate that incorporating short-term progress monitoring in the screening process leads to more appropriate identification of students for intervention (Compton, Fuchs, Fuchs, & Bryant, 2006; Deno, Reschly, Lembke, Magnusson, Callender, & Windram, et al., 2009). Although this practice does not preclude schools from using separate tools for screening and progress monitoring, using the same tool might save time and resources.

Progress monitoring tools must satisfy a unique set of requirements to be effective and useful (see http://studentprogress.org/tools). Like screening tools, those used for progress monitoring must have evidence supporting their reliability and validity, and they must be efficient and low-cost. In addition, progress-monitoring tools must have sufficient alternate forms at each difficulty or grade level so they can be given repeatedly without practice effects. Perhaps most important, the scores must be sensitive to change over a short period of time to allow for timely instructional changes.

Further, the progress-monitoring tool must have specified an expected rate of improvement (see Chapter 6) or benchmark to guide individual goal-setting. Finally, tools for progress monitoring should provide evidence that their use impacts teacher decision making and leads to student improvement. Having a rationale or logical expectation that a tool's use will result in a benefit to students is not quite the same as having research establishing that it actually does result in greater student achievement and improved teacher decision making (e.g., Fuchs, Deno, & Mirkin, 1984).

ECOLOGICAL PALATABILITY

Because universal screening by definition involves all children, administration and scoring of the measures must be low cost and efficient so as not to detract valuable resources away from instruction. Individually administered assessments must be short in duration, and group-administered tools must not be cost prohibitive or involve lengthy scoring procedures. Finally, teacher and staff buy-in is essential for effective use of the screening information. If the consumers of the information do not understand or use the data, its effectiveness will be limited or even undermined. Teachers may be wary of any new practice that impacts their workload, so initial skepticism itself need not automatically lead to a rejection of a tool under consideration. However, it is important to be aware of the skepticism and the teachers' point of view, so that if the tool is adopted despite any hesitancy, strategies can be employed to facilitate buy-in over time.

EFFICIENCY AND COST

Questions of efficiency and cost are essential in determining the impact of screening activities on a school's budget and delivery of instructional programs. In selecting a screening procedure, school decision makers should aim for procedures that yield the most valuable information in the shortest amount of time while minimizing the financial burden on the district. Efficiency refers to the amount of time required by teachers, administrators, and support staff to administer, score, summarize, analyze, and disseminate the screening assessment. Cost refers to the amount of money required for materials, training, and associated expenses. Although capturing the full impact of large-scale screening on budgets and workloads may be difficult to accomplish, consideration of the following factors can provide a basis for estimating this impact and assist districts in choosing a tool and planning its implementation.

Efficiency   Time is arguably a school's most valuable resource, so an estimate of the amount of time required for test administration, scoring, data entry/summarization, and dissemination is a key consideration in evaluating a screening tool. Time required for screening assessment should be considered in two ways: its cumulative impact on the personnel involved in data collection, and its impact on the instruction the students receive in the classroom. Features of tools that bear on efficiency include administration format (i.e., individual, group, computerized), scoring procedures and aids, and data management tools. Is the tool individually administered (given one-on-one with each child, such as a reading inventory) or group administered? If group administered, how much class time is required for administration, and how much additional time is involved in scoring? Are scoring aids available, such as computerized scan sheets or efficient answer keys?

If individually administered, estimate the average time needed per student to conduct the testing. With timed procedures, such as curriculum-based measurement, testing time required per student will be fairly consistent. Many of these measures involve one-minute samples. Untimed and dynamic procedures, such as reading inventories (e.g., Developmental Reading Assessment), will vary in testing time because additional tasks are given according to student performance. Additionally, some screening procedures do not provide standard administration protocols, leading to greater variation among examiners in the amount of time needed to conduct the assessment. In estimating the amount of time required per student, also consider time for establishing rapport, giving directions, scoring, and transitioning to the next student. Ultimately a one-minute measure may require three to four minutes per student.

Group-administered tasks often are more efficient because several students can be assessed at one time. If these tasks require more overall student time, they might require less teacher/staff time. However, group-administered procedures may have a greater impact on instructional time if they are considerably longer (e.g., 45 minutes) than individual assessments. A key factor to consider is time required for scoring. Although group-administered CBM tasks (e.g., CBM maze, math, spelling, and written expression) are administered very quickly and have very little impact on students' instructional time, they often involve substantial professional (or paraprofessional) time afterward in scoring, checking, and entering the data. Recent technological advances such as computer-based administration and scoring, handheld PCs, and data capture pens have increased the efficiency of scoring but often come at a higher cost and require more training and equipment than old-fashioned pencil-and-paper group-administered tests. However, as the technology becomes more affordable and user-friendly we are likely to see greater implementation of these tools.

Training of personnel to administer and score the assessment, enter data, generate reports, and use the data for decision making also requires substantial time. Training needs may vary according to the amount of skill required for standard administration and interpretation and use of the data. Some tools require follow-up training to ensure that examiners continue to adhere to standard administration procedures and to enhance personnel understanding and use of the information, especially if the information is used for multiple purposes. When considering a tool for adoption or planning your implementation, find out what typical training needs are for that assessment and be sure to plan adequate time for training. Consider how new staff will be trained every year and how those involved in screening will continue to sharpen their skills and understanding in collecting data accurately and using the information effectively. To maximize the efficiency of training, consider any differential involvement of personnel in the screening and plan the training accordingly. For example, if classroom teachers will not be entering data or generating reports because those tasks will be handled by an instructional leader and support staff, teachers do not need to participate in a training session on entering data. However, they might need training on interpreting reports and using the information to make appropriate decisions.

Cost   Any screening procedure will involve some monetary cost to the district. Some costs will be one time, such as the development or purchase of test manuals and reusable materials, and others will be yearly, such as consumable test booklets and renewable software licenses for data management. Even using locally created screening procedures will involve some cost for materials, copying, and considerable professional time for development and training. Training costs likely will involve honoraria and travel for an outside consultant, substitutes for any classroom teachers in attendance, purchase or reproduction of training materials not directly used in screening, and any meals or refreshments provided by the district for the training participants. The *Evaluating Potential Screening Tools* checklist provides for listing estimated costs in three areas: one-time costs for test materials, yearly costs for test materials, and training costs.

TEACHER AND STAFF BUY-IN

Often the biggest challenge in adopting universal screening is not in the selection and purchase of tools, the training of staff, or the compilation of the data so it can be usable, but in helping teachers understand, value, and use the information. Due to the ever-changing nature of education, with assessment and instructional systems coming and going, teachers often are appropriately skeptical about these changes when proposed. The current and likely future degree to which teachers will understand and use the information effectively is a key consideration in selecting a school-wide assessment system. However, initial skepticism is a predictable reaction to large-scale change and is not likely sufficient grounds to remove a tool from consideration. It is important to listen to teachers' expressed concerns and determine which of those reflect true limitations of the tool and which stem from apprehension of a more personal nature.

Common teacher concerns over assessment generally fall into one of three categories: concerns over how the assessment will add to their current workload and impact instructional time, whether the data will lead to unfair judgments of their teaching and/or their students' performance, and trepidation regarding whether using a particular assessment tool will lead to pressure to teach in a manner inconsistent with the teacher's philosophy or expertise. Teachers often need to be assured that the assessment (1) will yield information sufficiently valuable to justify their investment of time; (2) will lead to a fair evaluation of student performance and, by extension, their teaching; and (3) will not lead to punitive or undesirable administrative actions, such as a poor evaluation of their performance, mandated changes in curriculum and instruction, or rigid student retention criteria. Many of these concerns have little to do with the assessment tool itself but reflect a lack of trust in the decision makers' ability to fully consider their interests. Involving the teachers in the selection process is likely to alleviate some of these issues. Teachers can elect representatives to participate on selection committees and periodic reports can be made to the entire faculty during the process to solicit broader teacher input.

Even if the selection process is transparent and democratic, every school is likely to have a small number of teachers who continue to express concerns over the proposed assessment. Unanimous buy-in is not likely at the time a tool is chosen. Some teachers may oppose the undertaking of universal screening at all, in which case no amount of discussion over tools will sway their position. Understanding these teachers' concerns and showing them, rather than telling them, how the process will benefit their students might be necessary in bringing them on board. This can only be accomplished by collecting data and using it to improve decision making in the school. Sometimes teachers are pleasantly surprised that the data validates their preferred instructional approach rather than challenges it, or they find that the information really does help them make useful teaching decisions. Training, implementation, and time often are more effective in facilitating buy-in than any amount of discussion and debate.

Case Example

Lakeside Elementary, a K–5 building located in the suburbs of a medium-sized city in the Midwest, was introduced in Chapter 2. To review, it is one of nine elementary schools in the Woebegone Central School District, which also includes three middle schools and two high schools. In the Woebegone schools, the decisions about universal screening tools were made at a district level. The Assistant Superintendent for Instruction convened a working group with representatives from all nine K–5 buildings to research appropriate tools for use in universal screening of reading and early literacy. This group included classroom and special education teachers, literacy specialists, school psychologists, and building administrators. Individuals throughout the district introduced a variety of tools for consideration, including locally-created assessment materials, published reading inventories, norm-referenced tests, and curriculum-based measures. The group researched the evidence for reliability and validity of the various tools and examined the logistical aspects of adopting each tool. The team considered the budgetary and personnel costs of purchasing materials, training staff, and administering the assessment. They also considered how data would be managed and disseminated so that the information would be maximally useful.

In gathering information about specific tools, the group was able to eliminate a few choices based on lack of evidence for validity, prohibitive cost, or inappropriateness of the data for universal screening decisions. For example, the locally-created assessment was not ultimately considered because it lacked standardization and evidence for reliability. The team discussed the possibility of revising the assessment and collecting information for evaluating validity and reliability, but such a process would be time-consuming and involve a level of research expertise not found in district personnel. The team also removed several individually administered, published norm-referenced tests from consideration due to their excessive cost, time required to administer, and paucity of within-grade items at any level. The remaining choices included a variety of curriculum-based measurement systems and published reading inventories.

After narrowing the potential selection to a range of acceptable choices, team members met with the faculty and staff in their respective buildings to present the choices, answer questions, and solicit input. Although this step may be viewed by some as belaboring the process and inviting dissent, the Woebegone district administrators and universal screening working group members believed it was a necessary measure to facilitate ownership and buy-in once a tool was adopted. They wanted teachers engaged in the screening process, and worked to minimize teacher feelings of having the assessment imposed upon them. Additionally, knowing the specific concerns of teachers regarding any particular tool would be helpful in planning to respond to those concerns in a productive way. Team members led presentations outlining the features, costs, strengths and limitations of each tool under consideration. They recorded the questions and concerns raised by teachers and support personnel regarding the use of each particular tool, and shared those concerns with the district working group.

Not surprisingly, buildings varied in their responses to the list of options. In one building, the teachers were very skeptical about the need for universal screening and rejected every option presented. In other buildings, including Lakeside, the teachers accepted the idea of universal screening but expressed concerns about the options presented. Concerns ranged from why the district was considering universal screening at all, to very specific questions regarding the meaning of the scores produced by the various tools. In some cases, the team needed to research answers to questions raised by building personnel that had not been considered by the working group. Many of the issues centered on the impact of the data collection process on the teacher's role and available instructional time, the validity of the instrument for providing useful information with the potential to inform instruction, and the consequences the screening information for individual children and classroom teachers (e.g., will a child be retained in grade due to a low screening score? Would the data be used as part of the teachers' evaluation process?). The teachers and support personnel at some buildings tended to favor the reading inventories due to their more in-depth nature, and at others the curriculum-based procedures for their research base and efficiency.

The final decision for adopting an assessment tool was made in the spring, after considering information from the working group's own research process as well as the input from the schools. The process of researching the tools and gathering input took about six months, with the working group meeting approximately once every other week. Based on the group's recommendations, the administrators determined that one of the curriculum-based measurement systems under consideration best suited the needs of their district at the time. District administrators worked with building principals to arrange meetings with faculty and staff to introduce the new assessment process and to roll out their plans for implementing the assessment during the following school year.

Using Data to Make Decisions in General Education

DATA-BASED DECISION MAKING AT TIER 1

As reviewed in Chapter 3 there are a number of academic assessments that can be used for instructional decision making. Once the specific assessments are selected and the population to be assessed is identified (e.g., students in grades 1 to 3) a universal assessment plan can be created. This plan should identify the individuals to conduct the universal screenings, specify the training and continuing technical assistance to be provided, outline a schedule identifying when screenings will occur, and most important develop specific procedures for using the data to effectively improve student performance. This chapter will review important activities to be considered during the collection of universal or Tier 1 data, the establishment of student performance criterion, and the graphic illustration of the data. Lastly, a discussion will be provided related to the use of this data to (1) identify instructional priorities and improve instructional planning, (2) evaluate student's response to instruction, (3) identify students at risk for academic failure, and (4) evaluate the effectiveness of general education programming.

COLLECTING AND MANAGING DATA

In our experience most schools initially implementing RTI begin data collection with a limited number of educators and with a targeted student population. We have consulted with many schools that start with universal assessments in the area of literacy targeting students in the primary grades. In fact, this is the strategy employed by the widely implemented

Reading First Initiative. In order to begin, a group of educators (general education, special education, and reading teachers; school psychologists; administrators, etc.) receive training and ongoing support to conduct the universal screenings. All students in the targeted grade levels are typically administered the assessments at the beginning, middle, and end of the academic year. Ultimately, as RTI is diffused across a given school or district additional training and support may be provided for all teachers to conduct progress-monitoring assessments to students in their classrooms across basic skill areas and then into the secondary levels.

Once collected, student data are entered into a data management system at each assessment checkpoint. These results may then be compared to benchmarks, norms, and/or predetermined criterion to assess student performance levels (discussion of establishing performance criterion is presented later in the chapter). The data management system should allow for the results to be analyzed at multiple levels including that of the student, classroom, grade level, school, and/or district. In addition, classroom and/or grade-level results should be comparable across time to see if changes in instructional practices result in student performance gains. Examples of available subscription-based systems to manage this type of data include the DIBELS Monitor and AIMSweb. Free no-frills spreadsheets and graphing templates for managing DIBELS data in grades K to 6 are also available by clicking on the schooltoolz.us hyperlinks in the Resources CD. Among other functions, all three of these versions allow for the input of universal level data, illustrations of it at multiple levels, and comparisons across time.

Graphing Student Data

At Tier 1, data from class-wide or grade-level assessments is graphed to visually illustrate the performance of all students in a given cohort. The DIBELS is perhaps the most widely used primary grade assessment for conducting universal screening in academics (specifically literacy). To assist schools in illustrating and evaluating this universal data DIBELS scoring templates were developed at the State University of New York at Oswego. Graphing templates are Excel spreadsheets designed to perform prearranged functions, in this case to display DIBELS results. DIBELS scoring templates are available for grades K to 6 and include columns for input of student names and scores from appropriate DIBELS tasks according to grade level. Figure 4.1 is an illustration of a template displaying the data from a kindergarten benchmark assessment.

The templates can be accessed at http://www.schooltoolz .us/ (hyperlink provided in the Resources CD) by clicking on DIBELS scoring templates. To use these templates download the desired grade level, save to your computer, and read the instructions provided by clicking the "instructions" tab at the bottom of the spreadsheet. As specified, the blue area is for the input of student names and scores (delete contrived data in the blue section first but don't alter cells outside of it as these contain important formulas). When student scores are added descriptive ranges automatically appear in subsequent columns arranged by DIBELS task for each student. As illustrated by Figure 4.1, educators can easily identify and highlight at-risk students requiring intervention based on deficit range scores on one or more tasks.

In addition to displaying proficiency ranges by individual students, the templates also include graphs and tables illustrating the percent and frequency across students in each proficiency level for each task. This is helpful when assigning instructional priorities for the classroom and evaluating overall response to classroom instruction. With each template there are four sheets provided: (1) one for beginning of the year data, (2) one for mid-year, (3) one for end of the year, and (4) a results page that when printed will generate a four-page comparative report illustrating results from across the school year. Figures 4.2 and 4.3 illustrate in graphic and table format the overall second-grade DIBELS performance for one school across the academic year. It would appear from this information that one instructional priority for this class might hinge on increasing reading fluency since 68 percent of students scored in the deficient range during the first assessment.

Based on these data it also appears that while the number and percent of students reaching established ranges of performance increased across the school year (e.g., from 6.15 percent to 46.55 percent), the end goal of having roughly 80 percent of students at established levels of reading fluency was not achieved. This might

Figure 4.1 Universal Screening Data by Students in a Kindergarten Classroom

Student (name)	ISF	LNF	PSF	NWF	ISF Descriptor	LNF Descriptor	PSF Descriptor	NWF Descriptor	Areas Deficient
Jerry	20	31	34	10	Emerging/ Some Risk	Established/ Low Risk	Established/ Low Risk	Emerging/ Some Risk	
Mason	15	27	1	10	Emerging/ Some Risk	Established/ Low Risk	Deficit/At Risk	Emerging/ Some Risk	1 of 4
Tommy	4	27	1	4	Deficit/At Risk	Established/ Low Risk	Deficit/At Risk	Deficit/At Risk	3 of 4
Coleman	28	43	52	34	Established/ Low Risk	Established/ Low Risk	Established/ Low Risk	Established/ Low Risk	
Taneakwa	20	28	9	16	Emerging/ Some Risk	Established/ Low Risk	Emerging/ Some Risk	Established/ Low Risk	
Jason Lee	19	20	33	10	Emerging/ Some Risk	Emerging/ Some Risk	Established/ Low Risk	Emerging/ Some Risk	
Mickie	22	45	35	22	Emerging/ Some Risk	Established/ Low Risk	Established/ Low Risk	Established/ Low Risk	
Allen	17	22	0	5	Emerging/ Some Risk	Emerging/ Some Risk	Deficit/At Risk	Emerging/ Some Risk	1 of 4
Anna	15	19	2	3	Emerging/ Some Risk	Emerging/ Some Risk	Deficit/At Risk	Deficit/At Risk	2 of 4
Khira	21	14	38	25	Emerging/ Some Risk	Deficit/At Risk	Established/ Low Risk	Established/ Low Risk	1 of 4
Shyteka	5	12	0	0	Deficit/At Risk	Deficit/At Risk	Deficit/At Risk	Deficit/At Risk	4 of 4
Joey	6	6	0	0	Deficit/At Risk	Deficit/At Risk	Deficit/At Risk	Deficit/At Risk	4 of 4
Navtavone	21	39	38	42	Emerging/ Some Risk	Established/ Low Risk	Established/ Low Risk	Established/ Low Risk	
Justintime	20	23	12	13	Emerging/ Some Risk	Emerging/ Some Risk	Emerging/ Some Risk	Established/ Low Risk	
Monaray	21	28	44	21	Emerging/ Some Risk	Established/ Low Risk	Established/ Low Risk	Established/ Low Risk	
Alex	17	40	15	10	Emerging/ Some Risk	Established/ Low Risk	Emerging/ Some Risk	Emerging/ Some Risk	

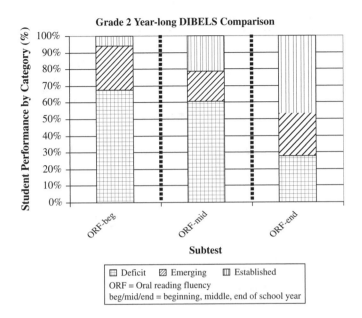

A graph from
the DIBELS
scoring
template

suggest the need for revisions in the curriculum and/or instructional practices prior to the next school year.

In addition to the DIBELS template the website has a norm generator that can be used to quickly analyze class or grade-level progress-monitoring data. The template includes a spreadsheet section where student data can be input at a given assessment checkpoint. After data entry is complete the user can click on the "graphing" button, which will graphically display the student data in addition to the mean score and demarcations for one standard deviation above and below the mean. This information

Figure 4.3 A comparative table from the DIBELS scoring template

Subtest	Descriptor	N	%
ORF-beg	Deficit	44	67.69%
	Emerging	17	26.15%
	Established	4	6.15%
ORF-mid	Deficit	40	60.61%
	Emerging	12	18.18%
	Established	14	21.21%
ORF-end	Deficit	16	27.59%
	Emerging	15	25.86%
	Established	27	46.55%

Figure 4.4

Norm
generator
graph
example

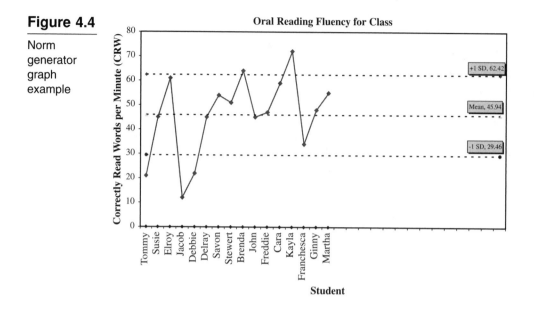

assts users to develop local norms (see discussion below) and to
identify at-risk students. An example of the norm generator graph
is included in Figure 4.4.

These basic graphic displays of student data allow educational teams to assess student performance across time, identify
and assist struggling students, and use data to improve instructional practices. While graphic displays of data are an important
element in a data-based decision-making process, another important consideration is the establishment of student performance
criteria. These criteria are specific performance goals to which
actual student performance can be compared. This allows for
focused goal setting as well as objective data-based decision
making. In the following section we examine the most poplar
methods for establishing student performance criterion.

ESTABLISHING STUDENT PERFORMANCE CRITERION

An important activity for school-based teams implementing RTI
models is the establishment of student performance criteria to set
instructional goals and to gauge the success of the RTI implementation. Three generally accepted procedures for setting performance criterion include the use of pre-established benchmarks,

norms (either national or local), and cut scores predictive of success on high-stakes state exams. Generally, schools or districts use a combination of these methods depending on availability and the purpose of the evaluation. Each of these areas is discussed below in terms of a review of the technique, the use of data gleaned from it, and the pros and cons of using each specific criterion.

Pre-Established Benchmarks   In general terms benchmarks are empirically based performance levels predictive of latter academic success. Perhaps the most widely applied benchmarks in contemporary models of school-based RTI are the DIBELS benchmarks based on the work of Roland Good and colleagues at the University of Oregon. As described by Good:

> the DIBELS benchmark goals are established not based on norms, but based on odds of achieving subsequent literacy outcomes. For students identified as needing intensive intervention the odds were 26% of achieving 40 or more words read correct on the end of first grade DORF [DIBELS Oral Reading Fluency] assessment. For students identified as strategic, the odds were 59%. Most important, for students meeting the middle kindergarten benchmark goals, the odds were 88% of reading 40 or more words correct per minute at the end of first grade on the DORF assessment. (Good et al., in press, p. 32)

Table 4.1 is an example of the DIBELS literacy benchmarks for first-grade students. As illustrated in the table, student performance ranges are presented for each of the first-grade DIBELS assessments across the beginning, middle, and end of the year checkpoints.

Use of Data   Comparing student performance levels to established DIBELS benchmarks allows for structured goal setting, the identification of students requiring additional instructional support, and the evaluation of core curriculum and instruction. For example, based on the first-grade benchmarks important instructional goals would be for 80 percent to 100 percent of students in a given school to identify 37 or more letters per minute

Table 4.1 First-grade DIBELS benchmark goals

First Grade DIBELS Measure	DIBELS Benchmark Goals and Indicators of Risk—Three Assessment Periods per Year					
	Beginning of Year Month 1–3		Middle of Year Month 4–6		End of Year Month 7–10	
	Scores	Status	Scores	Status	Scores	Status
DIBELS Letter Naming Fluency	LNF < 25 25 <= LNF < 37 LNF >= 37	At risk Some risk Low risk				
DIBELS Phoneme Segmentation Fluency	PSF < 10 10 <= PSF < 35 PSF >= 35	Deficit Emerging Established	PSF < 10 10 <= PSF < 35 PSF >= 35	Deficit Emerging Established	PSF < 10 10 <= PSF < 35 PSF >= 35	Deficit Emerging Established
DIBELS Nonsense Word Fluency	NWF < 13 13 <= NWF < 24 NWF >= 24	At risk Some risk Low risk	NWF < 30 30 <= NWF < 50 NWF >= 50	Deficit Emerging Established	NWF < 30 30 <= NWF < 50 NWF >= 50	Deficit Emerging Established
DIBELS Oral Reading Fluency			ORF < 8 8 <= ORF < 20 ORF >= 20	At risk Some risk Low risk	ORF < 20 20 <= ORF < 40 ORF >= 40	At risk Some risk Low risk

Source: Retrieved from the official DIBELS web site, May 5, 2008 at http://dibels.uoregon.edu/.

by the fall of first grade and by the end of first grade to identify 35 or more sounds per minute in PSF, 50 or more sounds in NWF, and 40 or more words per minute in DORF. Additionally, students scoring in the deficit or at-risk ranges could be offered additional assessment and instructional support to remediate identified skill deficiencies. The DIBELS offers instructional recommendations (e.g., need for strategic or intensive remediation) based on the student's pattern of performance on the beginning and mid-year assessments (see Good et al., 2002, for more information). Lastly, in terms of evaluating the core curriculum and instruction, the DIBELS benchmarks allow for end of the year results to be compared to the beginning of the year scores and the student performance goals set prior. If 80 percent to 100 percent of students reach end of the year literacy goals, then the first-grade program would be deemed to be effective; if not, steps would be taken to strengthen instruction. Other resources related to bench-mark assessments may be found at the National Center on Student Progress Monitoring (http://www.studentprogress.org/), The National Research Center on Learning Disabilities (http://www.nrcld.org/), and the Center on Instruction (http://www.centeroninstruction.org/index.cfm).

Pros and Cons   The strength of using pre-established benchmarks as the student performance criterion is that these levels of perform-ance have been shown to predict latter academic success. The DIBELS benchmarks have served as important literacy targets for thousands of primary grade students and allow for an assess-ment of general instruction, an identification of at-risk students, and intervention goals for targeted instruction. The primary weakness of the benchmark approach is that the research in academic areas other than reading and with students beyond the primary grade levels is less well established. In math, for example, there is less agreement on what constitutes appropriate curriculum at each grade level, making the establishment of performance benchmarks more difficult. Further, as students progress into intermediate and secondary levels, the required academic skills are more concep-tual and complex. This too makes establishing accurate progress-monitoring techniques and corresponding benchmark levels of performance more challenging at these levels.

Norms

Since the empirically validated techniques for progress monitoring are standardized with respect to administration directions, scoring procedures, and (to the extent possible) difficulty level, normative information related to student performance can be collected and used as a comparative criterion. Norms can be generated either at (1) a national/general level based on performance scores reported from research studies or demonstration projects or (2) at a local level using school or district data at each grade level sampled. Use of local norms allows for peer comparisons that may be more representative of student performance at a given school or in a given district. This may be of particular appeal to urban school districts or those with diverse populations or non-typical proportionality given the valid concerns with the appropriateness of national norms being applied to these types of student populations. More information related to the development of local norms can be found at Habedank (1995).

Schools and districts starting the RTI process will likely begin with CBM norms available from the literature. Table 4.2 comes from a technical report from the University of Oregon collapsing

Table 4.2 National Norms for Oral Reading Fluency (20 states, over 15,000 students)

Second Grade Descriptive Statistics for ORF Scores by Season			
Season	Fall	Winter	Spring
Mean	55.49	72.85	89.28
Standard Deviation	37	40.62	41.95
10th Percentile	11	18	31
20th Percentile	20	33	54
25th Percentile	25	42	61
30th Percentile	30	49	68
40th Percentile	41	61	79
50th Percentile	51	72	89
60th Percentile	62	84	100
70th Percentile	72	94	111
75th Percentile	79	100	117
80th Percentile	86	107	124
90th Percentile	106	125	142

Source: Technical Report 33, Oral Reading Fluency, 90 years of Measurement. Behavioral Research and Training, Eugene, OR, 2005.

results from multiple studies to offer national norms with respect to oral reading fluency by grade level and time of the year. While the report offers ORF norms for grade 1 to 8, the second grade information is used below for illustrative purposes.

These norms allow for a criterion to which the results of second grade ORF assessments from typical school districts may be compared. As with benchmarks, norms allow for structured goal setting, the identification of students requiring additional instructional support, and the evaluation of core curriculum and instruction. In addition to student performance levels, norms can be created to illustrate students' rates of progress across time.

In a widely disseminated study, Fuchs et al. (1993) identified the rates of student progress across time with a variety of CBM techniques. Table 4.3 is an adaptation of the Fuchs' findings illustrating expected rates of progress in the area of oral reading fluency. Here the mean slope indicates the average rate of improvement for the students sampled, the ambitious slope scores are rates of improvement that might be expected in response to effective supplemental instructional services. The latter slope scores are used in attempts to remediate low-performing students and to catch them up to peers in terms of performance. The standard deviations presented here are used to compute progress levels significantly below the mean. Students with progress assessed one or more standard deviations below the mean for their grade level could be flagged for more intense intervention services.

Table 4.3 Predictions for Rates of Weekly Reading Growth on One-Minute Oral Reading Fluency Assessments by Grade

Grade	Mean slope	Ambitious Slope	Standard Deviation
1	2	3	.8
2	1.5	2	.7
3	1	1.5	.5
4	.85	1.1	.3
5	.5	.8	.3
6	.3	.65	.3

Adapted from Fuchs, Fuchs, Hamlett, Waltz, and Germann, 1993. Means and SDs rounded off for clarity.

Use of Data   Fuchs and Fuchs (2001, 2006) outline an RTI model based on norms whereby students scoring below the 25th percentile on tests of achievement are monitored in terms of their response to classroom instruction (ideally weekly with CBM techniques) for eight weeks. For example, using the information in Table 4.2 when assessing a typical second-grade classroom for oral reading fluency, students scoring below 25 correct words per minute on the fall assessment (25th percentile) would ideally be progress monitored weekly for eight weeks. At the end of the eight-week interval a rate of improvement (slope) would be computed for each student. For Tier 1 instruction assessed growth over time that was above the 16th percentile (within one standard deviation of the mean) would be deemed as adequate. Students with progress below that level would be administered Tier 2 instruction. Based on the information in Table 4.3, then second-grade students with rates of progress at or below .8 words per week (mean 1.5 –SD .7 = .8) would be provided Tier 2 intervention, including daily instruction in group sizes of 3 to 1 and empirically based (standard protocol) procedures. Students continuing to demonstrate both performance deficits (scoring over one standard deviation below peers or national performance levels) as well as deficits in terms of their rate of progress (e.g., slope over one standard deviation below peers or national performance levels) would be referred for a comprehensive and individualized evaluation consistent with IDEIA procedural provisions.

Pros and Cons   Some advantages to using norms for performance criterion are that comparisons may be made both of student performance *and* rate of progress. These comparisons may be used to objectively identify students for more intense levels of intervention, and in the case of local norms these comparisons may be representative of the student population at a given school or district. As opposed to benchmark procedures, however, one distinct weakness that normative approaches have is uncertainty in predicting student success. For instance, while DIBELS benchmarks are established based on the odds of achieving latter important literacy outcomes, norms simply describe the performance of a given population. National norms may not be reflective of the performance of diverse student populations, whereas achieving performance levels within a standard deviation of local norms may not predict later student academic success. One procedure that has been reported in the literature to overcome this inherent weakness is to establish local cut scores predictive of success on high-stakes state exams.

Cut Scores

Given the national emphasis on high-stakes state assessments pursuant to No Child Left Behind legislation, an emerging body of research has investigated the establishment of criterion levels of student performance on CBM assessments that predict success on statewide assessments. As summarized by Deno (2003):

> Students reading at least 40 words correctly in 1 minute by the end of first grade are on a trajectory to succeed in learning to read, and students reading more than 110 words correctly in 1 minute by the beginning of third grade are most likely to pass their state assessments in Oregon (Good et al., 2001). Eighth-grade students who can read at least 145 words from local newspaper passages correctly in 1 minute are almost certain to pass the Minnesota Basic Skills Test in reading (Muyskens & Marston, 2002)." (p. 189)

These cut scores have also been referred to in the literature as target scores as they provide a criterion target to shoot for that, while not guaranteeing success on state assessments, certainly increases the likelihood of that outcome. Districts that have collected universal CBM progress monitoring information and have received the student's subsequent performance on state assessments are well poised to establish predictive cut scores.

McGlinchey and Hixson (2004) provide some direction for districts wanting to develop these cut scores. They compiled fourth grade CBM reading data on over 1,300 students over eight years of investigation. One goal of the study was to set criterion levels or cut scores for reading CBM performance that was predictive of passing the fourth grade Michigan state assessment in reading. The authors discuss how different cut scores can be established based on the desired level of confidence. For example, in their sample of the fourth grade students a cut score of 100 correct words per minute on the CBM reading task predicted 74 percent of students who passed the state assessment. Using a higher cut score can increase the probability of predicting a passing score on the state assessment, but it also decreases odds of predicting failure. For example, McGlinchey and Hixson found in their sample that by increasing the cut score to 140 CRWs on the CBM reading task, 84 percent of students at that level passed the state assessment. However, 39 percent of students not reaching that cut score also passed the state assessment. Obviously the goal here is to establish cut scores that best identify both students likely to pass the state assessments as well as those likely to be unsuccessful.

Use of Data   Districts establishing these types of cut scores have the ability to intervene with students early in the year (or even a year prior) given that predictive criterion levels can be established. Further, CBM goals can be established that assist educators in monitoring students toward success on high-stakes state exams. As an applied example the senior author collaborated with a local elementary school where student progress monitoring with CBM had been conducted over the course of three years. After analyzing the performance data it was found that students scoring 60 CRWs (correct read words) or higher on CBM assessments during the winter of third grade reliably passed the NYS English Language Arts (ELA) assessment in January of the fourth grade. Further, students reading at 110 CRWs in December of fourth grade had almost a 100 percent passing rate on the fourth grade NYS ELA exam given that following month. These cut scores were used to identify at-risk students and also to set specific target goals for students receiving literacy interventions; for third grade students the goal was 60 CRWs by mid-December, and for fourth grade students it was 110 CRWs for mid-December.

Pros and Cons   The obvious strength of this technique is that it directly relates the student progress monitoring data to the variable of most concern to educators: state assessment results. With early identification, students likely to fail these exams can be remediated across time and their progress charted. Cut scores or target scores provide a goal that predicts success on these high-stakes exams and allow for targeted instruction toward that goal. This technique is not without limitations however. As with other CBM-related criterion at the secondary level, student performance on these brief measures is less predictive of success on high-stakes exams. For example, one study found the relationship between oral reading fluency and state assessment success to be high in the third grade but only moderate by grade eight (Silberglitt, Burns, Madyun, & Lail, 2006). Further, in academic areas other than reading, less empirical support exists for this procedure. In math, for example, in order for CBM scores to predict state assessments the CBM probes would need to randomly sample curriculum from across the given school year and the sampled curriculum would need to be well aligned with the state standards upon which the state assessment was derived.

DATA-BASED DECISION MAKING: TIER 1

Thus far the chapter has discussed the collection and management of Tier 1 data and reviewed graphs commonly used to facilitate effective educational decision making. Further, we have high-lighted common methods for establishing student performance criteria including benchmarks, norms, and cut scores. For each of these techniques a description was offered along with common uses of the data, and pros and cons were identified. The perform-ance criteria selected will vary by student population, grade level, and the academic task being assessed, and often more than one technique will be implemented (e.g., benchmarks and cut scores).

Putting it all together to improve instructional practices and student performance will require that the data collected and graphed be reviewed by educational teams and compared to established performance criteria. This information will then in-form specific decision making at multiple levels including the classroom, the student, and ultimately across multiple years at school or district levels. At the classroom level, data will be used in the identification of instructional priorities and to assess progress toward desired levels of classroom proficiency. Further classroom data will be used to identify at-risk students and to periodically configure instructional groupings based on need. Decision making at the student level will include the identification of skill deficiencies to inform intervention design and the assessment of the student's RTI both in terms of performance as well as rate of progress. Given that Tier 1 instruction has been demonstrated to be effective, student performance, rate of progress, and level of instructional need can then be used to decide those students who require consideration for Tier 2 services. Specific use of student-level data is covered in some depth in Chapters 6 and 7. In terms of the bigger picture, annual goals can be evaluated with respect to increases in student performance on progress monitoring assessments and high-stakes state exams. This process assists with measuring the impact of improved instructional practices and with meeting the Adequate Yearly Progress (AYP) provisions of No Child Left Behind (NCLB) legislation. The use of Tier 1 data is discussed in some depth below as it pertains to the classroom and also to AYP provisions of NCLB.

Decisions Based on Classroom Data

Progress monitoring information collected on a given classroom during the beginning of the year assessment check point is typically reviewed to first identify at-risk students. This identification is largely based on the selected performance criterion as previously discussed. Options for designating students "at risk" include the use of benchmarks (e.g., DIBELS performance ranges), students scoring below a certain level on local or national norms (e.g., below 1 SD), and students with performance below pre-established cut scores predictive of latter success on state exams. Once an at-risk student is identified on progress monitoring assessments typically more in-depth skills assessments are conducted to verify that a given student indeed has skills in need of remediation and to assist in grouping the student with others with similar instructional needs. At this point in the process some school RTI models will refer low-performing students for Tier 2 supplemental services while other models provide at least one round of Tier 1 service in the classroom. This decision largely depends on school policy, availability of resources, the intensity of the instructional need, and perhaps the age or grade of the student. Subsequent benchmark assessments can be used to identify students who become at risk across the course of time and to periodically reconfigure instructional groupings based on need.

Classroom data can also be used to assist in the identification of instructional priorities. For instance, primary grade DIBELS benchmark assessments can be useful in determining the percentages of students reaching proficiency levels in important preliteracy skills. Since many of these skills are sequentially developed, teachers can use student data to focus instruction on, for instance, phonemic awareness and letter identification and then focus more on decoding when data suggests that these earlier skills were developing. Teachers conducting the progress monitoring assessment also have the opportunity to observe qualitative indications of missing skills such as patterns of errors that are consistent across students. For instance, if in a math CBM assessment several students demonstrate difficulties with a similar skill (e.g., division with a remainder), then a review of the material would be warranted.

Lastly, classroom data is reviewed across time to see if overall student proficiency is progressing according to plan. Goals for classroom-level progress depend on the assessments, grade level, and criterion used. Goals may include that 80 percent of students reach established pre-literacy levels on end of year DIBELS assessments, that 84 percent of students score within one standard deviation of the mean on national norms for CBM tasks, or that an increasing percentage of students perform higher than established cut scores on progress monitoring tasks and subsequently on the state exam.

THE BIGGER PICTURE: AYP

The use of proficiency goals for CBM tasks across years has been used as a model for districts to meet the Adequate Yearly Progress (AYP) provisions of NCLB. To develop this type of model a district would have to establish end-of-the-year CBM scores that indicated grade level proficiency (e.g., Fuchs, 2004). We have previously discussed the use of benchmarks, norms, and cut scores that would be suitable for this, though cut scores may best predict specific state exam performance. Once minimum proficiency scores are established for each grade and for the academic tasks of interest (e.g., reading, math), then the end of the year grade-level assessments are reviewed. The number or percentage of students meeting the proficiency level at each grade is computed. That number is termed the "initial proficiency status" as it represents the initial status of student performance and will serve as a baseline level. Next the discrepancy between the initial proficiency status and the universal proficiency level is computed. Universal proficiency is determined by NCLB, which stipulates that the goal for 2013–2014 school year is for 100 percent of students to meet or exceed a minimum proficiency level. Educators can easily determine the discrepancy between the initial proficiency status and universal proficiency, then divide that by the number of years they have to meet universal proficiency for the end of the 2013–2014 school year. This will allow them to chart their progress toward that long-term goal.

Data-Based Decision Making at Tier 1

Drawbridge Elementary School was particularly interested in increasing student performance on the third grade state literacy exam. With this goal in mind the administration, teachers, and support staff engaged in a structured process to improve student performance. This process included the establishment of performance criterion levels and reviewing universal screening results to establish instructional priorities and identify at-risk students. The process went on further to assess progress across multiple years the school established AYP goals. Each of these steps is described briefly in the following sections.

ESTABLISHING PERFORMANCE CRITERIA

In reviewing past CBM results the school developed predictive cut scores both for the fall and winter of third grade that predicted success on the state assessment given in the early spring. They found that students reading under 40 correct words per minute in third grade text in September were most likely to be unsuccessful on the exam. Additionally, they found that more than 90 percent of students scoring over 64 correct read words by mid-December were successful in passing the state literacy assessment. The school used this information to interpret the screening results obtained that fall.

REVIEW OF UNIVERSAL SCREENING RESULTS

Third grade screening results were reviewed that fall. The data indicated that 30 percent of students entering third grade performed below the predictive cut off of 40 correct read words (CRW) per minute and that several students had barely met the performance criterion. These results were used in two ways. First the teachers agreed that literacy instruction would be an instructional priority for them. They discussed ways to improve reading performance, including additional sight word instruction, an expanded literacy block for instruction, and peer-assisted learning procedures that had been shown to be effective in increasing students' reading fluency. Secondly, they agreed to conduct additional reading assessments on the at-risk students, those scoring below 40 CRWs on the fall screening. These students would be given extra small-group instruction in the classroom and monitored weekly to assess their response. The goal was for these students to get on a learning trajectory whereby they would achieve at or above the winter criterion of 64 CRWs by mid December.

AYP

In addition to the third-grade results discussed prior, the school also analyzed student CBM results at the end of the second grade. Not surprisingly they found that students with low oral reading fluency scores at the end of second grade (below 32 CRWs) could be accurately predicted to score poorly on the third grade state literacy assessment.

In reviewing 2009–2010 end-of-the-year CBM assessment results for second-grade students in the area of reading, the results suggested that 80 percent of these students obtained CBM scores at a minimum level of proficiency such that they were likely to pass the state reading exam administered in the winter of third grade. The discrepancy between the initial proficiency rate of 80 percent and the goal of 100 percent proficiency was determined to be 20 percent. This 20 percent was divided by four—the number of years before the conclusion of the 2013–2014 school year (the NCLB target for 100 percent proficiency). This suggests that for Drawbridge an annual increase of 5 percent is required to meet the universal proficiency goal. Therefore, annual goals were set up for each of the subsequent school years whereby at the end of the next year, 85 percent of second-grade students would reach proficiency, 90 percent by the year after, and so on. In addition to tracking the CBM proficiencies, the school also tracked student performance on the third-grade state exam to ensure that predicted success was actually achieved on state tests.

SUMMARY

In this chapter we have covered the use of data at the universal or Tier 1 level. This includes the establishment of student performance criterion, the visual display of data, and the use of this data. With respect to the use of data we discussed the establishment of instructional priorities and the identification of at-risk students using different common performance criterion and the establishment of AYP goals. Lastly, the chapter concludes with a case example that illustrates how one school used the data-based decision-making process to improve state literacy exam performance for their third-grade students.

This concludes the second section of our book focused on Tier 1 service within the RTI framework. What follows is the third part of the practitioners' guide focused on intervention and problem-solving activities that occur at the second tier of RTI service delivery. These activities would include the development of student interventions; goal setting, monitoring, and graphing; and Tier 2 data-based decision making.

TIER 2: TARGETED INTERVENTIONS AND PROBLEM SOLVING FOR STUDENTS AT RISK FOR FAILURE

III

PART

Developing Interventions

5
Chapter

A T ITS CORE, the RTI model depends upon schools having the ability to select the right evidence-based interventions and to implement them successfully with struggling students. Yet surprisingly, neither of the two pieces of federal legislation that have most encouraged school systems across the nation to embrace RTI—the No Child Left Behind Act of 2001 and the Individuals With Disabilities Education Improvement Act of 2004—provides a specific definition of the term "intervention." For the purposes of this chapter, we will use the definition adopted by the Wisconsin-based Responsive Education for All Children (REACh) initiative, which describes intervention as "the systematic use of a technique, program, or practice designed to improve learning or performance in specific areas of student need" (Dohrn, Volpiansky, Kratochwill, & Sanetti, 2007).

The term "intervention footprint" (Wright, in press) can be used to signify the cumulative effort required by a school to assess the educational needs of a struggling student, select one or more evidence-based interventions to match those needs, package the intervention(s) into a coherent plan, implement the plan, and verify the integrity with which that plan is carried out. Certainly, much research is still to be done on school-based interventions, including clarifying the intervention components that have the greatest impact on student achievement (Glover & DiPerna, 2007), identifying effective interventions in subject areas other than early reading (Fuchs & Deshler, 2007), and isolating those key variables that will increase the probability that interventions will be successfully implemented in typical school settings where resources are scarce (Kratochwill & Shernoff, 2004). Nonetheless, there is enough known at present about school-based interventions to allow us to describe in some detail how schools can use interventions most effectively. The remainder of this chapter describes the role that interventions play in the RTI model, provides guidance in the design and implementation of interventions in educational settings, and offers recommendations for evaluating the integrity with which those interventions are actually carried out.

MODELS FOR PLANNING INTERVENTIONS: STANDARD TREATMENT PROTOCOL VERSUS PROBLEM-SOLVING MODEL

If a student requires more assistance with academic or behavioral problems than classroom teachers alone can provide, more intensive interventions may be developed and delivered to that student in small groups (*standard-treatment protocols*) or in the form of customized intervention plans developed for just that student (*problem-solving model*). The current research base shows no clear evidence that either a standard protocol or problem-solving method results in more effective interventions (Glover & DiPerna, 2007).

STANDARD-TREATMENT PROTOCOL

A group-based intervention in which all students receive the same treatment is known as the *standard treatment protocol* (Daly, Martens, Barnett, Witt, & Olson, 2007). Groups of four to seven students can be an efficient vehicle for delivering interventions and may even result in better outcomes than one-to-one instruction (National Reading Panel, 2000). Because standard-protocol interventions are typically delivered in a uniform way to all children in the group, however, it can be difficult to modify specific variables in the collective intervention to match that intervention more closely to an individual student's needs (Daly, Martens, Barnett, Witt, & Olson, 2007).

Elementary schools can consider one of three options when scheduling group-based interventions (Burns & Gibbons, 2008). One option is for each classroom to schedule its own time for group interventions; the teacher is able to schedule those interventions to conform to the rest of the class schedule. A second possibility is for the school to schedule a single, daily building-wide time when *all* classrooms engage in group-level interventions. This shared time allows teachers to collaborate within and even across grades. Shared intervention time permits the school to pool all the students with a shared intervention need at a grade level and assign them to a single teacher who can run a reading group targeting their skill deficits. A third option, which Burns & Gibbons (2008) refer to as "floating RTI," is for schools to identify building personnel who support interventions across classrooms (e.g., reading teachers). These school-wide interventionists would schedule standing blocks of time each day when they would be available to assist all teachers at specific grade levels to run group interventions.

Emerging guidelines drawn largely from reading research suggest that standard protocol interventions should consist of at least three to five 30-minute sessions per week, in a group size not to exceed seven students (Al Otaiba & Torgesen, 2007; National Reading Panel, 2000). Standard protocol interventions should also supplement, rather than replace, core instruction taking place in the classroom.

PROBLEM-SOLVING MODEL

While the standard-treatment protocol is efficient, students cannot always be easily grouped for intervention services. For example, a student may present with unique academic or behavioral concerns that require an individualized treatment plan, have scheduling conflicts that prevent the student from receiving interventions in an existing group, or have failed to respond to a previous standard-protocol intervention.

The process in which student intervention plans are developed on a case-by-case basis is referred to as the *problem-solving model* (Fuchs, Mock, Morgan, & Young, 2003). The problem-solving approach has its origins in a teacher consultation model (Bergan, 1995) in which the student's academic or behavioral problems are identified and analyzed, one or more research-based instructional or behavioral strategies are implemented as a coherent plan, and the plan is evaluated to judge its impact on improving the originally identified student problem (Bergan, 1995).

Within the RTI framework, the problem-solving process is typically conducted by a multidisciplinary team that meets with the student's teacher(s) to develop the individualized intervention plan (e.g., Fuchs, Mock, Morgan, & Young, 2003). An advantage of the problem-solving approach is its flexibility; it can produce customized intervention plans for virtually any academic or behavioral concern. A potential drawback is that this method absorbs considerable resources, including the meeting time required for a multimember team to develop the intervention. Additionally, while research indicates that a team-based problem-solving process may have a positive impact on students with motivational or conduct problems, there is only limited information available at present about the effectiveness of problem-solving teams in developing plans to assist students with significant learning problems (Fuchs & Deshler, 2007).

In its general outline, the problem-solving model includes four steps:

1. *Problem identification.* The student is first identified as requiring intervention assistance through either a universal screening or through a referral from the teacher, other school staff member (e.g., administrator), or perhaps the parent. One goal at the problem-identification stage is to define student concerns in objective, specific, observable terms, because an accurate definition of the student problem substantially increases the probability of selecting an effective intervention (Bergan, 1995). A second goal is to collect information to document the degree to which the student's performance is discrepant from the grade-level instructional or behavioral expectations. A range of data sources can provide useful information at this stage, including direct observation of the student, teacher interview, and curriculum-based measurement.

2. *Problem analysis.* The problem-solving team collects additional information on the student. The team then develops a hypothesis that, in light of available evidence, best explains reason(s) for the student's academic or behavioral problems. The team's hypothesis generation is informed by the knowledge that virtually all student concerns can be best

framed as an interaction between the child and his or her instructional environment (Lentz & Shapiro, 1986). At this stage, the team may use formal tools, such as the Instructional Hierarchy or Brief Experimental Analysis (described later in this chapter), to aid them in their understanding of the student problem.

3. *Intervention planning.* A plan is developed that outlines interventions to be used with the student. Interventions included on the plan are written in a step-by-step "script" format with sufficient detail to allow interventionists to correctly carry out that intervention (Burns & Gibbons, 2008). If the intervention is recurring, the plan includes details about the frequency, session length, and group size of the intervention. If the intervention is contingency-driven, the conditions that will trigger the intervention are specified (Barnett, Daly, Jones, & Lentz, 2004). The problem-solving team also selects appropriate formative methods to monitor student progress during the intervention (e.g., curriculum-based measurement for basic academic skills; direct observation methods for inattention), sets a target goal for student improvement, and schedules a date to meet again to review that student intervention plan.

4. *Plan evaluation.* At the scheduled follow-up meeting, the problem-solving team reviews progress-monitoring data to determine if the student has reached the predetermined intervention goal. For those high-stakes cases in which the student has failed to make adequate progress despite several intervention attempts and is under consideration for a possible special education referral, the team applies decision rules to determine how to proceed.

The IDEIA 2004 federal regulations that provide guidance to schools on the implementation of RTI give no formal direction for evaluating a student's response to intervention. Commentary from the US Department of Education accompanying the 2006 publication of the final IDEIA regulations indicates that specific RTI details, such as plan-evaluation decision rules, are best left to states and school districts. This commentary also states that "what is important is that the group making the [special education] eligibility decision has the information that it needs to rule out that the child's underachievement is a result of a lack of appropriate instruction." (US Department of Education, 2006, p. 46656).

It falls beyond the scope of this chapter to provide a full discussion of the development and application of decision rules to be used by the problem-solving team. Before verifying that a student has failed to respond to intervention in the general-education setting, however, the school should be able to document that several intervention plans were attempted, that those plans were research based and matched appropriately to student concern, that the intervention had sufficient 'treatment strength' to adequately address the student problem, and that the intervention was implemented with integrity (Wright, 2007).

INTERVENTION SUPPORT: A THREE-TIER CONTINUUM

Under the RTI model, interventions are organized into levels or tiers of increasing intensity (Reschly, 2003; Vaughn, 2003). These levels form a continuum of intervention supports, with specific decision points at each tier to determine whether students are making appropriate progress or require referral to the next tier (Fairbanks, Sugai, Guardino, & Lathrop, 2007). Tier 1 interventions are universally available to the entire student body, Tier 2 interventions are individualized to meet the needs of selected students, and Tier 3 interventions are the most intensive available in a school.

Tier 1: Building the Intervention Capacity of the Classroom Teacher

Tier 1 interventions are those that can be delivered in the classroom or throughout the school and are available to all children to address student academic or behavioral concerns (Glover & DiPerna, 2007). Chapter 2 of this book presents guidelines for selecting effective academic programs to strengthen delivery of the core curriculum Tier 1, and Chapter 3 provides instruction in collecting school-wide screening data at Tier 1 that can help teachers to provide classroom instruction that better meets the needs of all students. In the present chapter, we revisit the question of effective Tier 1 instruction and intervention—focusing on how teachers can expand their capacity to consistently use effective whole-group and individual strategies to help the diverse learners in their classroom to achieve academic success.

Class-wide and school-wide interventions appropriate for Tier 1 can conceivably range from those shared teaching practices across classrooms tied to the local curriculum and instructional materials to the idiosyncratic collection of whole-group and individual strategies used by specific teachers. Schools should set up a systematic process to review the standard collection of Tier 1 interventions proposed for use across classrooms or throughout the school to ensure that they are empirically based (Fuchs & Deshler, 2007).

Teachers are expected to serve as the Tier 1 first responders for children who are not achieving academic success. Therefore, it is reasonable to expect that teachers will be responsible for identifying and documenting those research-based instructional practices that they use to differentiate instruction as needed for difficult-to-teach students. Yet schools may find that teachers within the same building vary widely in the quality and number of Tier 1 intervention strategies that they implement. One solution to this lack of consistency of practice across classrooms is to create a school-wide menu of Tier 1 strategies that all teachers would use for any children who show emerging educational difficulties.

There are several advantages to creating a consistent menu of Tier 1 interventions for teachers to use routinely for common academic or behavioral concerns. First, such a menu expands the capacity of teaching staff to appropriately meet the needs of students in their classrooms who present with a wide span of abilities. Second, the school can be assured that, before a student is referred for more intensive interventions, the teacher has first exhausted reasonable efforts in the classroom to remediate that student's area(s) of deficit. Third, teachers may well appreciate being given additional strategies to help them to achieve success with marginal learners.

Schools can create a uniform Tier 1 menu of intervention strategies by following these steps (Wright, in press):

1. *Generate a list of the top academic or behavioral concerns that lead to student referrals for more intensive interventions.* Every school has its own unique mix of reasons why students may commonly be referred for more intensive Tier 2 and Tier 3 interventions. The school can analyze past records of student referrals to compile a list of the most common six to eight academic and/or behavioral reasons why teachers tend to refer students. An elementary school, for example, may review meeting notes of the RTI problem-solving team from the previous year and discover that students were most likely to be referred in their building for poor reading fluency, slow math computation skills, failure to comply with teacher requests, lack of organizational skills, and limited homework completion.

2. *Create a Tier 1 classroom intervention strategies survey.* Once a school-wide list of the top student referral concerns has been generated, the school formats that list as a teacher Tier 1 strategies survey. The survey form lists the most common school-wide referral concerns and allocates space on the form under each concern for teachers to write extended responses.

3. *Survey teachers about effective strategies used in classrooms to address common referral concerns.* The school distributes their Tier 1 strategies survey to be completed by faculty. Teachers are directed to read each referral concern and to write down those whole-group or individual strategies that they use routinely in the classroom at the first sign that one or more students is experiencing difficulty in that academic or behavioral area. Teachers should be encouraged to include sufficient detail in their intervention descriptions to fully explain the strategies that they use.

4. *Collect and organize the strongest classroom intervention ideas into a school-wide Tier 1 intervention menu.* When all teachers have completed the Tier 1 strategies survey, the school collates and reviews the results. The best classroom strategies are collected into a Tier 1 intervention menu organized by referral concern. Before adding any teacher strategy to the Tier 1 intervention menu, of course, the school reviews that strategy to ensure that it is supported in the research as

an effective academic or behavior-management technique (Fuchs & Deshler, 2007). (The school may also choose to add ideas to this intervention menu drawn from research-based articles or other sources.) When completed, the Tier 1 intervention menu is distributed to all teachers in the school.

5. *Set the expectation that—before referring that student for more intensive interventions—teachers will use ideas from the Tier 1 intervention menu and document the student's response.* Students are often identified for Tier 2 services as a result of universal screenings. However, other children may be referred for more intensive interventions by their classroom teachers. For teacher-driven referrals, the school determines minimum expectations about what efforts teachers should make in using Tier 1 interventions for common student concerns prior to their referring the student for higher levels of support. A school may decide, for example, that teachers should attempt at least five ideas drawn from the Tier 1 intervention menu for any student with limited math computation fluency before referring that student for more intensive interventions. For students eventually considered for more intensive interventions, the teacher could be expected to produce classroom data to document those Tier 1 interventions previously attempted. Such documentation might include information about the implementation of each classroom intervention (e.g., When did the intervention begin? How frequently was it used? What was the group size? How long did each session last?) and progress-monitoring data demonstrating the student's response to those Tier 1 interventions.

This five-step approach can assist schools with the potentially tricky process of strengthening their core instructional practices by building a standard Tier 1 menu of intervention strategies that all teachers will use with consistency and confidence. Because the menu is initially built largely upon the current 'best practices' of the building's instructional staff, it acknowledges and capitalizes on teachers' existing intervention skills and expertise. Additionally, teachers who might be resistant to top-down directives about what Tier 1 interventions to use in their classrooms would presumably be more likely to regard ideas developed through such a teacher-driven process as doable. After all, Tier 1 strategies appearing on the school-wide menu would have been selected because they had been used successfully in other classrooms in the same school. And finally, schools can expand their capacity for teacher support by identifying staff who recommend good intervention ideas on the teacher survey and perhaps asking them to serve as peer coaches who can train their fellow instructors as needed in their "specialty" Tier 1 strategies.

Tier 2: Individualized Intervention Plans

Students who fail to make adequate progress with universally available interventions at Tier 1 are selected to receive more intensive intervention supports at Tier 2. Tier 2 interventions are available only to students who show emerging academic or behavioral difficulties and are matched to those students' needs. While the number of students who may receive Tier 2 interventions can vary by school and grade level, a general estimate is that approximately 15 percent of students in a school system may be referred at some point for a Tier 2 intervention plan (Reschly, 2003). However, noting that significant gaps in reading skills are very difficult to remediate after the end of first grade, researchers in early reading interventions recommend that proactive universal reading screenings be conducted in the early primary grades and that the lowest 30 percent of students be selected for group-based Tier 2 interventions (Al Otaiba & Torgesen, 2007).

Tier 2 interventions may be created and delivered either through group-based *standard-treatment protocols* or through the *problem-solving model* as customized student intervention plans. (These alternative intervention development processes are described later in the chapter.) It should be noted that, although in this chapter we describe both the standard-protocol and problem-solving methods as being suitable for Tier 2 interventions, some authors have a somewhat different view. Burns and Gibbons (2008), for example, limit Tier 2 to standard protocol interventions, reserving the problem-solving approach for the more intensive Tier 3 level. Small variations in RTI descriptions are not surprising; after all, RTI is still a fairly new model and there are a number of ongoing attempts to "operationalize" it for school implementation (Barnett, Daly, Jones, & Lentz, 2004).

Tier 3: Intensive Interventions

The final and most intensive level of intervention support under the RTI model is Tier 3. Services at Tier 3 are typically reserved for students with chronic and significant academic deficits or behavioral concerns. In one widely accepted version of the RTI model, students who have failed to make expected progress with those interventions provided in Tiers I (classroom) and 2 (standard-protocol or problem-solving methods) would be referred to special education to determine eligibility for Tier 3 services. That is, the initial discrepancy in academic skills and subsequent poor school performance of these students despite Tier 1 and 2 supports would be viewed as a failure to respond to intervention in the general education setting and thus be regarded as a possible diagnostic indicator of a learning disability (Fuchs, 2003). One widely reported estimate is that about 5 percent of a typical school's students may eventually qualify for Tier 3 support (Donovan & Cross, 2002). Longitudinal research studies of early reading intervention models suggest, however, that the incidence of reading disabilities—now the largest category of Specific Learning Disability—may decline to as little as 1 to 2 percent of the school population if schools are proactive in implementing sufficiently intensive and proactive reading interventions in grades K and 1 (Al Otaiba & Torgesen, 2007).

Alternatively, some school systems may view a general-education student as eligible for special education services despite the fact the student's high-strength intervention plan is successful—because the plan is so resource-intensive that the school requires special education funding to sustain the plan over time (Burns & Gibbons, 2008).

If a student is found to qualify for Tier 3 services, the actual interventions implemented by special educators will continue to be research-based. RTI logic recognizes that special education teachers have no 'magical' teaching strategies that differ qualitatively from those used in general-education classrooms (e.g., Martens, 1993). The main advantage that special education offers within the RTI model is the ability to carry out evidence-based interventions with greater intensity (e.g., smaller group size, longer and more frequent intervention sessions, etc.) than may be feasible in less resource-rich general education settings.

Because Tier 3 intervention plans are highly individualized to match student needs, there are no fixed guidelines for the intensity of services that the student is to receive. It is reasonable to expect, however, that Tier 3 services will at least match the level of intervention support recommended for Tier 2 (a minimum of three to five 30-minute sessions per week, with group size not to exceed seven students) and may well include one-to-one sessions with teaching staff. Along with manipulation of group size and session length, Tier 3 interventions also are likely to include "increasing the explicitness of instruction" (Al Otaiba & Torgesen, 2007, p. 213).

TOOLS FOR SELECTING THE RIGHT INTERVENTION: INSTRUCTIONAL HIERARCHY AND BRIEF EXPERIMENTAL ANALYSIS

Two related conceptual tools that can assist schools in selecting the most effective intervention are the Instructional Hierarchy and Brief Experimental Analysis.

Instructional Hierarchy

An essential task in RTI is to select those evidence-based interventions that best match a student's academic or behavioral needs. Yet students can appear so complex and their learning needs so individualized that the step of choosing the right interventions can seem daunting. The Instructional Hierarchy (Haring, Lovitt, Eaton, & Hansen, 1978) is one tool that can serve as a "dynamic interface between instructional activity and student competence" (Burns, VanDerHeyden, & Boice, 2008, p. 1153) by guiding educators to select appropriate academic interventions based on the student's current stage of learning.

All learners fall somewhere among the four stages of the Instructional Hierarchy—acquisition, fluency, generalization, adaptation—as they learn, practice, consolidate, and apply new skills or knowledge (Haring et al., 1978). Because the earlier stages of Instructional Hierarchy are the most central for schools when planning RTI interventions (Burns & Gibbons, 2008), we will discuss its first three stages. (Specific intervention ideas linked to the Instructional Hierarchy appear in Table 5.1.)

Table 5.1 Instructional Hierarchy: Matching Interventions to Student Learning Stage (Haring et al., 1978)

Learning Stage	Student "Look-Fors"	Which Strategies Are Effective
Acquisition: Exit Goal: The student can perform the skill accurately with little adult support.	• Is just beginning to learn skill • Not yet able to perform learning task reliably or with high level of accuracy	• Teacher actively demonstrates target skill • Teacher uses think-aloud strategy—especially for thinking skills that are otherwise covert • Student has models of correct performance to consult as needed (e.g., correctly completed math problems on board) • Student gets feedback about correct performance • Student receives praise, encouragement for *effort*
Fluency: Exit Goals: The student (1) has learned skill well enough to retain (2) has learned skill well enough to combine with other skills, (3) is as fluent as peers.	• Gives accurate responses to learning task • Performs learning task slowly, haltingly	• Teacher structures learning activities to give student opportunity for active (observable) responding • Student has frequent opportunities to *drill* (direct repetition of target skill) and *practice* (blending target skill with other skills to solve problems) • Student gets feedback on *fluency* and *accuracy* of performance

(*continued*)

Table 5.1   (*Continued*)

Learning Stage	Student "Look-Fors"	Which Strategies Are Effective
		• Student receives praise, encouragement for *increased fluency.*
Generalization: Exit Goals: The student (1) uses the skill across settings, situations and (2) does not confuse target skill with similar skills	• Is accurate and fluent in responding • May fail to apply skill to new situations, settings • May confuse target skill with similar skills (e.g., confusing "+" and "x" number operation signs)	• Teacher structures academic tasks to require that the student use the target skill regularly in assignments. • Student receives encouragement, praise, reinforcers for using skill in new settings, situations. • If student confuses target skill with similar skill(s), the student is given practice items that force him/her to correctly discriminate between similar skills. • Teacher works with parents to identify tasks that the student can do outside of school to practice target skill. • Student gets periodic opportunities to review, practice target skill to ensure maintenance.
Adaptation: Exit Goal: The Adaptation phase is continuous and has no exit criteria.	• Is fluent and accurate in skill • Applies skill in novel situations, settings without prompting • Does not yet modify skill as needed to fit new situations (e.g., child says "Thank you" in all situations, does not use modified,	• Teacher helps student to articulate the *"big ideas"* or core element(s) of target skill that the student can modify to face novel tasks, situations (e.g., fractions, ratios, and percentages link to the big idea of *the part in relation to the whole*; "Thank you" is part of a

equivalent phrases such as "I appreciate your help.")	larger class of *polite speech*).
	• Train for adaptation: Student gets opportunities to practice the target skill with modest modifications in new situations, settings with encouragement, corrective feedback, praise, other reinforcers.
	• Encourage student to set own goals for adapting skill to new and challenging situations.

Adapted from Wright, J. (n.d.). *The instructional hierarchy: Linking stages of learning to effective instructional techniques.* Retrieved October 4, 2008, from http://www.interventioncentral.org/htmdocs/interventions/genAcademic/instrhier.php.

In the *acquisition* stage of the Instructional Hierarchy, the student is in the process of acquiring a new skill and cannot yet perform it with accuracy. The learner at this stage benefits from such instructional strategies as modeling and guided practice. Instructor feedback should be immediate and focus on accuracy, as correct performance of the target skill is paramount. Students should receive praise or other positive reinforcement, with that reinforcement delivered contingent upon the student demonstrating on-task behavior. This "time-based" approach to reinforcement is more likely to encourage the student to apply the steady effort necessary to acquire the skill (Daly, Martens, Barnett, Witt, & Olson, 2007).

Having acquired the skill, the student's next learning goal is to become increasingly proficient in that skill. In this *fluency* stage of the Instructional Hierarchy, the instructor uses strategies that will promote the development of automaticity in the skill, such as structuring learning activities to give the student frequent opportunities for drill (direct repetition of target skill) and practice (blending target skill with other skills to solve problems). The student gets feedback on both fluency and accuracy in performing the skill. That performance feedback is increasingly delayed to allow the student uninterrupted time to practice the skill (e.g., a student may practice math computation problems for 10 minutes before using an answer key to independently check her work) (Burns, VanDerHeyden, & Boice, 2008). As fluency increases, the student receives praise or other reinforcement based on rate of correct performance, an accuracy-based contingency. This reinforcement pattern supports fluency building by explicitly rewarding high response rates (Daly, Martens, Barnett, Witt, & Olson, 2007).

As the student develops fluency in the skill, the teacher seeks to ensure that the student both retains that skill over time and is also able to apply that skill to new situations or settings when appropriate. In this *generalization* stage of the Instructional Hierarchy, the teacher may use such strategies as structuring academic tasks to require that the student use the target skill regularly in assignments and providing reinforcement to the student for using the target skill appropriately in new settings or situations. The instructor also provides the student with opportunities periodically to practice the skill (distributed practice) to ensure that the student maintains the skill over time.

The Instructional Hierarchy can be used flexibly to inform intervention plans. For example, in the area of reading decoding, a student may fall within the fluency stage on the Instructional Hierarchy and thus be assigned to meet daily with a peer tutor to engage in paired reading, a fluency-building strategy (Topping, 1987). Yet, because that same student may be at the acquisition stage in learning unfamiliar reading vocabulary, his intervention plan could also include individual sessions with a paraprofessional four times per week to use incremental rehearsal of vocabulary flashcards to learn new words (MacQuarrie, Tucker, Burns, & Hartman, 2002).

BRIEF EXPERIMENTAL ANALYSIS

One promising method on the horizon for the selection of reading-fluency interventions is Brief Experimental Analysis (BEA). In this approach, a series of intervention components are first identified that target instruction and motivation. In one widely used BEA protocol developed by Daly and colleagues (e.g., Daly, Murdoch, Lillenstein, Webber, & Lentz, 2002), students with reading-fluency delays meet individually with an examiner and are systematically administered each of a series of treatments for a brief period in a single session. Brief treatments used include strategies that target vocabulary development (Phase Drill) and decoding speed (Listening Passage Preview and Repeated Reading). One additional condition assesses motivation by offering the student a tangible reward for improved reading performance (McCurdy, Daly, Gortmaker, & Bonfiglio, 2006). Students are assessed immediately after each short treatment condition to determine if their decoding rate increases as a result of that brief intervention (Burns & Wagner, 2008), with the intervention that shows the greatest effect being selected for the student's intervention plan.

The student's response to the various interventions used in the BEA can provide insight into where that student falls along the Instructional Hierarchy (IH) (McCurdy, Daly, Gortmaker, & Bonfiglio, 2006). Students who do best with the Phased Drill vocabulary intervention, for example, may still be in the acquisition stage of the IH; those benefiting most from one of the two fluency-building treatments would fall in the fluency stage; and those whose reading performance responds most strongly to a reward condition are most likely in the generalization stage of the hierarchy.

BEA has been used successfully to select interventions for individual students (Daly, Murdoch, Lillenstein, Webber, & Lentz, 2002) as well as to choose the optimal intervention for groups of children with reading delays (McCurdy, Daly, Gortmaker, & Bonfiglio, 2006). A recent meta-analysis of Brief Experimental Analysis studies demonstrated a strong effect size (average effect size = 2.8) when the intervention identified as optimal through the BEA was compared to other intervention choices evaluated (Burns & Wagner, 2008).

These results suggest that BEA may eventually—but not immediately—be a helpful tool for schools to reduce guesswork in selecting reading-fluency interventions and to rapidly match students to academic treatments that are likely to be effective. To conduct BEAs, however, educators must first be trained in its fairly rigorous methodology and be able to implement the assessment procedures with a high degree of consistency. Additionally, there is not yet one universally accepted protocol for implementing BEAs, and to date, BEA methods have been developed for reading fluency concerns only (Burns & Wagner, 2008).

DETERMINING WHETHER AN INTERVENTION IS "SCIENTIFIC, RESEARCH-BASED": CHALLENGES

The federal regulations codifying the legislative changes of IDEIA 2004 that now guide districts in the implementation of RTI require that schools use only "scientific, research-based interventions" (U.S. Department of Education, 2006). However, it can be confusing for schools to attempt to judge whether a particular intervention has been sufficiently researched to permit its use under RTI. For interventions to meet RTI expectations, they must demonstrate positive outcomes in controlled research studies. Ideally, though, those interventions should also show evidence that they can be feasibly implemented in real-world educational settings, using only the resources typically available in public schools.

The first responsibility of a school when evaluating an intervention, then, is to judge the quality of the research that supports it. However, at present no universal guidelines exist in schools for identifying those interventions that are evidence-based (Odom, Brantlinger, Gersten, Horner, Thompson, & Harris, 2005).

One source that schools can turn to for objective information about research-based interventions is the What Works Clearinghouse (WWC; http://ies.ed.gov/ncee/wwc), a website sponsored by the Institute of Education Sciences, US Department of Education. Describing itself as "a central and trusted source of scientific evidence for what works in education," the WWC evaluates the efficacy of commercial intervention products by analyzing those studies that meet its guidelines for research quality. Advantages of the WWC are that it serves as an impartial judge of intervention effectiveness and uses a rigorous methodology to screen out flawed studies from its analysis. A significant disadvantage is that the WWC must depend upon existing studies of commercial intervention products for its analysis. An example demonstrates this drawback. In an August 2008 intervention report, the WWC summarized the results of its attempt to review Open Court, a K–6 reading program widely used in American schools (What Works Clearinghouse, 2008). Of 30 reports published or released on the Open Court reading series, WWC did not identify a single one that met the organization's standards of acceptability. As a result, the WWC was "unable to draw any conclusions" about the effectiveness of Open Court (What Works Clearinghouse, 2008, p. 1).

Another constraint on the goal of making evidence-based interventions available in schools is that the research base is uneven. While the body of research supporting early reading interventions is large and growing, academic strategies targeting mathematics, science, and other content areas are not yet as well studied (Glover & DiPerna, 2007; Vaughn & Fuchs, 2003).

Yet another major research question looms for educators striving to implement evidence-based interventions: To what degree is an intervention 'transportable' from the sheltered conditions of highly controlled and often well-resourced research studies to real-world school settings that are often resource poor (Kratochwill & Shernoff, 2004)? A research-supported intervention may demonstrate efficacy—strong effects under research conditions—but fail ultimately to show efficiency—widespread adoption in typical classrooms (Walker, 2004). For example, Al Otaiba and Torgensen (2007) note in their review of intensive early reading intervention studies that "to date, most of the intensive interventions have been conducted by well-trained project staff rather than school personnel and even researchers who did train classroom teachers to implement intervention provided considerable support" (p. 220).

Kratochwill and Shernoff (2004) propose a four-part continuum of research intended to study 'evidence-based interventions' (EBIs) as they move through the implementation pipeline from initial development to full use in applied settings. *Efficacy* studies are carried out using a tightly controlled research protocol. The goal at this initial stage is to establish clear experimental control to determine whether the intervention shows promise as an academic or behavioral treatment. *Transportability* studies examine the intervention in applied settings such as schools, paying close attention to such implementation variables as treatment acceptability, cost, and training requirements. *Dissemination* studies focus on intervention agents, such as reading teachers or school psychologists, and practices that will promote the successful adoption of the intervention in a school environment. *System evaluation* studies attempt to evaluate the intervention supported only with the resources typically available in a school. Their purpose is to determine those system variables that may support or hinder use of the intervention in natural school settings. While the EBI movement shows promise in building a research database with the capability to capture a full range of EBI implementation variables, that work is still in its formative stages (Kratochwill & Shernoff, 2004).

At present, then, educators must deal with a lack of agreement in public education about how to define evidence-based interventions, limited data regarding effectiveness of many commercial curriculum and intervention products, an uneven research base on interventions other than reading, and uncertainty about the transportability of interventions to applied educational settings. Schools can address these research limitations in three ways. First, they should regularly update their knowledge of current research into effective interventions. Second, they should not depend solely on publishers' assurances that commercial instructional or intervention products are "evidence-based." Rather, schools should use local RTI data collected on group and individual student academic performance to formatively evaluate core instruction and interventions and discard those practices that appear ineffective. For example, if a school's universal screening data show that the median student at a given grade level is performing below benchmark in reading fluency, the school should consider revamping the reading curriculum (Burns & Gibbons, 2008). Finally, schools should be knowledgeable of basic components of effective academic interventions and screen published materials to ascertain whether they make use of those components (Burns, VanDerHeyden, & Boice, 2008).

ACADEMIC INTERVENTIONS: KEY RESEARCH-BASED BUILDING BLOCKS

When considering commercial intervention materials, educators must set aside time and wade through often-flawed or limited studies to investigate claims of publishers that those materials are indeed research-based. In addition, schools are frequently presented with students whose unique learning needs cannot easily be addressed by an off-the-shelf intervention product. A solution in both instances is for schools to understand basic components, or building blocks, of effective academic instruction that are particularly suited for struggling learners. Before purchasing commercial materials, schools can verify that they incorporate basic instructional practices that promote student academic growth (Burns, VanDerHeyden, & Boice, 2008). If commercial materials do not exist or are not readily available to address a student's academic problems, schools can customize their own intervention plans using these essential academic intervention components as a guide. Here are six "big ideas" that research supports for academic interventions with whole groups and individual students:

1. *The student is motivated to do the work.* Before selecting an intervention, the school assesses the student's motivation on the academic task to determine if that student *can't do* or *won't do* the work (Skinner, Pappas, & Davis, 2005). To discern whether motivation or skill issues explain the student's poor academic performance, the student is asked to complete equivalent academic tasks without and with positive reinforcement. If the student performs substantially better on the task when provided with reinforcement, motivation strategies should be included in the student's intervention plan.

2. *The student's stage of instruction is identified using the Instructional Hierarchy.* The school uses the Instructional Hierarchy (discussed earlier in this chapter) to determine whether the student is performing at the acquisition, fluency, generalization, or adaptation stage of learning (Martens & Witt, 2004). Linking the student's stage of learning to the Instructional Hierarchy allows the school to generate a focused problem-identification statement. A well-defined problem-identification statement increases substantially the probability that a teacher or problem-solving team will select appropriate and effective interventions (Bergan, 1995).

3. *The student is working at the appropriate level of "instructional match."* The student is placed in instructionally appropriate material that guarantees a high success rate (Gettinger & Seibert, 2002; Skinner, Pappas, & Davis, 2005). On reading comprehension tasks, students in the acquisition stage

should work on passages with 93 to 97 percent known words, while other basic skill area tasks (e.g., math computation worksheets, spelling lists, vocabulary flashcards) should contain no less than 50 percent known material (Burns, 2004).

4. *The student receives explicit instruction.* New skills are presented in small steps in an explicit, detailed manner (Burns, VanDerHeyden, & Boice, 2008, p. 1153). When first introducing a new academic skill, the instructor describes and demonstrates the skill, has students try out the skill in large- or small-group format with teacher performance feedback, and observes students to assess for understanding. Students are then given an opportunity to practice the skill supported by teacher feedback and praise (Carnine, 1994).

5. *The student is required to respond actively to instruction.* Students must *show what they know* in instructional activities through "active, accurate academic responding" (Heward, 2003; Skinner, Pappas, & Davis, 2005). Active student responding is effective because it provides students with practice in emerging skills as well as giving the teacher observable information about student skill development. Frequency is an important additional dimension; as students accelerate the number of correct active responses, rates of learning and retention increase as well (Heward, 1996; Skinner, Pappas, & Davis, 2005).

6. *The student receives performance feedback.* Feedback to students about their instructional performance should be timely. Students just learning new skills should get frequent feedback to shape those skills. As students shift to working to build fluency, teachers delay feedback somewhat to allow the students uninterrupted periods of skill practice (Burns, VanDerHeyden, & Boice, 2008). Providing students with praise and perhaps other forms of positive reinforcement contingent on increased accuracy (for students learning a new skill) or fluency (for students practicing an established skill) can also be an effective form of student feedback (Martens & Witt, 2004).

MEASURING THE INTEGRITY OF THE INTERVENTION PLAN

When a struggling student fails to respond adequately to a series of evidence-based interventions, that student is likely to face significant and potentially negative consequences, such as failing grades, long-term suspension from school, or even placement in special education. It is crucial, then, that the school monitor the integrity with which educators implement each intervention plan so that it can confidently rule out poor or limited implementation of the intervention as a possible explanation for any student's "non-response" (Gresham, 1989; Gresham, Gansle, & Noell, 1993).

Intervention integrity is best assessed through direct observation (Roach & Elliott, 2008). The key steps of the intervention are defined and formatted as an observational checklist. An observer watches as the intervention is conducted and checks off on the checklist those steps that were correctly carried out. The observer then (1) adds up the number of steps correctly completed, (2) divides that sum by the total number of potential steps in the intervention, and finally (3) multiplies the quotient by 100 to find the percentage of intervention steps done correctly.

While the chief advantage of direct observation is that it yields objective information about the integrity of the intervention, the method does present several drawbacks. Direct observation is time consuming to carry out. Also, teachers who serve as interventionists may at least initially regard observations of their intervention implementation as evaluations of their job performance, rather than as a child-focused RTI "quality check" (Wright, 2007).

Another limitation is that an intervention-implementation checklist typically does not distinguish between—or differentially weight—those intervention steps that are more important from those that are less so. If two teachers implement the same 10-step intervention plan, for example, with one instructor omitting a critical step and the other omitting a fairly trivial step, both can still attain the same implementation score of steps correctly completed (Gansle & Noell, 2007).

Supplemental ways to assess intervention integrity include having the interventionist complete regular self-ratings of the intervention implementation and evaluating permanent products created during the intervention. As a form of self-monitoring, directing interventionists to rate the integrity of their own interventions may prompt higher rates of compliance (e.g., Kazdin, 1989). However, because teacher self-ratings tend to be upwardly biased (Gansle & Noell, 2007, p. 247) they should not be relied upon as the sole rating of intervention integrity. One suggestion for collecting regular teacher reports on intervention implementation in a convenient manner is to use Daily Behavior Reports (DBRs; Chafouleas, Riley-Tillman, & Sugai, 2007). DBRs contain brief descriptions of student academic or behavioral goals; teachers use these forms to rate student behaviors daily. DBRs provide useful information about student academic and behavioral targets from the teacher's perspective; they can also be customized to include one item requiring that the teacher rate the degree to which he or she was able successfully to implement the student's intervention plan that day. The school can monitor DBRs and provide additional support if teacher self-ratings of intervention implementation fall below an acceptable level. (The Behavior Reporter, a free online application that creates customized Daily Behavior Reports, can be found at http://www.interventioncentral.org.)

If an intervention plan naturally yields permanent products (e.g., completed scoring sheets, lists of spelling words mastered, behavioral sticker charts), these products can be periodically collected and evaluated as another indicator of intervention integrity. In fact, schools should consider monitoring intervention integrity through a mix of direct and indirect means, including direct observation and permanent products (Gansle & Noell, 2007), as well as interventionist self-ratings (Roach & Elliott, 2008).

While schools certainly want to assess intervention integrity with accuracy, the more pressing question is how to increase the *quality* of teacher interventions. Gansle and Noell (2007) note that, when teachers are provided with adequate training prior to their starting an intervention and also receive periodic performance feedback about how well they are implementing that intervention, the intervention is likely to be carried out with a higher level of integrity. These authors also suggest that schools provide closest attention to intervention integrity when students are first acquiring a skill (in order to promote accuracy).

EXPANDING INTERVENTION CAPACITY: IDEAS FOR SCHOOLS

This chapter reviewed important concepts in intervention selection, implementation, and evaluation. Following are two additional practical ideas to assist problem-solving teams in expanding their capacity to implement interventions (Wright, in press).

CREATE AN INTERVENTION BANK

When creating student intervention plans, problem-solving teams are obligated to use research-based instructional or behavior management strategies. One idea to ensure that teams have sufficient empirically supported intervention ideas from which to draw when developing intervention plans is to assemble an *Intervention Bank*. First, the problem-solving team generates a list of the most common academic and behavioral problems that occur in their school. The team next makes up a three-ring Intervention Bank binder separated into tabbed sections—with each section labeled with one of the school's common student problem areas (e.g., reading fluency). Over time, the team reviews reputable sources of research-based intervention ideas, such as peer-reviewed journals, published commercial materials, and web sites. Whenever the team identifies a useful intervention strategy that addresses one of the common referral concerns, it makes a copy of that strategy and files it under the appropriate tab in the Intervention Bank binder. Incrementally, the problem-solving team builds a comprehensive library of intervention strategies that it can routinely review at problem-solving meetings to speed the development and improve the quality of its individualized intervention plans. Larger districts may consider creating standard Intervention Bank binders to be distributed across all of their schools as one way to help buildings to be more consistent in the quality and range of intervention ideas that they recommend.

INVENTORY BUILDING AND DISTRICT INTERVENTION RESOURCES

The RTI model is unlikely to be funded with many resources beyond those already present in a school system. To plan effective, high-strength interventions using existing resources, then, the problem-solving team must be able to identify and access all available intervention resources throughout the school. To collect information about the school's intervention capacities, the team should conduct an Intervention Resource Inventory within the building to include the following:

- Printed materials or software accompanying textbooks designed for classroom instructors to provide additional or remedial instruction for lower-performing students.
- Supplemental commercial materials such as computer software purchased by the school to improve academic skills.
- Staff members whose specialized knowledge or skills (e.g., an advanced degree in reading instruction or training and experience working with children with behavioral disorders) can be put to use as a consultant on the problem-solving team or as an intervention coach willing to train staff in the use of specific strategies.
- Staff members who have flexible schedules or pockets of available time in their daily or weekly schedule during which—with proper training—they might assist with implementation of interventions, collect student progress-monitoring data, serve as student mentors or tutors, and so on.

Once the inventory is complete, the problem-solving team should organize their intervention resources into a comprehensive list. That list would be available for the problem-solving team to consult at student problem-solving meetings when they need to identify additional resources for a student's intervention plan.

READING INTERVENTION ACROSS THE TIERS:
A CASE EXAMPLE

The following student case example illustrates how one school flexibly addressed the needs of a struggling reader through successive tiers of RTI support. Christina is a third-grade student who started the year with delays in reading fluency. Christina's teacher, Mr. Arnold, constructed a strong class-wide Tier 1 foundation in reading by using a number of literacy instructional strategies such as modeling of fluent reading, daily student reading practice, and encouragement of students to engage in wide reading beyond classroom texts. The instructor also set up reading centers (Kosanovich, Ladinsky, Nelson, & Torgesen, n.d.) to accommodate the broad range of reading abilities represented in his classroom. Additionally, the instructor trained his students in Peer-Assisted Learning Strategies (PALS) in reading (McMaster, Fuchs, & Fuchs, 2006), a program in which all children in the class pair off to provide structured tutoring to each other. The PALS program took place three times per week for 30 minutes per session.

While more than 80 percent of Mr. Arnold's students performed at or above expected levels in reading fluency with these Tier 1 supports, Christina continued to lag behind her peers. The four third-grade classrooms in her school all scheduled RTI Tier 2 supplemental support at the same time. Christina and four other students with similar delays in reading fluency were recruited from across the four classrooms and placed in a daily Tier 2 supplemental reading group led by Mrs. Thomas, another third-grade teacher. For the group-based intervention, Mrs. Thomas implemented Corrective Reading, a sequenced and scripted program that addresses reading fluency as one of its instructional targets. Students' reading fluency rates were assessed twice per month, using Curriculum-Based Measurement oral reading fluency (ORF) probes. The school consulted research norms in ORF (Tindal, Hasbrouck, & Jones, 2005) to compute Tier 2 student reading fluency goals, because it found that those outside norms were more ambitious than the school's own local norms.

At the beginning of the Tier 2 supplemental group intervention in January, Christina was reading 50 correct words per minute (WPM) in third-grade text. The research norms for reading fluency used by the school indicated that by the middle of the school year (winter), typical reading rates for grade 3 ranged from 62 WPM (25th percentile) to 120 WPM (75th percentile). The school therefore decided to set 62 WPM as a realistic short-term intervention goal that would help Christina to begin to close the reading gap with her peers. It was anticipated that this intermediate goal would be attained within eight instructional weeks, representing an average weekly growth rate of 1.5

words. Christina and other students in the group were to be administered Oral Reading Fluency CBM probes twice per month to track progress with the intervention. A review of Christina's reading-fluency data at the conclusion of the eight-week Tier 2 intervention period showed that she had indeed made promising gains but had not reached her reading fluency goal. As a result of the intervention, Christina had added a word per week to her reading fluency, raising her reading rate from 50 to 58 WPM in third-grade text.

The school's RTI problem-solving team met with Mr. Arnold, Christina's teacher, to develop a more intensive Tier 3 intervention plan to help this student catch up with peers. Because the Tier 2 intervention had led to promising improvements in Christina's reading speed, it was decided to retain this pull-out group as part of Christina's Tier 3 intervention plan. Additionally, the RTI team and teacher agreed that Christina should be tutored by a para-professional three times per week for 30 minutes to allow more opportunities for reading rehearsal. The tutor was trained by the school's reading specialist to engage Christina in paired reading (Topping, 1987), a simple but effective fluency-building strategy that allows the student to read aloud with adult encouragement, assistance, and corrective feedback. The reading specialist also supervised the adult tutor during the intervention to ensure high rates of intervention integrity.

Christina's reading rate when beginning the Tier 3 intervention was 58 WPM. Because the school had now moved into the spring portion of its instructional calendar, however, the RTI team consulted the spring research norms for reading fluency to revise Christina's intervention goal and found that the 25th percentile in the third grade spring norms was 78 WPM. So the RTI team set the expectation that at the end of eight instructional weeks, Christina would increase her reading speed from 58 to 78 WPM—an ambitious goal. During this Tier 3 intervention phase, Christina was administered Oral Reading Fluency CBM probes two times per week (Burns & Gibbons, 2008) to track progress.

At the end of the eight-week Tier 3 intervention phase, the RTI team and teacher met once again to review Christina's intervention and progress-monitoring data. It was discovered that, with the addition of individual tutoring to the supplemental group instruction, Christina had increased her reading fluency rate by approximately two words per week, bringing her new reading speed in grade 3 material to 74 WPM. The student had fallen just short of her reading fluency goal of 78 WPM. However, the RTI team and teacher were greatly encouraged that Christina's actual rate of improvement exceeded typical rates of reading growth for third-grade students (Tindal, Hasbrouck, & Jones, 2005) and indicated that Christina was likely to attain and surpass the reading goal of 78 WPM well before the end of the school year. The RTI team and teacher concluded that they had created an effective intervention package for the student, as Christina was now making quite substantial gains in reading speed and was closing the gap with peers. The RTI team therefore decided to maintain and monitor the present Tier 3 intervention through the end of the school year.

Setting Goals, Monitoring Progress, and Graphing Intervention Outcomes

I NTERVENTIONS ARE MOST effective when monitored. Yet what does it mean to "monitor" an intervention? Often this term is used without the specificity required in understanding which aspect of the intervention is monitored and how the monitoring is accomplished. Two types of monitoring are instrumental in facilitating intervention success: evaluating the outcomes of the intervention (i.e., student learning, also referred to as progress monitoring) and monitoring the fidelity/integrity of the implementation of the intervention (i.e., whether the intervention is being carried out as planned). These types of monitoring complement each other and when used together and often lead to greater student success.

To illustrate the distinction between outcome assessment/progress monitoring and implementation fidelity monitoring, imagine you have undertaken a modified diet and exercise program out of a desire to improve your overall health and appearance. One of the first things a person does when embarking on this kind of program is to set a goal. Typically the goal is defined in terms of reduction of body weight in pounds. For example, a person desires to lose 30 pounds. Often this goal is associated with a time frame—they want to lose 30 pounds in six months. Then, as the person makes the diet/exercise modifications, he or she frequently uses a scale to determine whether the desired weight loss is occurring on schedule. Some people weigh daily; others weigh once to a few times per week. However, most people are eager to step on the scale to see if their program is working. If so, they can celebrate their success and continue their program as intended. If not, they might get discouraged and give up, or they might make some changes to their program in an attempt to produce the desired outcome

6

Chapter

(i.e., weight loss). This portion of monitoring a personal health program's effectiveness is analogous to outcome/progress monitoring.

In addition to stepping on that scale, successful dieters often keep track of the food they eat and/or the exercise they perform on a daily basis. This helps them to analyze their actual food intake and exercise output in the event that they do not see the desired results on the scale. It allows for daily reflection on the degree to which they are following the program as prescribed, and it can help them identify any trouble spots they might encounter during the day. This daily reflection can help them make informed decisions about what to do differently the next day. This tracking of one's own behavior is analogous to monitoring the fidelity of intervention implementation.

This chapter will define the key components of both types of monitoring with a primary focus on the first type: monitoring student progress. First, considerations for setting individualized goals and a process for writing effective goals for progress monitoring will be discussed. This includes the specifics of the goals—what materials to use for progress monitoring, how to determine a time frame and goal criterion, how frequently to assess the student, and conventions of graphing progress data and using decision rules. The latter part of the chapter will outline the various aspects of monitoring intervention fidelity and some methods for accomplishing this monitoring. The chapter will conclude with case examples illustrating how the two types of monitoring are used together to facilitate effective intervention delivery.

STUDENT PROGRESS MONITORING

Progress monitoring is just becoming widely implemented and therefore is a very young field. At this point, the most well-established and research-supported system for progress monitoring uses Curriculum-Based Measurement (CBM). This may change as interest in and knowledge of progress monitoring spreads through the scientific and educational community. Already test developers and researchers are working on alternatives to CBM for use in progress monitoring. However, to date few, if any, alternatives have generated a sufficient research base to warrant inclusion in a how-to book like this one, so much of the discussion in this chapter is based on procedures for monitoring progress using CBM. If you or your district are not interested in using CBM and wish to pursue another alternative, the discussion that follows may be helpful in determining what to look for in a progress-monitoring tool as well as considerations in using the alternative tool(s). In addition, the National Center for Student Progress Monitoring (http://www.studentprogress.org) provides a wealth of information about the nature and purpose of progress monitoring, including standards for effective progress-monitoring tools and reviews of existing tools and systems available to conduct progress monitoring.

DEVELOPING INDIVIDUALIZED GOALS

The first step in progress monitoring involves setting a goal. In doing so, practitioners must make a variety of decisions. What skill is the intervention aimed at increasing? How will that skill be measured? What level of performance do we want the child to achieve before deeming the intervention a success?

According to IDEIA, goals must be measurable and data based. These data-based goals involve four key components (Shinn, 1989): the behavior measured, the person doing the behavior (i.e., the student), the measurement conditions under which progress will be monitored (e.g., specific materials used, level of materials, time frame for goal), and the criterion (i.e., specific level of performance desired by a given date). Some of these components are self-evident (e.g., the student, sometimes the time frame). Others require some decision making on the part of the teacher, practitioner, or team.

SURVEY-LEVEL ASSESSMENT

When using CBM or a similar measurement system to set goals, the process can be informed by beginning with a survey-level assessment (SLA). This involves assessing students' skills in successively lower grade levels until a level is reached at which the student is successful. The survey-level assessment results can be used to (1) quantify the child's performance in terms of grade-level expectations, (2) choose an appropriate curriculum level for progress monitoring, (3) set an appropriate goal criterion, and sometimes (4) identify an appropriate instructional level for the student.

To conduct a survey-level assessment, the examiner should have probes available from several levels of the curriculum or monitoring program, beginning with the student's grade level and successively lower levels until approximately a grade level below the child's estimated performance. For example, if the student is in fifth grade, and his teacher estimates his reading at a third-grade level, then the examiner should have at least three probes available from the fifth-, fourth-, third-, and second-grade levels of the reading probes used for progress monitoring. Begin assessing the student's skills with the probes at the student's grade level, unless the student had already completed grade-level probes as part of a benchmark assessment within the past two weeks. Score the probes and summarize the data. If the student performed unsuccessfully (see next section), continue testing in successively lower levels until the child does perform within an acceptable range, or until the lowest level of the curriculum or monitoring program is administered.

Often educators will ask why a survey-level assessment begins with the higher-level materials and works backward instead of the other way around. Conducting the SLA in this manner will ensure that the examiner determines the highest level at which the student is successful. If beginning with a lower level and working to higher levels, an examiner may stop the assessment prematurely and not test the child to his or her upper limits. This might lead to inappropriately low expectations and insufficiently ambitious goals. In addition, when working backward, the most difficult materials are administered first, presumably when the student is fresh, and then tasks gets easier as the testing goes on. This gradual increase in success can help the child stay motivated to keep working. By working down to the level where the child is successful, the survey-level assessment concludes on a positive note rather than with frustration and failure.

A possible exception to beginning at grade level is when the student's estimated performance is so far below his or her grade placement that beginning with grade level would cause undue frustration and significantly add to administration time. In this situation, a good starting point would be one or two grade levels above the student's estimated performance level. For example, if the student's primary subject teacher estimates the student's performance as second-grade level, begin with third- or fourth-grade probes. If the student performs successfully at the first level administered, administer the next higher grade level until the student performs unsuccessfully. If the student is unsuccessful at the first level administered, move down in level until success is reached. In short, a survey-level assessment will identify the *highest* level at which a student performs successfully.

DETERMINING SUCCESS

When conducting a SLA, successful performance can be defined in a number of ways. The most common definitions of successful performance using CBM involve either norms or instructional placement standards. The approach you choose may depend on availability of norms and the type of decision you wish to make. It is sometimes helpful to be aware of where the student stands according to several of the various criteria, because some criteria are more appropriate for specific kinds of decisions. For example, local norms might be more useful than instructional placement standards in defining a performance discrepancy and setting goals, and instructional placement standards might be more appropriate for specific intervention planning decisions (i.e., level of materials to use for instruction).

NORMS

When using norms, the student is successful when his or her performance falls within the average range for a given level of the assessment materials (i.e., at or above the 25th percentile using either local or national norms). Figure 6.1 contains an example of SLA using local norms. Although many practitioners would express an almost knee-jerk preference for national norms, local norms have several advantages that warrant consideration, especially in light of the purpose of the SLA. First, local norms provide a clear operational definition of the academic expectations in any

Figure 6.1

Aaron's
Survey-Level
Assessment
Using Local
Norms

LEVEL	DATE	PASSAGE 1	PASSAGE 2	PASSAGE 3	MEDIAN	PERCENTILE
3	9/15/08	26/4	42/3	35/4	35/4	13th
2	9/15/08	48/3	40/5	53/2	48/3	57th
1	9/15/08	68/1	73/4	55/2	68/2	97th

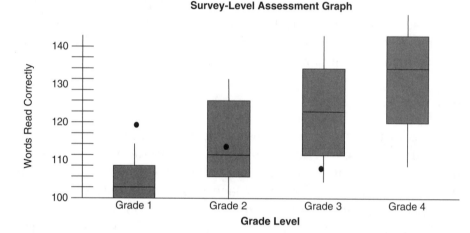

Survey-Level Assessment Graph

given school. These expectations are important when determining the magnitude of a student's problem and the desired outcome of intervention. National norms may result in expectations that are too high for a given school, resulting in overidentification of students as needing additional support when classroom instruction might meet their needs and keeping those students in remedial or intervention programs longer than necessary, or they may be too low, resulting in too few students receiving support and too many being released from intervention programs before they are ready to meet classroom expectations.

The second advantage of local norms is that practitioners usually have more information about the nature of the norms, including students tested, materials used, examiner qualifications and training, dates of assessment, and other pertinent factors that might impact the results. Although normative information is available through online data management programs such as AIMSweb (http://www.aimsweb.com) and the DIBELS Data System (https://dibels.uoregon.edu/benchmark.php), and national norms have been published in the literature on CBM (e.g., Hasbrouck & Tindal, 2006), to date no carefully constructed set of national norms is available for CBM data. The data provided by AIMSweb and the DIBELS Data System are aggregates of scores from all school users in the system. The degree to which these school users are representative of schools nationally is unknown. Further, some schools choose to use such systems for a subset of their students, and the degree to which this is a factor also is unknown and may vary with grade level and/or specific measure used. For example, a given middle school may choose to use the AIMSweb writing and math measures with its students in special education and other remedial programs, and therefore provide a disproportionate amount of data from these students. If a substantial portion of schools engage in this practice, average ranges would be artificially lowered and could result in ineffective decision making. Although these aggregates can be useful for decision making when limited normative information is available, practitioners should be aware of their potential drawbacks.

EXPERT JUDGMENT

Another option for defining successful performance is to use instructional placement standards (Burns, VanDerHeyden, & Jiban, 2006; Deno & Mirkin, 1977). Instructional placement ranges for CBM reading, mathematics computation, written expression, and spelling are summarized in Table 6.1. These standards were created based on expert judgment and are most often used to determine the appropriateness of instructional material for a student. They represent how challenging the instructional material should be based on student performance. For example, if a child reads a passage flawlessly and with automaticity, that material is not likely to challenge the student enough to enhance their decoding skills. On the other hand, if the child reads the passage at an extremely low rate and/or makes a lot of errors, the material is likely to be frustrating and the student may lose motivation to complete the task. Between these two extremes is the recommended instructional placement range. It represents the amount of challenge appropriate for a child given *teacher-led* instruction. If looking for material for independent work, then

Table 6.1   Recommended Instructional Placement Ranges for CBM Reading Aloud[a], Mathematics Calculation—Mixed Probes[b], Written Expression—Total Words Written, and Spelling—Correct Letter Sequences[c]

Grade Level	Reading (WRC)	Mixed Calculation (CD)	Written Expression (TWW)	Spelling (CLS)
1	40–60	10–19	15	20–39
2	40–60	14–31	28	20–39
3	70–100	14–31	37	40–59
4	70–100	24–49	41	40–59
5	70–100	24–49	49	40–59
6	70–100	20–39	52	40–59

[a](WRC, Fuchs & Deno, 1982)
[b](Deno & Mirkin, 1977 for G1 and G6; Burns et. al for G2–G4)
[c](Shapiro, 2004a, 2004b)

materials selected using instructional placement standards might be too challenging.

The procedure for SLA is the same whether using norms or Instructional Placement Standards. Simply begin at the student's grade level and test in successively lower levels until the student's performance falls within the recommended instructional placement range for that level of materials. See Figure 6.2 for an example.

Using SLA to Determine Time Frames, Measurement Materials, and Criteria

Once the SLA has been completed, the next step in progress monitoring is to use that information in determining timelines, measurement materials, and goal criteria. This information is crucial in setting up a progress-monitoring graph and using the data to determine intervention effectiveness.

Time Frame   A typical goal time frame begins at the time of assessment and ends with the current school year. When used for IEP evaluation, the time frame may be annual and extend into the following school year. Teams using this approach need to

LEVEL	DATE	PASSAGE 1	PASSAGE 2	PASSAGE 3	MEDIAN
3	9/15/08	26/4	42/3	35/4	35/4
2	9/15/08	48/3	40/5	53/2	48/3
1	9/15/08	68/1	73/4	55/2	68/2

Figure 6.2

Aaron's Survey-Level Assessment Using Instructional Placement Standards

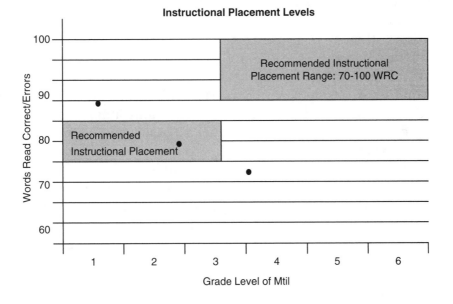

consider that the student will be in a higher grade level at the end of the goal time frame and choose their measurement materials and criteria accordingly. Shorter time periods may be appropriate when progress monitoring is not expected to continue or when the team anticipates switching to higher-level measurement material before the end of the school year.

Measurement Materials Another important decision is the level of materials to use for frequent progress assessment. Often educators will assume (incorrectly) that because a student needs easier material for instruction, he or she also needs easier material for progress monitoring. This is rarely the case. If a student has some skills in performing the assessment on grade-level material, that level might be the best choice for progress monitoring. Grade-level material represents the general education expectations for the student's grade placement, and it is most closely associated with the ultimate goal for the intervention: to help the student achieve at a level commensurate with same-grade peers. Monitoring at a lower level will not provide that reference point.

In some cases, however, it may be beneficial to monitor progress using lower-level materials. If a student's performance on grade-level tasks is so low that real improvements in learning may not be reflected in the material because the task is much too difficult, then it is appropriate to use easier material until the student has adequate skills for grade-level performance (in this case the team might select a shorter goal timeline). For example, a second-grade student who is working on mastering basic decoding skills, such as phonemic awareness and letter-sound correspondences, but is yet unable to read passages of connected text, might experience a great deal of growth in early literacy with a particular intervention but still not be able to read passages after several weeks. If that student's progress was monitored using second-grade CBM passages, a team might conclude the intervention is not effective and make changes to a program that is working. Instead, the team might use an early literacy measure such as Nonsense Word Fluency (Good & Kaminski, 2002) or an isolated word reading measure such as Word Identification Fluency (Fuchs, Fuchs, & Compton, 2004) and set a short-term goal for the student. As the child gains skills, progress monitoring can continue with higher-level material when appropriate.

Criterion   Selecting the criterion, or level at which the student should be performing by the end of the timeline, is probably the most complex decision in the goal-setting process. As is the case with determining success on SLA, selection of a criterion is based on logical and/or empirically based practices. Practitioners may use normative performance, expected rates of progress, or benchmarks based on established linkages to future outcomes to guide the selection of a criterion. Often the most informed goal criterion can be based on a combination of these options.

Norms   Using normative performance is a straightforward option for selecting a criterion. Depending on the severity of the student's performance discrepancy, a practitioner or team would select a percentile level at which they would like to see the student perform by the end of the measurement timeline. This level would represent a reduction in the current discrepancy. For example, if the student is currently performing below the 10th percentile compared to grade-level peers, a criterion would be set to bring the student's performance to the 15th or 20th percentile. A very ambitious criterion would aim for the average range (i.e., above the 25th percentile). When using norms to set the criterion it is important to use the norms table representing the end of the time frame, not the one used to find the student's beginning percentile. If the student was assessed initially in September, the fall norms would be used to establish current performance, and if the time frame ends in June, the spring norms are used to set the criterion. For example, Aaron, a third-grade student, is currently performing at the 13th percentile using his district's local norms. His team decided that a successful intervention would have him performing in the average range (i.e., at or above the 25th percentile) by the end of the school year. According to the spring norms for the district, he will need to be reading at least 74 WRC by the end of the year to be performing in the average range.

Because percentile scores are based on ordinal data, increases in percentile ranks require greater absolute increases at the lower levels than is required when student performance is closer to the average range. For example, a child is likely to need to gain more WRC in reading to move from the second to the 10th percentile than s/he would need to move from the 10th to the 20th percentile. The absolute gain in behavior (e.g., WRC) should be considered in setting goals using normative data. In Aaron's district, for a third-grade student to move 8 percentile points from the second percentile in the fall to the 10th percentile in the spring would require a gain of 44 WRC. To move 10 percentile points from the 10th to the 20th percentile in the same district at the same grade level would require a gain of 38 WRC.

Although using norms can be a useful and efficient method for setting goal criteria, it has some limitations. First, regardless of whether the norms are national or local, normative performance might not represent proficiency on an absolute scale. Performing in the average range does not guarantee a student's success in meeting later objectives. Second, effective goal setting requires a criterion that is achievable for the student yet ambitious enough to result in an accelerated rate of learning. Choosing a level based solely on desired percentile level might result in goals that are either unrealistic (i.e., too high) or not sufficiently ambitious (i.e., too low).

Expected Rates of Progress

Early CBM researchers recognized the problems inherent in choosing a goal based on normative levels of performance. How would we know those goals are achievable? To find out, a group of researchers assessed all children in grades 1 to 6 on a weekly or monthly basis to get normative information on growth rates (Fuchs, Fuchs, Hamlett, Walz, & Germann, 1993). One of the outcomes of this study was a set of norms on student growth rates across grade levels and CBM measures. These growth rates can be helpful to current practitioners in deciding whether a goal is reasonable and sufficiently ambitious. See Table 6.2 for a summary of the growth rates reported in Fuchs et al.

Although the growth rates reported here are useful, their limitations must be acknowledged. These rates were obtained on a sample of students in one geographic area and could be more idiosyncratic than universal. Growth rates ostensibly are influenced by the quality of the curriculum and instructional programs in place in the participating schools, and the quality of these programs was not assessed as part of the study. However, the growth rates shown are achievable at the least. Therefore, they are not likely to result

Table 6.2 Expected Rates of Growth across Grade Levels and CBM Measures

Grade	Reading CBM		Mathematics CBM		Spelling CBM	
	Realistic	Ambitious	Realistic	Ambitious	Realistic	Ambitious
1	—	—	0.30	0.50	—	—
2	1.50	2.00	0.30	0.50	1.00	1.50
3	1.00	1.50	0.30	0.50	0.65	1.00
4	0.85	1.10	0.70	1.20	0.45	0.85
5	0.50	0.80	0.70	1.20	0.30	0.65
6	0.30	0.65	0.45	1.00	0.30	0.65

Fuchs, Fuchs, Hamlett, Walz, & Germann (1993)

in goals that are unrealistic. Setting goals reflecting growth rates lower than these, however, might not be ambitious enough to lead to a maximum learning rate for the student.

The growth rates from the Fuchs et al. (1993) study reflect student progress in general education. However, the degree to which these expectations are appropriate for students with learning disabilities is not known. Deno, Fuchs, Marston, and Shin (2001) examined growth rates for students identified as having a learning disability and receiving special education services. The resulting growth rates for students receiving special education was about half that for their peers in general education up through fourth grade. In fifth and sixth grades, when growth rates typically decrease for students in general education, the growth rates for students with learning disabilities was equal that of grade-level peers. These were disturbing findings considering how these students' performance was already significantly below that of grade-level peers. Making less growth over time as compared to typical peers obviously would result in their falling further behind rather than catching up. Even in fifth and sixth grades when growth rates for the two groups were equal, the level of performance for students in special education was less than half the level for those in general education. In the best-case scenario, the students were not falling further behind, but they also were not catching up to their grade-level peers.

However disappointing the findings, they represented an estimate of the current rate of growth given existing special education practice. Deno et al. (2001) argued that given the widespread criticism of the effectiveness of the current special education system, existing practices should not be considered as representing the outcomes that *could* be achieved given effective interventions. So they examined the published scientific literature on interventions for students with learning disabilities to see how much growth these students *can* make when given highly effective instruction. Findings from this search yielded more optimistic growth rates for R-CBM than those obtained by simply observing growth given current practices. These growth rates, summarized in Table 6.2, may be more appropriate for use in goal setting than the substandard rates of growth currently observed with students in special education.

To use expected rates of progress in determining a goal criterion, choose a growth rate based on the previous discussion. If using the growth rates from Fuchs et al., use that which corresponds to the grade level at which the child is currently performing (i.e., success level) instead of the student's grade placement level. Because Aaron was successful on second-grade passages, a growth rate based on typical progress for second-grade students was chosen for him.

Once you have determined the expected rate of progress, multiply the growth rate by the number of weeks in the time frame and add the result to the student's initial performance on goal-level material. In other words, criterion = initial performance + (growth rate × number of weeks). If norms are available, practitioners can look up the criterion in the appropriate norms table (the one corresponding to the end of the time frame and the level of progress-monitoring materials used) and make sure the goal reflects a reduced discrepancy between the student and their grade-level peers. Typically if an ambitious rate of progress is used, the goal, if achieved, will result in a reduced discrepancy. If this reduction is not apparent (bearing in mind that if a child's performance is below the 5th percentile more gains will be needed on CBM to see a modest reduction in the discrepancy), the goal can be adjusted upward until a reduced discrepancy would be achieved.

Aaron's team chose an ambitious growth rate of 2.0 WRC in setting his goal criterion. His current performance on the goal-level (i.e., third-grade) passages is 35 WRC, and the goal time frame is 35 weeks. Given the formula for setting his criterion, [criterion = initial performance + (growth rate × number of weeks)], Aaron will need to gain 70 (35 × 2.0) WRC over the 35 weeks to achieve his goal. Adding 70 to his current performance of 35 WRC would result in a criterion of 105 WRC. According to the spring norms in his district, that would place Aaron's reading performance at the 69th percentile. The team could have set a more conservative goal using a 1.5 words-per-week growth rate. This would have resulted in a criterion of 45 + (1.5 × 35) = 87.5 (round to 90), which corresponds to the 49th percentile using spring district norms. However, the team determined that a more ambitious criterion was warranted for Aaron because they were optimistic that the intervention they selected was effective and suited Aaron's particular skills and attributes.

It is clear from this illustration that in Aaron's district, using local norms to set goals resulted in a less ambitious criterion than using the expected rates of progress. Recall that choosing the 25th percentile resulted in a criterion of 74 WRC, or an overall gain of 39 words, which amounts to just over 1 WRC per week rate of progress.

Benchmarks   A third option for setting the goal criterion is to use established benchmarks based on empirical linkages between the progress-monitoring measure (e.g., R-CBM) and a future success-ful outcome (often defined operationally as achieving a passing score on a state high-stakes test). These linkages can be made at a local level using advanced procedures that are beyond the scope of this chapter, or school teams can use previously published linkages. A prominent example of this approach is the bench-marks associated with the Dynamic Indicators of Basic Early Literacy Skills (DIBELS; Good & Kaminski, 2002). To establish the DIBELS benchmarks, Good, Simmons, and Kame'enui (2001) examined the association between end-of-the-year scores in third grade and student performance on the statewide high-stakes test. They identified a level at which the vast majority of students went on to pass the test (i.e., 110 WRC) and worked backward from there. Next they identified the level of performance on their oral reading measure (DORF) in the winter of third grade that pre-dicted their achieving at least 110 WRC at the end of third grade, then the fall DORF predicting their achieving the winter bench-mark, and so on right down to the students' phonemic awareness in the beginning of kindergarten. The DIBELS benchmarks can be found on the University of Oregon website, http://dibels .uoregon.edu.

Advantages of this approach include that setting a goal criterion is relatively straightforward once the benchmarks are identified. In addition, the benchmarks are established empirically and may result in more meaningful goals than those based on normative performance or expected rates of progress alone. Dis-advantages are that unless a school develops its own benchmarks, which requires some level of statistical skill and data analysis software that might not be available to most practitioners, it must rely on benchmarks created elsewhere, with potentially different populations and outcome measures. It is assumed that a similar relationship exists in any particular district, but the assumption has not been tested. This approach also might set up the expectation that if a child achieves the benchmark he or she is guaranteed to succeed on the outcome measure, which is not the case. Even in the studies establishing the benchmarks some students achieved the benchmark but did not pass the test. The percentage is small, but it is large enough that in any school some students will show that pattern.

If Aaron's school district used DIBELS benchmarks to set his goal, his criterion would be 110 WRC. It is advisable to check the expected rate of progress for this criterion to determine how ambitious this goal might be. For students whose performance is significantly below grade-level expectations, a lower criterion might be more appropriate than the established benchmark.

The Goal Statement

After all goal components have been determined, practitioners then summarize the goal in a single statement. A complete goal statement identifies the student, the behavior measured, conditions under which the behavior is measured (i.e., time frame and measurement materials), and the criterion. The goal statement could read as follows: "In (time frame) weeks, when given (measurement material, including specific level used), (student) will (behavior) at least (criterion) (unit of measurement)." For example, Aaron's goal statement would be "In 35 weeks, when given a passage selected randomly from the third-grade level of the district's current reading series, Aaron will read at least 115 words correct per minute."

Often, goal statements also reflect a degree of accuracy as well as the behavior (e.g., WRC) measured. For reading goals, an accuracy of at least 95 percent is desired. Depending on the criterion, a team can specify a maximum number of errors as part of the goal statement. For Aaron, with a criterion of 105 WRC, an error rate of 5 or fewer would represent accuracy that is greater than 95 percent. To add a component of accuracy to the goal statement, simply add the clause "with 5 or fewer errors" to the end of the goal statement.

MONITORING PROGRESS AND GRAPHING PERFORMANCE

Once a goal is in place, practitioners can begin to monitor student progress. Logistical decisions regarding who does the assessment and/or graphing and how frequently to measure need to be settled. Practitioners not using an established graphing program, such as AIMSweb, also need to know how to construct a progress graph and use it to make decisions.

Who Should Be Responsible for Progress Monitoring? Choosing the person to conduct the progress monitoring will depend on the resources and expertise in each particular school. In many cases, the person doing the intervention is the ideal person to do the monitoring. This person typically is able to work the monitoring into the intervention time with the student because s/he will have frequent contact with the child. In addition, this is the person who needs to use the data to make instructional adjustments as necessary. Therefore, the progress monitoring should be seen as an integral part of the intervention. Finally, most of the research on formative evaluation involves the teacher as the person who sets goals, monitors progress, and adjusts interventions (e.g., Fuchs, Deno, & Mirkin, 1984).

Despite the advantages of having the teacher monitor progress, in some situations it might be more beneficial for someone else to conduct the assessments and graph the results, especially when a school is just beginning to implement progress monitoring. When the interventionist does not understand the purpose and value of the measurement, does not know how to conduct the assessments, or is otherwise reluctant to engage in progress monitoring due to time or other concerns, it might be beneficial for someone else to conduct the monitoring until the teacher is more comfortable with the process. This "someone else" could be a school psychologist, who can work in consultation with the teachers to facilitate the transition to having them do the monitoring. A school also might consider hiring a paraprofessional to collect progress-monitoring data and enter it into a graphing program. If taking this approach, a school should set up procedures to ensure that teachers are regularly examining the graphs and making decisions accordingly. Be sure not to fall into the trap of collecting data solely to satisfy some procedural requirements and not using the data to enhance instruction and student achievement.

Frequency of Measurement   Another common question regarding progress monitoring is "How often should I assess?" The simple answer is twice per week. Studies examining the optimal measurement frequency for CBM (e.g., Shinn, Good, & Stein, 1989) found that measuring progress more than twice per week did not substantially increase the timeliness of instructional decisions. However, measuring progress less than twice per week may lead to delays in obtaining enough data to accurately estimate a student's rate of growth. Approximately 6 to 8 data points are needed to establish a stable trend (Shinn, Good, & Stein, 1988). With measurement occurring twice per week, sufficient information for deciding whether instruction needs modification can be obtained within four weeks. Although twice per week is an optimal measurement frequency for CBM, a school may not have enough resources to maintain this schedule with every child receiving intervention. Therefore, school teams need to decide how best to allocate their progress-monitoring resources. Students performing significantly below their grade-level peers, or those receiving special education services, are most likely to require and benefit from the optimal progress-monitoring schedule. For students whose performance discrepancies are less severe, a less frequent monitoring schedule might be acceptable. Keep in mind that 6 to 8 data points are needed for a reliable trend, so a less frequent schedule results in less timely decisions. With less frequent data collection it also is advisable to increase the reliability of the assessments by administering multiple probes at each assessment time. This would be recommended for schedules involving less than weekly measurement.

Constructing Student Progress Graphs   Although teachers can use numbers to evaluate whether a student is making adequate progress, graphing the data increases the effectiveness of formative evaluation (Fuchs & Fuchs, 1986). Several tools for graphing progress are available. Most commercially available assessment tools include some kind of graphing program. Generic tools, such as the "Chart Dog" application found on www.interventioncentral. com and the graphing templates on www.schooltoolz.us, also are available. A practitioner with a basic understanding of Excel can also create progress graphs on the computer. Additionally, graphs can be drawn the old-fashioned way: by hand using graph paper, a pencil, and ruler. Whichever way one chooses to construct the graph, an understanding of the basic conventions of graphing student performance will facilitate the effectiveness in using the data.

Student performance is typically charted on a time-series graph. These are line graphs where the horizontal (*x*) axis represents equal-interval units of time (usually instructional days or weeks), and the vertical (*y*) axis represents the behavior measured (e.g., number of words read correct). Each axis should be clearly labeled to facilitate communication and interpretation by others. For example, the *y*-axis label should read "Number of words read correctly" rather than a more generic "Reading performance." Likewise, the *x*-axis should specify the unit of measurement of time (e.g., instructional days, weeks, etc.). Finally, the entire graph should have a brief title that is specific enough to communicate its content (e.g., "Aaron's Reading Progress"). See Figure 6.3 for an illustration of the various components of the graph.

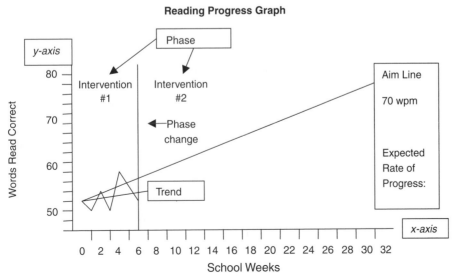

Figure 6.3

Sample Progress Graph

The axes, labels, and title comprise the structure in which the graph is created. Each point on the graph represents the student's performance at any given date, and this should be clear. Points are recorded using a dot or other small character (e.g., square, diamond, star) at the intersection of the appropriate date and score. Adjacent data points are connected by a straight line to demonstrate continuity of programmatic conditions.

The student's initial performance is usually drawn from the survey-level assessment. This and any other data collected prior to the implementation of the intervention is the baseline performance. The student's goal is represented on the graph using an aimline. The aimline connects the student's baseline performance to his or her goal, and the slope of the aimline corresponds to the student's expected rate of progress. The aimline becomes the reference against which the student's performance is interpreted, and it will assist teachers or teams in deciding whether an instructional change is warranted. Construct the aimline by plotting the goal performance at the date on the graph corresponding to the end of the time frame and connecting it to the median of the survey-level assessment results (i.e., initial performance).

When the intervention is implemented and progress monitoring begins, draw a vertical line between the last baseline data point and the first progress monitoring point. Do not connect the data points across this line. This is called a "phase change" line, and its purpose is to delineate the various instructional conditions the student receives. A phase change line is drawn whenever a change is made to the student's intervention. Each phase is labeled briefly to identify the intervention, and a more thorough description of each intervention can be attached, either below the graph or on a separate page. This is important for documenting what instructional programs or strategies have been tried for a student, and it will facilitate decision making when changes are needed.

USING DECISION RULES

Use of decision rules leads to increased student achievement (Fuchs & Fuchs, 1986). Decision rules help to ensure that the progress-monitoring information is used constructively. It helps to keep teachers and teams move beyond admiring the problem to making a positive change in the student's program. It also reduces ambiguity about what to do when a child is not making expected progress. Two common types of decision rules are data point analysis and trend line analysis. A third type of decision rule, the dynamic approach, is a variation on the trend line analysis and involves procedures for raising goals when student performance exceeds the original expectations.

The data point analysis is the simplest to use and most appropriate when graphing by hand. If three consecutive data points fall below the aimline, make an instructional change. So long as data points are falling above and on the line, continue the intervention. The main advantage of this approach is its lack of complexity. It does not require any special skills or equipment beyond the ability to construct a basic time-series graph. However, it may seem a little *too* simple, and it might be too easy for teachers or teams to wait "just one more week" before acting on the decision rule. There may be a tendency to explain away individual samples of performance, such as noting extreme passage difficulty or a student's apparent lack of focus on a given day. Another disadvantage is that the data point analysis does not lead to a numerical estimate of the student's current rate of progress. When student performance exceeds expectations, teams may be less likely to raise goals without an estimate of the current rate of progress or a trend line they can extend to the end of the time frame.

The trend line analysis involves summarizing the student's progress data with a straight line, called a trend line, and comparing its slope and level to the aimline. If the trend line is flatter than the aimline, an instructional change is warranted. Trend lines increase in stability as more data are collected. As noted earlier, CBM trend lines tend to stabilize after 6 to 8 data points (Shinn, Good, & Stein, 1988). Drawing a trend line before 6 data points are collected may lead to inaccurate decisions.

The dynamic approach is an enhanced version of the trend line analysis. Using the dynamic approach, if the trend line is steeper than the aimline, the student's goal would be raised. For example, if Aaron's rate of progress after six weeks of data collection showed him to be on track to achieve 120 WRC by the end of the goal time frame, the teacher or team would raise his goal from the original 75 WRC to 120 WRC. This approach is advantageous because it corrects for goals initially set too low. It also keeps the teachers interacting with the data, by encouraging them to either change the intervention or raise the goal on a regular basis. Finally, raising goals has been shown to lead to increased student achievement.

CREATING SLOPES AND TREND LINES

Trend lines either can be drawn by hand or constructed using a computer program such as Microsoft Excel. Drawing a trend line by hand is usually accomplished using the split-middle method. Briefly, this method involves dividing the data points into two equal sides by date, then finding the intersection of the median date and median rate of behavior (e.g., WRC) for each side. Finally, the trend line is drawn connecting those two intersections, using a ruler or straight edge. The computer-generated method involves using ordinary least squares regression to summarize the data and then plot the line accordingly.

MONITORING IMPLEMENTATION FIDELITY

As illustrated at the beginning of this chapter, monitoring the fidelity of implementation is the second key component to monitoring interventions. The fidelity, or integrity, of the implementation of the intervention refers to the degree to which an intervention is carried out as planned. Implementation fidelity was introduced in the previous chapter because questions of implementation arise during the intervention development process. Intervention selection is influenced by considerations of fidelity, including the resources available for the intervention, the skills of the intervention provider, his or her willingness to implement the intervention, and the level of intrusiveness of the intervention given competing demands on the interventionist (for example, a classroom teacher being asked to implement one-on-one instruction for a student while simultaneously being responsible for teaching and supervising 23 additional students). By planning for implementation fidelity monitoring at the intervention development stage, teams can attend to and try to minimize potential implementation problems from the beginning. In addition, developing specific indicators of implementation fidelity requires teams to attend to the details of the intervention, which, in turn, leads to greater fidelity of implementation. Thus, attending to implementation issues during intervention development may increase the likelihood that the intervention is implemented with fidelity.

STRATEGIES FOR INCREASING FIDELITY

A few related strategies for increasing fidelity may be established after the intervention has begun. A number of strategies for assessing fidelity were discussed in the previous chapter. These include direct observation, teacher self-report, Daily Behavior Reports, and examining permanent products. Each strategy has strengths and limitations, and combining them might yield the most accurate and useful information in evaluating implementation and adjusting interventions as appropriate.

Using Teacher Checklists   An important component of a well-written intervention plan is an outline of the specific steps involved in carrying out the plan. These steps can be arranged into a checklist for teachers to follow as they learn to implement the procedures. A detailed checklist is useful for at least two purposes. First, it gives the interventionist a detailed guide to follow during instruction. Second, it can be used as a direct observation and a self-report measure of implementation fidelity. Teachers can complete the checklist as a self-assessment, and outside observers can corroborate the teacher's self-assessment by using the checklist to observe one or more sessions. Checklists are also useful in identifying specific components of the intervention which the teacher may find problematic or have difficulty in following. If a teacher is consistently forgetting Step 5 of the intervention, the teacher or team can devise specific strategies to help the teacher remember to include that step. Or perhaps the teacher rates herself as performing Step 5 but the outside observer notices the teacher makes mistakes that might impact the student's learning. The observer can give the teacher specific feedback and recommendations for following the plan more closely.

The 24-Hour Check-In   It is important to have someone check in with the interventionist within a very short time after the intervention has begun. Teachers are likely to have the most questions as they are beginning the intervention, as it may involve a new skill or activity for them. If nobody is available to answer their questions, teachers will need to devise their own answers, which may or may not be aligned with the intent of the plan. Another reason to check in immediately is that the interventionist may be more amenable to feedback at the beginning before settling into a routine. After some time has passed and the interventionist is more comfortable with the procedures, being told they are making mistakes and changing the plan can be irritating. Aside from being asked to make changes, again, they might be frustrated by the amount of time spent incorrectly implementing the intervention. A 24-hour check-in can help ensure the intervention is implemented correctly from the beginning, reducing unnecessary frustration later if the intervention is not implemented as planned.

Using Fidelity Data to Inform Interventions

Assessing implementation fidelity is a dynamic process that serves multiple purposes. In addition to informing whether a student's non-response is due to implementation problems, it provides useful feedback in making adjustments to interventions when necessary. If the progress-monitoring data indicate that the student is not making adequate growth toward the established goal, implementation fidelity data should be the first consideration. Was the intervention implemented as planned? If not, what changes can be made to the intervention to increase fidelity? Perhaps the intervention *might* be effective but is too intrusive to be carried out without additional support. Perhaps the interventionist has a philosophical issue with the instructional methods and is having trouble implementing them without further discussion. Perhaps the intervention requires skills the interventionist has not quite mastered yet or requires too much time. Data on implementation fidelity can help teams identify the problem(s) and act accordingly.

Commonly school personnel learning methods for goal setting and progress monitoring express concern over knowing what and how to change when the data indicate changes are needed. This is rarely an issue when interventions are well-planned and carried out with an eye to implementation issues. Through the process of implementing and evaluating the intervention, the teacher and others gather a great deal of ancillary information about what is working well and what might need some adjustment. When the time comes for changes to the intervention, teachers and teams often have clear ideas about what and how to adjust the intervention. The literature on formative evaluation supports a conclusion that often changes made to programs result in greater achievement gains for the students. Although there is no "magic bullet" intervention program, there does appear to be great power in the process of monitoring and evaluating interventions.

Rebecca

Rebecca is a fourth-grade student at a suburban elementary school in the Northeastern region of the United States. She currently receives special education services under the category of Other Health Impaired on the basis of a medical diagnosis of AD/HD, Primarily Inattentive Type. According to her IEP she currently receives 90 minutes per day of instructional services in language arts, and an additional 120 minutes per week of assistance with science and social studies. Further examination of her actual services indicates that she spends the majority of her time in the general education classroom with special education assistance. However, she does receive some pull-out reading services.

Classroom observations indicated Rebecca is less engaged in academic tasks than her peers. She spent a good deal of time looking around and playing with small objects within her reach. She received a great deal of individual attention, which increased her engagement temporarily. However, she did not seek assistance at her own initiative. A teacher interview revealed that Rebecca receives most of her services in the general education classroom, and that the primary strategy for keeping Rebecca engaged and successful was to read all written material out loud to her.

A Survey-Level Assessment was conducted with Rebecca using R-CBM probes from the AIMSweb® system. She performed in the well-below-average range (<10th percentile) on fourth- and third-grade materials, in the at-risk range (between 10th and 25th percentiles) on second-grade materials, and in the above-average range (between 75th and 90th percentiles) on first-grade materials. Based on this performance, her reading skills appeared to be similar to those of a typical first-grade student. Further

(continued)

(continued)

assessment into her specific reading skills revealed that her primary difficulty was in decoding using alphabetic word-identification strategies. An intervention was developed aimed at helping Rebecca increase her decoding accuracy and fluency. Rebecca's special education teacher would provide 30 minutes daily of decoding instruction using the SRA Reading Mastery program. This program includes procedures for monitoring implementation, such as documenting student mastery of each lesson's content and keeping a record of the lessons taught. These procedures would be implemented and used for evaluating the implementation of the program.

To evaluate the effectiveness of this intervention, the team set an initial goal for Rebecca using second-grade R-CBM passages, on which she had read a median of 28 WRC with 5 errors during her SLA. Fourth- and third-grade passages were not used because Rebecca read fewer than 20 WRC at these levels. First-grade passages were not used because the team wanted to measure her progress using the highest-level passages likely to detect her reading growth. The team used a realistic growth rate from Fuchs et al. (1993) for first-grade students, because Rebecca's SLA performance most closely approximated first grade. The time frame for Rebecca's goal was the remainder of the school year, which happened to be 32 weeks. Therefore, Rebecca's goal statement read as follows: In 32 weeks, when given a second-grade AIMSweb R-CBM passage, Rebecca will read 92 words correct per minute with at least 95 percent accuracy. The expected rate of progress for this goal was two words per week.

Rebecca's progress was monitored twice weekly using the second-grade AIMSweb probes as planned. After five weeks of data collection, the team reconvened to review the data and determine whether to continue or modify the intervention. Rebecca's rate of progress, based on 10 data points, was 1.2 words per week. She was showing improvement in her skills, but was not on track to reach her goal.

An examination of the implementation data showed that Rebecca was not receiving the intervention daily as had been planned, mostly due to school holidays, special events, and teacher and student absences. She received the intervention an average of three days per week. In addition, the teacher was moving Rebecca through the program even when she did not achieve mastery on a lesson, rather than reteaching the lesson as recommended by the program's authors. The team discussed ways to increase the frequency of Rebecca's instruction given the complexities of the school's schedule, and it developed a plan to ensure she received instruction every school day. This plan included strategies to increase Rebecca's attendance. In addition, the team addressed the teacher's hesitancy to reteach lessons so the teacher would ensure Rebecca mastered the content. These modifications were implemented immediately. Rebecca's progress and plan implementation were monitored as before, and in another five weeks the team reconvened again to review the data. This time Rebecca's rate of progress was 2.3 words per week. She received the intervention four to five days per week, and when she did not master the content of a lesson her teacher taught it again the following day. The team determined to continue the intervention as planned until the end of the school year unless Rebecca's progress data indicated she was no longer progressing toward her goal.

Making Decisions after Intervening

7

Chapter

THE DECISION REGARDING which students need Tier 2 intervention is likely one of the easier data-based decisions that has to be made within the RTI process. For one thing, schools typically have access to numerous sources of data (e.g., Curriculum-Based Measurement, standardized group-administered tests, state-mandated tests) that provide reliable and valid predictions regarding which students need supplemental intervention services (Ardoin et al., 2004). Furthermore, one of the only truly negative repercussions of identifying students in need of Tier 2 instruction, who actually do not need Tier 2 instruction, is the unnecessary use of school resources. Providing quality Tier 2 intervention services to a student not in need of Tier 2 intervention is unlikely to result in any harm to the student. Our biggest mistake with regard to identification of students needing Tier 2 intervention is the failure to identify those in need. Such mistakes should however be preventable through the use of multiple and valid sources of data and an unbiased decision-making process.

Although decisions regarding whether students need supplemental Tier 2 instruction maybe fairly straightforward and risk free, decisions regarding the effectiveness of Tier 2 instruction are not as simple. Decisions regarding the effectiveness of Tier 2 instruction for an individual student are fairly unique to the RTI model and thus are not decisions that schools are currently accustomed to making. In the past most decisions concerning students' academic needs have been made based upon static data, or data that provides information pertaining to the student at one specific time. When examining static data, a student's performance is generally compared to either local peers (e.g., grades) or to national norms (e.g., standardized achievement tests). Although analysis of a student's achievement level relative to some sample of other students remains important when making decisions regarding the impact of Tier 2 services, we must also consider changes (non-static) in academic performance of the individual student. To state it another way, it is not only a student's level of performance that must be evaluated but the rate at which the student's level of achievement is changing. Data must therefore be collected that provides an estimate of the change in student achievement across time, and based upon these data high-stake educational decisions are made. The first decision that must be made is whether the intervention is resulting in adequate rates of change in achievement. If the intervention is resulting in sufficient change, it then has to be decided whether the intervention should be continued to allow for further accelerated rates of gain or if supplemental services should be faded. On the other hand if the data suggest that the intervention is not resulting in sufficient rates of change, teams must decide what type of modifications should be made and/or whether more in-depth assessment is needed to proceed with a more intense evaluation of a student's needs with special education as a possibility.

Unlike the decision whether or not to provide supplemental instruction, the decisions made by intervention teams regarding whether a student is responding adequately to Tier 2 services have potential negative consequences. For instance, misinterpreting the data to suggest that the student is making adequate progress may result in the early removal of an intervention and the student falling further behind peers and experiencing unnecessary failure. Potentially more damaging for students is when data are mis-interpreted to suggest that a student is not responding, when in actuality the intervention is resulting in adequate rates of growth. Such inaccurate decisions have the potential of mislabeling a student as having a learning disability. For these reasons it is vital that multiple sources of data across a sufficient period of time be used to evaluate each student's response to each Tier 2 inter-vention provided to him/her.

The purpose of this chapter is to provide the reader with information regarding making decisions for students once Tier 2 services have begun. Although greater attention is provided to the individual student with the implementation of Tier 2 services, we must continue attending to the context in which services are being provided. Thus, we first provide suggestions on the subject of how summative evaluation data should be incorporated into the evaluation of individual students' response to intervention. Summative evaluation provides information about the effects of intervention on groups of students. We then discuss factors that must be considered when determining what sources of data should be collected for making formative evaluations. While summative evaluation data provide us with information concerning what expectations we should have for the target student, formative evaluation data provide information regarding whether the established expectations were met. Although at this time, in the infancy of RTI, we cannot provide clear evidence-based guidelines on how long interventions should be implemented and what exact rates of gain can be used as evidence of a student's response or nonresponse to intervention, we have provided some suggestions. The chapter provides recommendations on when (1) to begin fading interventions, (2) to increase the intensity of an intervention, and (3) sufficient data has been collected to be a formal evaluation for Tier 3 services.

FORMATIVE VERSUS SUMMATIVE EVALUATIONS

Although measures used for summative evaluation can be identical to those used in formative evaluation (e.g., curriculum-based measurement), the manner in which the data are used differs. Formative evaluation data are used to evaluate individual student performance. The effects of an intervention are evaluated by examining the extent to which the intervention has changed performance within an individual child over time. A student's performance is compared to his/her previous performance, and the performance of other students is somewhat, although not entirely, irrelevant. Summative evaluation on the other hand involves the evaluation of group-level data. Summative evaluation data are used to evaluate whether instruction is resulting in improvements in a group of students receiving the same instruction. Summative evaluation data could and should be used to evaluate the benefits of all tiers of instruction being provided within a grade level/building/district.

Formative versus Summative Evaluation Data

- *Formative Evaluation Data:* Data that provides information on the effects of intervention for a specific child.
- *Summative Evaluation Data:* Data that provides information on the effects of instruction for a given group of individuals and therefore provides information concerning the general quality of instruction provided to students in the specified group.

When perusing the literature on evaluating the effects of intervention, substantial attention is given to the importance of conducting continuous (e.g., weekly) progress monitoring as a means of evaluating the effect of intervention on the individual (i.e., formative evaluation). Continuous collection of data allows for the ongoing evaluation of student progress, thus providing schools with near constant information on whether intervention modifications are necessary (Deno, Fuchs, Marston, & Shin, 2001; Fuchs & Fuchs, 1986b). Failure to collect such information might result in the continual implementation of ineffective instruction, whereas collection of such data should minimize the length of time that an ineffective intervention is implemented. Research suggests that the use of formative evaluation by teachers leads to improved academic performance by students (National Center on Student Progress Monitoring, 2006), possibly as a function of the reduced time during which ineffective intervention is provided. Within an RTI model these data also play a key role in the process of determining whether a student should continue receiving Tier 2 instruction, exited out of Tier 2 instruction, or whether a student is eligible for special education services (Ardoin, Witt, Connel, & Koenig, 2005; Barnett, Daly III, Jones, & Lentz, 2004; Burns, Appleton, & Stehouwer, 2005; Fuchs & Fuchs, 2006).

Although quality formative evaluation data are essential to the effective implementation of an RTI model, the data are not necessarily sufficient for making Tier 2 level decisions for a student. A critical component of RTI models is consideration of the context in which students are being instructed and formative evaluation data do not provide such information (Ardoin et al., 2005; Barnett et al.,

2006; Brown-Chidsey & Steege, 2005; VanDerHeyden & Snyder, 2006). In order to examine the context in which a student is learning, data must be collected on all or at a minimum a representative sample of students within the setting. If an intervention is not leading to sufficient gains for the large majority of students within a school/grade/classroom, it should not be expected that an individual identified as at risk could make acceptable rates of gain (Ardoin et al., 2005). For this reason, summative evaluations must be conducted within a school. Summative evaluations provide information regarding the general effects of intervention on a larger group of students (Ardoin et al., 2005; Brown-Chidsey & Steege, 2005; Marston, 2005). Examples of summative evaluations include universal screenings using curriculum-based measurement procedures, state-mandated test, and computer-based programs such as the Measures of Academic Progress (Northwest Evaluation Association, n.d.). Summative evaluation data are important to evaluation of both the quality of Tier 1 instruction and Tier 2 supplemental instruction.

USE OF SUMMATIVE EVALUATION DATA AT TIER 1

Although schools across the nation are adopting RTI models, it is critical that RTI models not be viewed simply as a replacement procedure for identifying students with special education needs. Unlike the IQ-achievement discrepancy model, which simply requires experts in test administration and analyses (e.g., school psychologists), implementation of an RTI model requires the commitment of both regular and special education teachers in the evaluation and use of valid data and empirically based instructional practices. In fact before implementing an RTI model it is necessary that quality Tier 1 instruction has been in place for a sufficient amount of time so that the vast majority of students are succeeding with Tier 1 instruction alone. In the absence of effective Tier 1 instruction the number of students in need of Tier 2 instruction is likely to exceed the resources available within a school building (Ardoin et al., 2005; Barnett et al., 2006; Vaughn & Fuchs, 2003). Furthermore, in the absence of evidence-based Tier 1 instruction, it will be difficult to develop a Tier 2 intervention that actually supplements Tier 1 instruction.

For instance, let us imagine a school where the primary source of reading instruction involves each student weekly choosing a library book and reading that book on their own, with the teacher occasionally listening to the student reading the book. Within such a school, there are no evidence-based interventions to supplement Tier 1 instruction because Tier 1 instruction is antithetical to what we know about quality reading instruction. In schools that fail to provide students with empirically based core reading (Tier 1) instruction, empirically based Tier 2 intervention might contradict the philosophy of instruction within Tier 1. When Tier 2 instruction does not supplement quality Tier 1 instruction, the impact of Tier 2 instruction is likely to be minimal. RTI models can only be successful in schools where Tier 2 interventions supplement Tier 1 instruction as opposed to functioning as the only source of the quality instruction. It is therefore essential that summative evaluation data be used as a means of evaluating Tier 1 instruction.

USE OF SUMMATIVE EVALUATION DATA AT TIER 2

The use of summative evaluation data does not end with the evaluation of whether Tier 1 instruction is beneficial for most students. Summative evaluation data continue to be useful in determining whether a student is adequately responding to Tier 2 instruction. In continuing with the idea that it is essential to evaluate the context in which a student is learning, it is important to evaluate the general effectiveness of Tier 2 instruction. This can be achieved by simply extracting the data of the students who receive Tier 2 instruction from the summative evaluation data collected for making decisions at Tier 1. If the majority of students receiving Tier 2 instruction are not making adequate gains, one must question the sufficiency/quality of Tier 2 instruction. When most Tier 2 students in a school are not making adequate gains, the school should question whether (1) enough time is being devoted to Tier 2 instruction, (2) appropriate empirically based Tier 2 interventions have been selected, and (3) Tier 2 interventions are being implemented as designed. Having Tier 2 instruction in place is not sufficient to produce gains in student achievement. Tier 2 instruction should be provided with sufficient intensity (i.e., appropriate group size, duration, frequency), conducted with fidelity, and target skills that promote academic achievement. Schools should therefore develop interventions that result in permanent products that will provide evidence of when interventions were implemented and whether they were implemented with fidelity (Witt, Daly, & Noell, 2000).

RESPONSE REMAINS DEPENDENT ON TIER 1

Another purpose of summative evaluation data for evaluating a student's response to intervention is to determine whether an individual student is making sufficient gains in comparison to his/her peers. When evaluating the gains of a student receiving Tier 2 instruction using formative evaluation data, it is important to remember that the student's core instruction is being provided through Tier 1 instruction. A student receiving 30 minutes of supplemental Tier 2 instruction should still be receiving the same 90 minutes of daily reading instruction that is being provided to his/her peers. Supplemental instruction should be in addition to, not in replacement of, Tier 1 instruction. The primary source of instruction provided to Tier 2 students must remain Tier 1 instruction and thus the academic gains made by students receiving Tier 2 instruction should remain heavily influenced by Tier 1 instruction.

Considering Tier 1 instruction should remain the core source of instruction, fluctuations in student growth will occur with fluctuations in the quality and quantity of Tier 1 instruction. It is therefore important that when we evaluate a student's response to instruction that we compare the student's rate of growth to peers receiving identical Tier 1 instruction. In Example 7.1 Mike's rate of growth during the spring semester increased just slightly above his rate of gain from the fall. However, analysis of summative evaluation data revealed that the rates of gain made by his peers decreased substantially. Thus while the student's rate of growth relative to his own rate of growth was minimal, his rate of growth relative to his peers increased.

Example 7.1 Using Summative and Formative Evaluation Data in the Tier 2 Decision-Making Process

Mike was identified as needing Tier 2 instruction based upon results of data collected during a fall universal screening. His level of oral reading performance and his classroom performance, based upon multiple in-class assignments and tests, were discrepant from his peers in the area of reading. Soon after being identified as at-risk, Mike was provided Tier 2 supplemental instruction three times weekly for 30 minutes each session in the form of group repeated readings. Results of CBM progress-monitoring data collected between October and December suggested that Tier 2 instruction was not exactly meeting his needs. The data suggested that he was making only 0.9 word gained per week, which fell short of the established goal of 1.6 words gained per week—approximately the rate of gain made by the students in his grade. Evaluation of other students receiving the same or similar interventions to Mike suggested that they were making comparable or greater gains than students receiving only Tier 1 instruction. A decision was therefore made to provide Mike with an adult tutor on the two days during which he was not involved in intervention.

Formative evaluation data collected between mid-January and April indicate that Mike's rate of gain increased to 1.1 words gained per week. In the absence of summative evaluation data of students receiving Tier 1 instruction, these results would suggest that the added intervention did little to improve the rate at which Mike was making global gains in reading achievement. Summative evaluation of Mike's second-grade peers, however, indicated that during the spring semester those students were only making 0.8 words gained per week. Thus, although Mike's rate of gain in the spring differed relatively little from that observed in the fall, his rate of gain during the spring relative to his peers was substantial. When judging Mike's response to intervention very different decisions would likely be made depending upon whether consideration is given to the summative data of second-grade students receiving identical/similar Tier 1 instruction.

Consideration should not only be given to variation in rates of growth across the academic year, but also to variation in rates of growth between classrooms. Just as all students are not made alike, the quality of instruction across classrooms is not necessarily equivalent. For instance, I once worked in a school where a teacher, for medical reasons, missed a large portion of the fall semester. The rates of gain made by her students were substantially less during this period than gains made by students within other classes at the same school. Similarly, in another school the gains made by the students in one teacher's classroom far exceeded that made in another teacher's classroom. One might attribute these differences in the two teachers' classrooms to variations in the level at which students began the school year, but universal screening data from the beginning of the year suggested that the skill levels of all classes were relatively equal. What differed between these classrooms was the amount and quality of reading instruction provided to students. In summary, to appropriately determine the effectiveness of Tier 2 instruction for an individual student it is essential to know what sort of gains should be expected of the student. Measures such as CBM that can be administered to large groups of students multiple times during the academic year provide summative evaluation data that should enable teams to develop evidenced-based expectations of rates of growth.

ENSURING YOU ARE MAKING APPROPRIATE COMPARISONS

High-stakes decisions regarding whether a student qualifies for special education and whether intervention should be discontinued should not be made in the absence of multiple sources of data including summative evaluation data. Furthermore, it is important that when making high-stakes decisions using estimate of student growth as compared to other students that those comparisons are made using the same instruments. For instance, we would not want to compare a student's estimated rate of growth using biweekly CBM progress-monitoring data to estimated rates of growth of peers established using their universal screening data. Rather, we should use the target student's universal screening data to estimate his/her rate of growth as we did for the peer group (Ardoin & Christ, 2008).

Example 7.2 Using Summative and Formative Evaluation Data

Tina, a first-grade student, was identified as needing Tier 2 supplemental intervention based upon several sources of data. These data included (1) January oral reading fluency scores falling 1.5 standard deviations below that of her classmates, (2) a follow-up CBM performance conducted one week later also falling 1.5 standard deviations below her classmates, (3) failing grades, and (4) a standard score of 76 on a group administered standardized test on which the majority of her classmates exceeded a standard score of 85. The culmination of these data provided strong evidence that Tina was struggling in

(*continued*)

(*continued*)

reading despite being provided with instruction from which her peers were benefiting. Based upon a more thorough assessment of Tina's skills, it was determined that she lacked both accuracy and fluency in oral reading of first-grade materials. It was therefore decided to provide Tina with intervention services three times weekly in 35-minute sessions.

One of Tina's short-term goals was for her to make 1.4 words gain per week when monitored using AIMSweb first-grade oral reading fluency progress-monitoring probes. This goal was based upon the fact that during the previous year, first-grade students on average made this rate of gain, thus it was a goal that many other students achieved/exceeded the previous year with similar instruction. At the end of seven academic weeks, Tina's progress-monitoring data were examined. The data suggested that she was gaining only 0.7 words per week, half of the established goal. Data from three other students who were receiving identical Tier 2 instruction suggested that they were making rates of gain above 1.3 words per week. These data along with continual poor performance in the classroom suggested that Tina was in need of a more intense intervention.

Critical Uses of Summative Evaluation Data

- Summative evaluation data must be used as a means of evaluating Tier 1 instruction.
  - Provides information regarding the context in which the target student is learning. If Tier 1 instruction is not beneficial for most students, it should not be expected to be beneficial for the target student.
- Summative evaluation data must be used as a mean of evaluating Tier 2 instruction.
  - Provides information regarding the context in which the target student is receiving Tier 2 instruction. If Tier 2 instruction is not beneficial for most students receiving Tier 2 instruction, it needs to be revised and evaluated at the group level.
- Summative evaluation data should be used as a means of estimating whether the target student is making similar gains to students receiving Tier 1 instruction.
  - Rates of gain made across an academic subject area are not necessarily consistent across districts, classrooms, or within an academic year. Summative evaluation data can provide insight

regarding what levels of performance Tier 2 students should be expected to make.

- When comparing a student's rate of growth to peers, when possible this rate of growth should be compared using the same measurement instruments/assessment probes (e.g., CBM passages). Variation in the difficulty of materials can impact estimated rates of growth.

FORMATIVE EVALUATION

Parents, teachers, and school staff are unlikely to want an intervention implemented for an entire year only to find out that the intervention has been ineffective. Decisions whether interventions should be continued or discontinued are unfortunately not simple ones to make, and there is not a single manner by which these decisions should be made. Prior to providing suggestions on how to make these decisions, several factors need to be considered in the selection of measures used in formative evaluations. First, RTI teams must plan for the type and amount of data that will be desired when it comes time to decide whether an intervention should be continued as is or modified. Planning is important because failure to do so might result in inadequate sources of data to make reliable, valid, and objective decisions. For instance, when it comes time to evaluate a student's response to intervention, we are not only interested in a student's level of performance but also rate of growth. In order to determine a student's rate of growth, data are needed regarding a child's level of performance prior to intervention (i.e., baseline data). Failure to collect baseline data might relegate teams to using sources of data that are only remotely related to the skills targeted through intervention. If RTI teams do not decide what type of data must be collected prior to decision-making time, teams are more likely to selectively choose the data that supports the desired outcome.

PLANNING DATA COLLECTION PROCEDURES

In selecting measurement devices for making decisions regarding whether intervention modifications are necessary, RTI teams must use multiple sources of data. No measurement instrument is perfect. There is measurement error involved regardless of the measurement device chosen, and thus teams should not be confident in a decision unless there are multiple sources of supporting data. This is especially true when attempting to evaluate changes in skills within an individual child, sometimes referred to as absolute changes, as opposed to changes in a person's skills relative to a group (Christ, 2006). Data might suggest that a student made absolute changes in performance, but his/her standing in relation to other students might not have changed.

Another important factor to consider when selecting a measure to evaluate a student's response to intervention is that generalization of intervention effects do not necessarily occur automatically and are unlikely to occur immediately. When examining the effects of an intervention using global measures of academic performance, such as CBM measures in reading, teams should not expect intervention to have an immediate effect on the student's performance. Thus, in addition to global measures of achievement, RTI teams should select assessment tools that are likely to capture the effects of an intervention within a relatively short period of time (6 to 8 weeks) (Ardoin, 2006).

Many schools mistakenly choose to use CBM progress-monitoring procedures in reading as their sole source of data for evaluating all reading-based interventions. Although extensive evidence exists demonstrating the sensitivity of CBM (Hintze, Shapiro, & Lutz, 1994; Shinn, Deno, & Espin, 2000), the effects of an intervention targeting comprehension skills is unlikely to have an immediate impact on a student's CBM reading performance. In addition to using CBM, teams should therefore use assessment measures that directly assess the skills being taught during intervention sessions. Evaluation of intervention effects using global measures of academic performance should only be used as part of the assessment decision. The decision to evaluate only global gains in academic performance would be similar to evaluating a behavioral intervention implemented at home to increase a child's homework completion and on-task behavior during homework completion time by evaluating classroom grades and classroom behavior. Although the intervention is likely to positively impact these measures, effects are unlikely to be immediate. Intervention effects are more likely to be observed if assessments that directly assess intervention effects are selected. Thus, in the case of the homework intervention we would be more likely to recognize the benefits of intervention if data were collected on the percent of homework completed by the student and if observations of on-task behavior were conducted. Only if changes in these two variables are observed should changes in grades or behavior at school be expected. By only assessing global gains in performance schools are likely to terminate interventions that are having positive direct effects and if given time might result in sufficient global gains.

Factors to Consider in Planning for Decision Making

- Prior to intervention implementation, decide and plan for what type of data will be needed to objectively evaluate intervention effects.
- Error is involved in all sources of data collection, and multiple sources of data must be collected.
- Generalization does not occur naturally and therefore immediate gains should not be expected when using global measures of achievement for evaluating intervention effects. Measures should be used that directly assess those skills being targeted through intervention.

DIRECT ASSESSMENT

Let's now return to the difficult question of how to decide whether an intervention should be continued as is or modified. As stated previously, summative evaluation data are typically only collected three times across an academic year, allowing for only two comparisons of the target student to his/her peers, which lacks sufficient frequency. Assessment measures, however, are available that would allow for ongoing evaluation of all students within a building. For instance, schools might choose to administer maze probes on a monthly basis either through computer-based administrations or through group administration. Even if mazes were administered only monthly, these data would allow for an ongoing evaluation of the progress of all students within a building and/or classroom. Unfortunately not all schools will choose to conduct frequent assessments of all students within their building, but other options for determining whether intervention modifications are necessary are available and should be employed regardless of whether school-wide progress-monitoring data are available.

One source of useful data for determining whether intervention modifications are necessary is to simply evaluate whether an intervention is having a direct impact on the materials on which the intervention is being implemented. Although this may seem simplistic, such assessment must be formalized and therefore planned for prior to intervention implementation. Evaluation of direct intervention effects must be conducted systematically to prevent the use of subjective assessments. Multiple procedures are available for assessing direct effects.

Student Responses

One form of direct assessment is the formal evaluation by teachers of students' responses to questions/problems presented in class. When providing students with opportunities to practice skills taught through question and answering, teachers should formally evaluate each student's proficiency in responding to the questions presented. Every time a student is asked a specific question type, the teacher can record whether the student answered the question correctly and, on a scale of 1 to 5, what level of support was required to assist the student in answering the question correctly. These procedures could be employed during supplemental instruction as well as during regular classroom instruction as a means of evaluating whether the student is generalizing skills across settings. In addition to these data being useful in determining whether or not intervention modification is necessary, the data would be useful in determining when it was appropriate to move to the next skill within the hierarchy of skills to be taught (Hosp & Ardoin, 2008). Having teachers collect data on students' responses to questions presented during Tiers 1 and 2 instruction might also help teachers to ensure that they (1) are providing all students equal opportunities to practice all question types, (2) recognize the skill(s) with which each particular student is having the greatest difficulty, and (3) allow students the opportunity to practice answering questions correctly even when they at first miss a question. Outcome data could also be used as a means of providing feedback to both students and parents regarding instructional outcomes.

CURRICULUM-BASED ASSESSMENT

A second form of direct academic assessment is the continual/ repeated assessment of student performance on probes that sample the skills being taught to a student (Ardoin, 2006). Although CBM probes intended to assess global gains in academic performance are useful, the probes being referred to here differ in that they are not intended to necessarily measure global skills but rather the specific skills being taught to a student. Such probes are oftentimes referred to as curriculum-based assessment probes. Again they differ from CBM probes in that they directly assess the skills being taught and are thus developed using the specific curriculum being used during instruction. The development of such probes first requires an assessment of what skills will be taught during a given time period (2 to 3 months). Probes can be developed by either writing questions/problems that represent the skills being taught or by sampling from existing problem sets that are provided with the curriculum in which instruction is being provided. Each of the probes should contain problems that represent all or most of the skills that will be taught across the specified time period and problem types should be randomized within probes. Ideally all probes developed would be equivalent in level of difficulty; however, it is likely that there will be some variability in probe difficulty, and for this reason multiple assessments should occur weekly. The purpose of these assessments is not to provide students with instruction but rather to provide information regarding RTI. Thus, these assessments should be developed so that they require minimal administration time and thus do not drastically detract from instructional time. It would be expected that at baseline a student would not be able to perform all/most problems on the probe and that they might be relatively slow in completing problems presented. Once the skill(s) has been taught and the student has received sufficient practice on the skill(s), it would be expected that a student would complete probes with high levels of accuracy and speed (Fuchs & Fuchs, 1986a; Hosp & Ardoin, 2008).

By developing probes derived from the curriculum in which instruction is being provided, improvement in performance should be more rapid than on probes that assess global gains in progress (Ardoin, 2006). If gains are not being observed on the materials in which instruction is being provided, then it is unlikely that the instruction being provided will result in global gains and thus modification should be made to the intervention. Given that these measures should be developed to require minimal administration time, teachers could also occasionally administer these probes to Tier 1 students. Administration of the probes to Tier 1 students would allow for goals to be established regarding level of performance and could also be used to establish expected rates of gains (see Chapter 11 on establishing short-term IEP goals). If these probes are not administered to students receiving only Tier 1 instruction, then each student's performance can be compared to the other peers who are receiving identical Tier 2 instruction.

Classroom Performance

A second valuable source of data, which should be readily available, are data collected as part of the evaluation of daily Tier 1 instruction. If Tier 2 instruction is supplemental to Tier 1 instruction, then the time spent in Tier 2 instruction should have beneficial effects on a student's Tier 1 classroom performance. Impact of Tier 2 instruction might however take some time to be noticeable depending upon the overlap between Tier 1 and Tier 2 instruction. Measures that should be considered include performance on teacher-developed tests, in-class assignments, homework assignments, and the active engagement of the student within Tier 1 instruction. When considering these sources of data, it is important to remember several factors. First, the context of instruction remains important. For instance, if we are considering the amount of the student's participation or on-task behavior during Tier 1 instruction, these levels must be considered in relation to the context of instruction. Thus as opposed to examining a student's performance in isolation, student performance should be compared to the other students in the classroom as well as to the student's baseline performance.

Classroom tests are generally not meant to evaluate student growth but rather a student's acquisition of newly taught material. Since the content and difficulty level of tests vary, it generally would not make sense to plot test scores on a graph as we might with progress-monitoring assessments. It however might be appropriate to evaluate whether a student's performance changes in relation to peers. The student's performance may even remain at the bottom of the class, but compared to earlier performances the student might not be as far away from peers in the level/quality of test performance.

SUMMATIVE DATA USED IN FORMATIVE EVALUATIONS

The final group of useful measurement tools for making decisions regarding intervention effectiveness that will be discussed are those measurement devices that allow for ongoing formative evaluation as well as summative evaluations. Despite summative evaluation data only allowing for a direct comparison of a student's performance to his/her peers twice yearly, estimates of desired levels and rates of growth can be drawn based upon data from previous years. For instance, if CBM-Reading data from the 2007–2008 academic year suggest that second-grade students within a school made rates of gain equivalent to 2.3 words gained per week, this rate of gain can be used as a basis for establishing goals for Tier 2 students during the 2008–2009 academic year. Since these data are being used for making relatively low-stakes decisions, it is better to assess frequently and modify potentially ineffective interventions than to maintain the implementation of an intervention that might be doing little more than wasting school resources.

DECIDING TO FADE THE CURRENT INTERVENTION

A primary purpose of Tier 2 instruction is to give students the necessary skills needed to succeed in Tier 1 instruction in the absence of Tier 2 instruction. Fading of Tier 2 instruction should not begin until the data collected provide strong evidence that this has in fact been achieved. Although there might be a temptation to remove Tier 2 instruction once data simply indicate that the student is responding, it is essential to remember that the purpose of Tier 2 instruction is to do more than determine a student's special education eligibility. Deciding to withdraw intervention simply because a student's data suggest that he/she is a responder and thus will not be eligible for special education is likely to result in the student again needing Tier 2 instruction. Fading of Tier 2 instruction should not begin until it is clear that the student no longer needs Tier 2 instruction to succeed in Tier 1 instruction.

Prior to beginning the fading of Tier 2 intervention, decisions regarding the effects of Tier 2 instruction on student skills and performance must be evaluated using multiple sources of objective data collected prior to and following intervention implementation. Data should first be examined to determine whether the student is currently experiencing success in Tier 1 instruction. If the student is not succeeding in Tier 1 with the assistance of Tier 2, the student will not succeed in the absence of Tier 2 instruction. Relevant sources of data for making this decision include classroom grades, amount and quality of classroom participation, and the amount of support needed by the student for accurate responding. The second question to address is whether the student has obtained mastery of the prerequisite skills needed to succeed in Tier 1 instruction and/or that the student's level of proficiency in prerequisite skills is nearly equivalent to that of his peers. If during Tier 2 instruction the student is being provided with assistance in skills considered to be prerequisite to those being taught during Tier 1 instruction, the student will not be able to succeed in the absence of Tier 2 instruction and therefore Tier 2 instruction should not be faded. Relevant sources of data might include assessment of the student's skills on single-skilled math probes and reading fluency and accuracy in materials drawn directly from the student's curriculum. Essentially, what is being asked in questions 1 and 2 is whether Tier 2 instruction has provided the student with the skills necessary to benefit from Tier 1 instruction to the same degree as his/her peers.

If the student is succeeding in Tier 1 and has mastered prerequisite skills, then data must be examined to determine whether the student's level and rate of gain in the skills being taught during Tier 1 instruction are commensurate with Tier 1 peers. This is not to suggest that the student's level of performance has to be at the average level of his/her peers, but it should not be substantially different from peers. Similarly, the student's rate of growth does not necessarily need to exceed or even be at the mean level of his/her peers to begin the fading of Tier 2 intervention. However, it is important to consider that with the gradual withdrawal/fading of Tier 2, the student's rate of growth may decrease. Tier 2 intervention should provide increased opportunities to respond, which should accelerate growth, thus with the decrease in these opportunities to respond the student's rate of growth is likely to decrease (Szadokierski & Burns, 2008).

Is It Time to Begin Fading?

1. Is the student succeeding in Tier 1 with the assistance of Tier 2?
   - If "yes," move to question 2. If "no," continue implementing Tier 2 as designed and/or increase intensity of Tier 2.
   - Examples of useful sources of data: grades, classroom performance, ability to respond to questions posed during Tier 1 instruction, level of support need to accurately and fluently respond to Tier 1 questions.
2. Has the student mastered prerequisite skills?
   - If "yes" to questions 1 and 2, move to question 3. If "no," continue implementing Tier 2 as designed or increase intensity of Tier 2.
   - Examples of useful sources of data: Subskill analyses of test administered in the class, direct assessment of prerequisite skills using CBM measures, criterion measures of performance at grade level, criterion measures of performances administered to students in lower grades.
3. Does the student's level of performance approximate his peers?
   - If "yes" to questions 1 to 3, move to question 4. If "no," continue implementing Tier 2 as designed or increase intensity of Tier 2.

> ○ Examples of useful sources of data: CBM survey level assessment data, accuracy scores as compared to peers on class-administered tests, criterion referenced measures.
> 4. Does the student's rate of growth exceed or approximate his peers?
>   ○ If "yes" to questions 1 to 4, begin fading. If "no," continue implementing Tier 2 as designed or increase intensity of Tier 2.
>   ○ Examples of useful sources of data: CBM survey level assessment data, accuracy scores as compared to peers on class-administered tests.
>
> *Ultimately, it must be determined whether Tier 1 instruction alone will be sufficient to allow the student to continue his current rate of growth and whether that current rate of growth will allow the student to continue to succeed in Tier 1 instruction.

How to Fade

Once the decision has been made that the student is adequately responding to Tier 2 instruction, that Tier 2 instruction has resulted in the student's mastery of prerequisite skills of Tier 1 instruction, and the student's level and rate of growth are commensurate with peers, fading can begin. Plans regarding how Tier 2 instruction will be faded should be determined at the time of initial intervention development. Considering how an intervention might be faded, when initially developing an intervention, will increase the probability that the intervention will train the student in skills that will later promote independence and success in Tier 1 instruction.

Fading options include but are not limited to decreasing the number of days of intervention per week, decreasing the length of sessions, and decreasing the level of support provided during Tier 2 instruction. If an effective fading plan is developed, toward the conclusion of the fading process Tier 2 instruction might not look any different from the format of Tier 1 instruction. As opposed to systematically practicing skills that are prerequisites of Tier 1 instruction during faded Tier 2 instruction, faded Tier 2 instruction might include explicit opportunities to practice skills previously learned in Tier 2 instruction within the direct context of Tier 1 instruction. Such practice is important to effective fading because it helps to ensure that students not only know how to implement the skills, but also to implement the skill automatically in the context of general education. The skills taught during Tier 2 instruction are of little use to a student if the student cannot easily employ them so that he/she can succeed in Tier 1 instruction.

Let us consider how an empirically based intervention might be faded in a group of second-grade students struggling with phonics, reading fluency, and comprehension. The Tier 2 instruction selected for the students is an adult tutoring version of the Peer Assisted Learning Strategies (PALS) with a group of third-grade students (Fuchs, Fuchs, & Burish, 2000; Fuchs et al., 2001; McMaster, Fuchs, & Fuchs, 2006). The initial reading skills of students in the group required that they work on materials at the first-grade level. After four months of intervention, two of the three students seem to have mastered the skills taught during adult tutoring. The first step in fading this intervention might be to have students spend an increasing amount of time working together without the direct support of the Tier 2 adult tutor. Another important step would be to gradually employ increasingly difficult material until the students are able to work successfully and independently from the adult tutor in materials at the second-grade level. Once students have mastered employing these procedures in their classroom materials, sessions could be reduced in number. The students, however, should continue to receive opportunities to work together to practice these skills as well as be given time to work on their own with some Tier 1 teacher supervision. Parents could also assist in this process by encouraging their child to practice and employ the skills at home.

The fading procedures described above are not likely to occur during a short period of time. This is intentional and important for multiple reasons. First, the quick withdrawal of services from full intensity to no services is likely to lead to failure by the student and less likely to promote a student's employment of skills learned during Tier 2 instruction within Tier 1 instruction. Failure to employ appropriate fading procedures might also expend valuable resources that are not necessary. If fading is designed to occur rapidly, teachers might insist on the intervention being implemented at the highest levels of intensity for longer periods of time to increase their confidence that the student will be able to succeed in the total absence of Tier 2 instruction. Finally, slowly fading an intervention will allow schools to use ongoing assessment data to determine a student's likelihood of continued academic success at each of the varying levels of Tier 2 support. Close monitoring of a student's level of performance and rate of gain should not be discontinued until way beyond the time period during which intervention is entirely faded. Premature discontinuation of an intervention and monitoring of student progress can potentially result in a student quickly falling substantially behind his/her peers and Tier 2 services again having to be provided. Services and assessments must continue until the severe discrepancy between the student and his/her peers is eliminated and evidence suggests that complete removal of supplemental services will not result in the student again being discrepant from his/her peers when the next summative evaluation is conducted.

DECIDING MORE SUPPORT IS NEEDED

The first level of Tier 2 intervention will not result in the necessary gains needed for all students identified as needing Tier 2 instruction, and for some Tier 3 instruction will be necessary. However, before deciding that a student needs Tier 3 instruction, multiple levels of Tier 2 instruction should be evaluated, with each level somehow resulting in the student being provided with more explicit instruction and more opportunities to respond. Just as with the decision to begin fading, multiple sources of data should be used to address multiple questions before determining that more intervention is necessary. The first question to address is whether intervention is being implemented as designed, as it is inappropriate to suggest that a student is not responding if intervention is not being provided as specified. Interventions might not be implemented as designed for reasons such as the person implementing the intervention not implementing it with fidelity, student absences, and/or behavior interrupting intervention implementation. Sources of data that can address this question include permanent products that provide evidence of intervention implementation and the gains made by other students receiving the same Tier 2 instruction. If other students receiving the same intervention services are not making improvements, it may be that the intervention is simply not being implemented as intended. Another question that should be examined is whether or not the intervention targets any or all of the appropriate skills/behaviors that need to be targeted. Further assessments may need to be conducted to determine if the student has the prerequisite skills to benefit from the instruction being provided (Hosp & Ardoin, 2008). Because the first level of Tier 2 interventions are generally targeted toward small groups of students, they are not necessarily specific to the individual needs of a given student. To address this question it may be necessary to conduct a task analysis of the skills being taught during Tier 2 instruction in order to make a list of necessary prerequisite skills. Then an assessment should be conducted to determine whether the student has the prerequisite skills. Again, as with the first question of whether intervention is being implemented as directed, it is important to consider the student's behavior. A student's inability to attend to directions, difficulty following directions, and/or lack of motivation to succeed will impact growth. A final question to address is whether there is sufficient overlap between what is being taught during Tier 1 instruction and that being taught during Tier 2 instruction as well as the skills being assessed/monitored. If there is inadequate overlap between any of these areas, rates of growth are likely to be minimal. Lack of overlap between Tier 1 and Tier 2 instruction means a lack of opportunities to practice skills being taught across settings, and it is likely to result in a lack of improvement in the student's grades and classroom participation. Similarly, if progress is assessed only using global measures of performance, it is likely to take a considerable amount of time for changes to be noticeable. For instance, the effects of repeated readings are likely to take a considerable amount of time to impact a student's observed level and rate of gain when assessed using CBM reading progress-monitoring procedures. CBM reading probes are not drawn from the same curriculum and thus may contain few of the words practiced during repeated reading sessions. Although repeated readings improve students' reading of the intervention materials, research indicates that even the immediate impact on materials containing many of the same words may not be that substantial (Ardoin, Eckert, & Pender, 2008). Using multiple sources of direct and indirect assessment information will more often result in correct decisions regarding the need to continue or modify instruction.

Only after multiple interventions have been implemented and evidence exists that interventions were implemented with integrity and sufficient frequency and intensity should Tier 3 instruction be considered for a student. Unlike the decisions to modify, fade, and withdraw supplemental instruction, the decision to qualify a student as needing special education services is a high-stakes decision. This decision should therefore not be made unless multiple sources of data indicate that Tier 2 intervention is extremely unlikely to result in the student's skills becoming commensurate with his/her peers. In addition to considering sources of data that were discussed in regards to deciding when modifications are necessary (e.g., classroom performance), it is essential that measurement tools be considered that have strong evidence of reliability and validity. In making decisions regarding a student's response to intervention the greatest attention should be given to summative evaluation measures that were administered multiple times across the academic year during the implementation of Tier 2 instruction. Although many studies have demonstrated the utility of progress-monitoring data, the majority of CBM research has focused on the evaluation of students' relative levels of performance. Therefore as opposed to attending to weekly progress-monitoring data, attention should be given to universal screening data. Other sources of data might include reliable and valid standardized tests administered to all students in the schools (e.g., Measures of Academic Progress) and norm referenced tests, if it has been determined that Tier 1 instruction provided to the student has been adequate.

In addition to considering the reliability and validity of the data collected for making decisions, several other factors should be considered that are frequently ignored by intervention teams. First, when comparing a student's level and rate of growth to peers it is important that the same data sources be used to compare the target student to Tier 1 peers. Recent evidence suggest that the type of CBM reading passages (e.g., DIBELS or AIMSweb) as well as the order of passages administered can produced significantly different estimates of a single student's rate of growth (Ardoin & Christ, submitted; Francis et al., 2008). Similarly, data collected through weekly progress monitoring should not be compared to triannual universal screening data when making high-stakes decisions. Comparison of a student's biweekly progress-monitoring data to universal screening data of peers is akin to using different measurement instruments to compare students' skills as different probes are used during universal screenings and weekly progress monitoring (Ardoin & Christ, 2008). A final consideration in evaluating a student's response to intervention is that when estimating a student's rate of growth it is important for an intervention to have had the opportunity to impact the data collected. For instance, if a student was identified based upon fall universal screening data but intervention was not commenced for four weeks after screening, it would not be appropriate to use the change in level of performance from fall to winter to spring as an estimate of growth. There were six weeks during the period from fall to winter during which the student was not receiving Tier 2 supplemental instruction. Thus, there were six weeks during the time period when the student was not able to benefit from Tier 2 instruction. While these data might be useful for making low-stakes decisions, it would be inappropriate for making a high-stakes decision such as the final determination of whether a student is eligible for special education.

Although problem-solving models have been employed by districts across the last two or three decades, the use of a student's response to intervention for determining special education eligibility is relatively new. There are many questions that have yet to be answered regarding this decision-making process. One thing, however, is certain and that is that caution should be used in determining a student's special education eligibility. Thus, multiple levels of intervention should be employed and multiple sources of data should be used to assess intervention effects. Furthermore, once a decision has been made, that decision should never be considered final. When intervention intensity is increased or decreased to any level, monitoring of the student's progress must continue. Every effort must be made to prevent a student from falling further behind peers. Both the decision to remove Tier 2 services and the decision to place a student in Tier 3 services could negatively impact a student and thus multiple sources of data evaluating level and rate of growth should continually be collected.

SUMMARY

This chapter unfortunately could not and did not provide any clear-cut RTI rules regarding how long to implement a Tier 2 intervention, how long to fade an intervention, or how many data points must be collected before making a decision. We also did not provide suggestions as to how much discrepancy is needed to qualify a student for special education services. These questions were not addressed because the research literature to date has not provided supporting evidence to definitively answer these questions. However, we must remember that despite the IQ-Achievement model seemingly having clear-cut rules and guidelines, students that quality for special education in one school district under the IQ achievement discrepancy model do not necessarily qualify in another district. Thus, it is not necessarily the case that these rules are set in stone, and there is certainly no research to support the benefits to using one set of IQ achievement discrepancy rules over another.

So then how is the RTI model better given that many important questions are left to be answered by school evaluation teams? It is an improvement because decisions are made based upon the context in which the student is receiving instruction. The goal is not to label a student but to determine what type/level of instruction will assist the student in making optimal rates of academic achievement. Unfortunately, even under an RTI model wrong decisions regarding whether to continue, fade, or qualify a student for special education might be made. The probability of making the wrong decision can be minimized, however, if multiple sources of data are collected for extended periods of time. Decisions also can be rectified by continually collecting data to evaluate the impact of a decision on student performance. The response of a student to Tier 2 instruction should not mean the complete discontinuation of the student from supplemental services at any level. Likewise, the identification of a student as needing special education should not mean that the student will receive special education for life or even until a triennial evaluation is conducted. Continual evaluation of the student's level and rate of progress should aid in determining if special education remains necessary.

TIER 3: INTENSIVE INTERVENTIONS/INDIVIDUAL EDUCATION PLAN CONSIDERATION AND DEVELOPMENT

IV

PART

Moving to Tier 3: Eligibility Determination

T HIS CHAPTER BEGINS Part 4 of the *practitioners' guide*, which describes the process and procedure for moving to Tier 3 activities. This includes the process for special education decision making within an RTI model. The specific focus of this chapter is on articulating the decision making required for determining student eligibility for special education services within the RTI model. Two caveats are required prior to this discussion. First, in moving to Tier 3 eligibility determinations, educators must ensure that Tier 1 and 2 supports and services are in place and have demonstrated efficacy. Effective core instruction, universal screening, timely and effective supplemental services, and ongoing progress monitoring must be in place prior to deeming that students are "nonresponsive" to intervention. The Resources CD offers educators a Tier 3 worksheet that may be used by school teams to determine whether they are ready for Tier 3 activities including eligibility determinations.

The second caveat worth mentioning here is that there is no one *right* procedure for determining student eligibility for special education within an RTI model. The model we propose below is based largely on guidance from the Iowa Department of Special Education and from the work of Doug and Lynn Fuchs at the National Research Center on Learning Disabilities. While these two models differ somewhat, we have proposed a merging of conceptual ideas here. Essentially we believe that important decision-making criteria here would include a discrepancy in student performance and rate of progress, and demonstration of instructional need consistent with the Iowa model. We also support a subsequent comprehensive individual evaluation for nonresponders consistent with recommendations from the Fuchs. The

8

Chapter

model outlined below is based largely on the personal preference of the authors. Implementation across actual states and districts will likely vary, though most if not all of the components described below will likely be included.

A MODEL FOR DECISION MAKING

The Iowa Department of Education has developed a rather detailed process for determination of special education eligibility based on RTI procedures (Iowa Department of Education, January 2006). This model incorporates a team-based decision-making process that includes the parents and emphasizes the importance of adopting an ecological perspective. Multiple sources of data from a variety of sources are reviewed to assess the student's educational progress, the magnitude of the performance discrepancy, and his or her level of instructional need. Based on Iowa's model, student disability is demonstrated by a rate of progress and a performance discrepancy that is significantly behind that of peers or other expected rate and level of performance. A need for service is demonstrated by instructional (need) data demonstrating that the student fails to respond to scientifically research-based interventions that are feasibly implemented in the general education setting. In the Iowa model this would be the information required for an eligibility decision. In our model we have also incorporated a referral for a comprehensive evaluation into the eligibility process. This evaluation would include a valid cognitive measure and potentially social-emotional assessment, interview and observation information, and social and medical history. Figure 8.1 illustrates the requirements for eligibility within this adapted model.

Figure 8.1

A model for determining special education eligibility incorporating RTI procedures

Thus, this eligibility model based on the Iowa Special Education Eligibility Standards delineates a dual discrepancy (student performance and rate of progress) for eligibility as well as the additional component, that of instructional need. Unlike Iowa and in keeping with the concerns articulated by Fuchs and others (i.e., Fuchs, Mock, Morgan, & Young, 2003) we have incorporated a referral for a comprehensive evaluation including a cognitive assessment. This will allow for a continued understanding of learning disabilities and assist in the differential diagnosis of students with varied and/or multiple barriers to learning. Each of the components of this eligibility process is discussed in more depth below. The chapter ends with case examples to further illustrate this process.

PROGRESS

As discussed in Chapters 4 and 6, students' rates of progress are assessed across all tiers of RTI. At Tier 3 the student's progress or response to instructional interventions would have been assessed for some period of time and across two or more well-implemented, scientifically based interventions. Progress is most often operationalized by weekly slope estimates. These slope estimates illustrate the student's weekly growth on a valid and agreed upon performance indicator (i.e., fluency on correctly computed digits in math). To assess a discrepancy in this area the student's rate of progress is compared to either (1) their own historical rate of progress and/or (2) to the rate of progress of a normative group (that of peers or a larger sample).

Figure 8.2 is a graphic representation of a target student's progress (student A) compared to the progress of peers at that grade level. The selected progress-monitoring technique (performance indicator) in this case is the number of correctly read words per minute collected over the course of time with CBM oral reading fluency procedures. Based on the data illustrated in Figure 8.2 we can see that the rate of progress for student A is significantly below that of grade-level peers. This student therefore evidences a current discrepancy with respect to his or her progress in the development of oral reading fluency as compared to peers at the same grade level. We can see by the graph that given the

Figure 8.2

A comparison
of the rate of
progress for
student A and
that of grade-
level peers

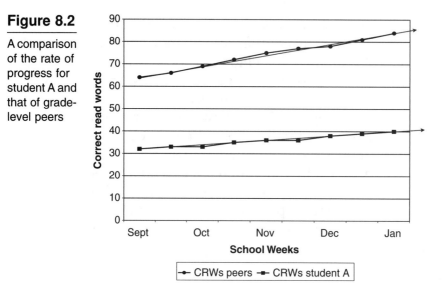

same rate of progress student A will continue to fall further behind peers in this reading skill and therefore will require additional intervention in hopes of improving the rate of progress.

Objective strategies for determining discrepant rates of progress include the following: (1) graphed slopes that suggest the student is consistently falling behind peers in skills acquisition, (2) slope estimates one or more standard deviations below peers or expected rates, and (3) slope estimates below one-half that of peers or expected rates. The first strategy is the least objective but fairly straightforward. It only requires that educators view graphed data to determine that the student's current rate of progress is consistently below expected rates and that they will likely continue to fall farther behind without additional intervention or support. The second strategy requires that the slope for expected rate of progress be computed along with the standard deviation for that population (e.g., grade-level peers). Recall that Table 4.3, back on page 85, suggests that an average rate of progress for reading fluency in third grade is one word per week with a .5 SD. Given this data, then any student with a weekly slope of .5 (1-.5=.5) or less would be considered significantly discrepant in terms of their rate of progress. The last strategy for identifying significantly delayed rates of progress is a more simplistic albeit less statistically sound version of strategy 2. Here the mean slope for improvement is divided in half, and that is taken as the indicator of significantly delayed progress. So if the mean weekly slope of progress for second grade ORF is 2 words per week, then students with progress of one or less words per week would be identified as discrepant with respect to their rate of progress.

While illustrations of a referred student's rate of progress is a major component of RTI decision making, there are several other considerations that should be addressed here, many of which come directly from the Iowa Special Education Eligibility Standards manual. First, given a student's baseline level, a progress goal and a decision plan should be developed prior to intervention and data collection. The goal should be realistic yet ambitious, and the decision plan should include criteria for expected rates of progress and levels that would be considered significantly delayed. The student's historic growth (e.g., prior to intervention) and phase changes should be noted on the monitoring graph so that response to different instructional techniques or intensities may be assessed. A sufficient amount of data collected over a significant amount of time should be used for decision making. Generally at least 8 to 15 data points and weeks of intervention for each phase would be warranted. Further, to the extent possible, interventions should be scientifically research based, have been implemented with documented integrity, and have evidence that they work with similar students in the setting where they were applied. Lastly, other sources of data should be reviewed such that a convergence of evidence exists that can be used to substantiate decisions related to students' rates of progress. These data sources would include standardized tests, report card grades, test and quiz scores, interview information, and information obtained from educational records.

Relevant questions for educational teams to ask related to student rate of progress would include the following:

1. Have sufficient data been collected over a significant period of time?
2. Are the implemented interventions scientifically research based? Have they been shown to be effective with students with similar needs at the given setting? Does sufficient documentation exist that suggest the intervention(s) was implemented with integrity?

3. Has the rate of progress for the referred student been compared to an expected rate or that of peers? Does this comparison suggest that the rate of progress of the referred student is significantly below expectation?

4. Under what conditions does the individual demonstrate the most progress?

PERFORMANCE

In addition to a referred student's rate of progress, their performance at a given point in time is also reviewed to inform eligibility decisions. Here performance would refer to the student's level of performance compared to expected performance or that of grade-level peers at a single point in time. The focus here is to assess the performance discrepancy between the referred student and that of peers or other comparisons. Figure 8.3. illustrates the performance discrepancy between student A and grade-level peers in mid-December. Based on the data illustrated in Figure 8.3 we can see that the performance level for student A appears significantly below that of grade-level peers. This student therefore evidences a

Figure 8.3

The performance discrepancy between student A and grade-level peers in mid-December

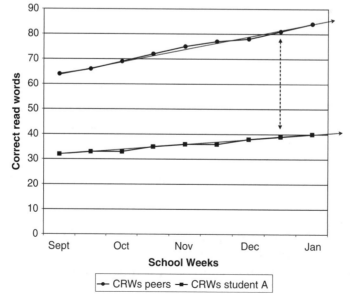

current discrepancy with respect to their performance level in oral reading fluency as compared to peers at the same grade level.

Objective strategies for determining performance level discrepancies include the following: (1) performance levels near or below the 10th percentile, (2) performance levels one or more standard deviations below peers or expected levels, (3) performance levels expressed in the amount of time or years behind in a given curriculum, and (4) performance levels discrepant from generally agreed upon medical or developmental standards. The first strategy for assessing a performance discrepancy requires that the measurement technique include normative percentile rankings. In Chapter 4, for instance, oral reading fluency norms were presented for a large sample of second-grade students (Table 4.2). Based on this information the 10th percentile for winter ORF assessments would be 18 correct words per minute. Therefore, based on the first strategy here students scoring near or below 18 CRWs per minute would be identified with a performance discrepancy in reading fluency. Information from the same table indicates that the mean winter performance of second-grade students is 73 CRWs with a standard deviation of 41. Therefore, to apply the second strategy here one would subtract 41 (the SD) from 73 (the mean) to establish a performance discrepancy criterion of near or below 32 CRWs. As illustrated by this example different methods of computing discrepancy levels will result in different criterion scores.

The third strategy here involves assessing the student's performance discrepancy based on the amount of time or number of years they are behind in a given curriculum. Care should be used here as it would be unwise to withhold early literacy support until the student is two years behind in the curriculum. Likewise, a high school student assessed one grade level behind in literacy development may not be demonstrating a significantly discrepant level of performance. Districts would need to develop guidelines for identifying discrepancy levels for different curriculum and across different grade levels that would suggest a level of performance that warranted consideration for special education services.

The fourth strategy here incorporates the standards used in the medical profession and with respect to other service-related providers. Some disciplines have established levels of performance that dictate their work such as assessments of physical development, adaptive behavior, social and communicative development, and so on. These are also considered when assessing a student's performance level.

In considering a performance discrepancy for a given student, data would be evaluated in one or more formats discussed earlier. Again a convergence of evidence is sought here across a variety of sources and measurements. For example, student A assessed with a performance discrepancy in reading fluency may also evidence low performance levels on state reading exams, standardized tests, classroom assessments, and with respect to performance in the curriculum. Performance measurements below the 10th percentile or 1 SD below peers, in addition to delays in curriculum and in observed developmental level, could all be used to make the case for a performance discrepancy. While this criteria is an important component of the eligibility process, documentation must also exist that the student has a lower-than-expected rate of progress as well as an instructional need that requires special education in order to be referred for a formal evaluation.

Relevant questions for educational teams to ask related to student performance levels would include the following:

1. What sources of data were used to assess the student's current performance level?
2. Do multiple sources of data indicate that the student's level of performance is significantly discrepant as compared to peers or other standards?
3. In what way(s) was the magnitude of the performance discrepancy assessed? How large is the discrepancy?
4. Has this performance discrepancy been demonstrated to persist despite well-implemented, scientifically research-based intervention?
5. Under what conditions or in what areas does the individual demonstrate the best performance?

Instructional Need

The third area of consideration in regards to eligibility is that of instructional need. In short this consideration would review the evidence to determine whether the student requires special education services to be successful in school. Instructional need requires consideration of the student performance and rate of progress, the types of interventions implemented, the age of the student, the length of time interventions were provided, and of course other school and background information. Several strategies can be employed to demonstrate that a student's instructional needs are special education in nature. First, educators can document a lack of response to several well-implemented Tier 2 interventions that have been shown to work with other students with similar needs. Additionally, some schools provide a Tier 3 level support for a course of time to demonstrate that the student responded to a service that is special education in nature due to the intensity of the service. Figure 8.4 displays student A's response to two Tier 2 interventions as well as a Tier 3 intervention briefly implemented by the school resource room teacher. As illustrated by the graph in Figure 8.4, this student did not demonstrate significant response to the two Tier 2 interventions that were implemented. Given that these were well-implemented, scientifically based interventions that had been shown to be effective with other students with similar needs, this student had demonstrated a resistance to intervention. This data in itself may have provided a basis for considering the student's instructional need to be special

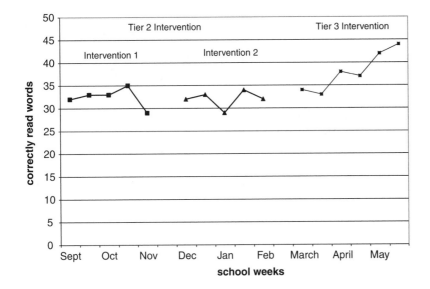

Figure 8.4

Demonstration of instructional need

education in nature. Also displayed here are the results of a Tier 3 intervention implemented in a format consistent with special education resource room services. As demonstrated by the graph, the student has responded to this level of service. This Tier 3 trial may be used as further evidence that the student requires special education services and gives considerable insight into the instructional practices and level of intensity required for the student to make progress.

Relevant questions for educational teams to ask related to student instructional need would include the following:

1. Has adequate data been collected to demonstrate that the student's needs require special education?
2. What environmental variables contributed to the student's lack of response to intervention?
3. What specific needs of the individual cannot be met in general education?
4. What specific special education services are required for the student to progress?
5. Does a convergence of the information on the student suggest that his or her instructional needs are at this time special education in nature?

COMPREHENSIVE EVALUATION

The model of eligibility articulated here includes a referral for a comprehensive evaluation as well as a series of educator meetings to determine the student's special educational classification and programming needs. In the scheme previously illustrated by Figure 8.1, the comprehensive evaluation is the last step prior to decision-making meetings to determine the student's eligibility for special education. At this point to the extent possible a lack of appropriate instruction has been ruled out as the primary cause for the student's academic delays. This has been systematically ruled out by progress monitoring across two tiers of scientifically based interventions that have been well implemented over a substantial amount of time. These interventions have demonstrated effectiveness for students with similar needs, and the referred student's performance and rate of progress has been determined to be significantly different than that of peers or grade-level expectations. Further, there has been a demonstrated instructional need for services that have a level of intensity beyond what can be provided in general education.

Given that instructional accommodations did not result in the desired level of student improvement, the focus of the comprehensive evaluation now turns to identifying student-centered characteristics that likely interfere with learning. While successful RTI implementations in Iowa and Minneapolis do not include this step we feel that it is important for three primary reasons. First, while the RTI eligibility process does a fine job of identifying students who are not responding to educational accommodations it does little to identify why they are not responding. We believe there is some merit in trying to identify the characteristics of students not responding to otherwise effective interventions. This may include, for example, assessments of memory, language, cognition, emotional, and behavioral regulation. A better understanding of student-centered reasons for diminished academic and behavioral performance and progress may assist in the development of more effective Tier 3 accommodations.

Secondly, and on a related note, we agree with Fuchs (i.e., 2001) that there is also merit in preserving our traditional distinctions between special education classifications like MR, LD, and EBD. This information is again useful in accommodating students in special education. Furthermore, in the future maintenance of these categories may assist us toward the development of more effective interventions to assist individuals in specified groups or subgroups.

The third rationale for comprehensive assessment is pragmatic in nature and related to the definition of SLD in the 2004 Individuals with Disabilities Education Improvement Act (IDEIA). As illustrated by the following federal definition of SLD, it requires both the identification of a disorder in one of the basic processes involved in learning as well as the exclusion of other disorders that might result in the observed delays in learning.

> i. General. The term means a disorder in one or more of the basic psychological process involved in understanding or in using language, spoken or written, that may manifest itself in an imperfect ability to listen, think, speak, read, write, spell, or to do mathematical calculation, including

conditions such as perceptual disabilities, brain injury, minimal brain dysfunction, dyslexia, and developmental aphasia.

ii. Disorders not included. The term does not include learning problems that are primarily the results of vision, hearing, or motor disabilities, of mental retardation, of emotional disturbance, or of environmental, cultural, or economic disadvantage. CFR300.7(c)(10).

While RTI may represent an adequate process for identifying students with learning delays, it would likely not be useful for identifying intraindividual processing skills nor in excluding the presence of other disorders as required by the current regulations. While the authors of this text agree with Reschly and Shinn that research on the relevance of cognitive processing tests for the identification of effective academic interventions is "inconclusive" (Chamberlin, Nov 2005), we believe the additional information gleaned is important in meeting the intentions of the regulations and in studying the student-centered difficulties that may be hampering their performance. While a detailed description of a comprehensive evaluation is beyond the scope of this text, the evaluation should represent a multiple measure, multifaceted assessment to the extent appropriate to satisfy the special education regulatory requirements related to identification and to more fully understand the individual's unique pattern of strengths and weakness in cognition, language, memory, emotion, academics, and so on. For more information on the integration of comprehensive assessment and RTI readers are referred to a two-part special issues series of *Psychology in the Schools* edited by Nancy Mather and Nadeen Kaufman (2006), entitled "Integration of Cognitive Assessment and Response to Intervention."

Relevant questions for educational teams to ask related to the student's comprehensive evaluation would include the following:

1. What unique pattern of strengths and weaknesses may explain the student's lack of academic progress?
2. Does the individual present with assessed delays in areas associated with academic performance including but not limited to memory, language, cognition, and emotional regulation?

3. Given the results of the comprehensive evaluation what evidence suggests that the student's observed academic delays would best be explained by the presence of a SLD?
4. With respect to the student's specific learning problems have other possible explanations (e.g., sensory, motor) been ruled out to the satisfaction of the team?
5. What instructional strategies, accommodations, and supports would likely improve the referred student's performance?

Macenaw Elementary School

Macenaw Elementary School had collected two years of progress-monitoring data on their students using grade-level oral reading assessments. With this data they were able to develop local norms for each grade level by inputting student CBM scores at each benchmark assessment point—fall, winter, and spring. The data was analyzed to compute the mean (M) and standard deviation (SD), then the SD was subtracted from the M to obtain a discrepancy score. Students scoring below this discrepancy score at a given benchmark are designated as low performing. Table 8.1 illustrates the student performance data for third-grade students at Macenaw Elementary School.

Table 8.1   Third-Grade Oral Reading Fluency Benchmark Data

Benchmark	Sept	Jan	May
Mean	71.07	92.89	107.54
SD	31.19	32.55	31.07
Discrepancy Score	39.88	60.34	76.47

The district also computed rate-of-increase (ROI) levels for each grade level. The ROI is computed by subtracting the fall benchmark score from the winter benchmark score and dividing by the number of instructional weeks. This gives a weekly rate of progress between these two benchmark points. Similar to the analysis above, the mean ROI, SD, and a discrepancy score was computed for this indicator of student progress. Table 8.2 illustrates student rate-of-increase data for third-grade students at Macenaw Elementary School.

Table 8.2   Third-Grade Oral Reading Fluency Rate-of-Increase Data

Time Frame	Fall	Spring
Mean	1.15	.78
SD	.56	.43
Discrepancy Score	.59	.35

The student performance data illustrated in Table 8.1 and the rate of progress data illustrated in Table 8.2 will serve as the criterion for the following two case examples.

Julie

Julie, a third grader, was identified as a student in need of Tier 2 reading services based on her September benchmark score of 32 CRWs. Her performance level was below the September discrepancy score for third grade of 39.88. Teacher reports and additional reading assessment confirmed that Julie had poor fluency in text and a limited sight word vocabulary. Julie continued with the core instruction in the classroom and was included in an extra reading remediation group. Her progress was to be monitored weekly and her case was to be reviewed by a grade-level RTI group at mid-year. In early January Julie's case was reviewed. Her performance was largely unchanged, 35 CRWs at the last assessment, and her rate of progress slope was −.17 across the fall. At mid-year Julie demonstrated dually discrepant scores in that her last CBM score of 35 CRWs was well below the 47.34 third-grade discrepancy score for January, and her −.17 slope was well below the third-grade fall discrepancy score of .59. A review of the intervention implementation, however, indicated that the remediation groups were often canceled due to teacher illness, snow days, and field trips and school assemblies. In addition the interventionist suggested that Julie appeared to require training in decoding strategies in addition to text fluency and sight word development. Her intervention was revised by including a training component for decoding and by identifying another teacher who could cover in the case of teacher illness. The team also agreed that if Julie missed a session during the week for whatever reason that the session would have to be made up as soon as possible. A follow-up meeting was scheduled for May.

Julie's progress and response to the two interventions implemented from September through May are illustrated in Figure 8.5. Over the course of the second intervention Julie's weekly slope was 1.07, which when compared to the third-grade rate-of-increase table for spring suggests better than average growth. In comparing her last May assessment score of 61 to the May discrepancy score of 76.47, it is obvious that her

Figure 8.5

Julie's Reading Progress

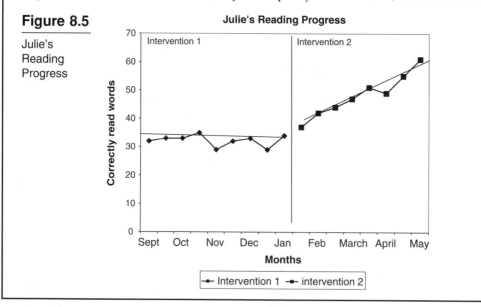

performance remains discrepant from classmates. In terms of instructional need based on her response to the second Tier 2 intervention, the team felt that Julie did not require an evaluation for special education services at this time. She was, however, deemed to be significantly behind peers and so the team recommended six weeks of reading services over the summer, collaboration with the parents to implement a home-based intervention, and further intervention and monitoring in the fall.

Robert

Robert was also in third grade and identified as a student in need of Tier 2 reading services based on a September benchmark score of 29 CRWs. His performance level was also below the September discrepancy score for third grade of 39.88. Teacher reports and additional reading assessment confirmed that he, too, had reading delays and also that he had received Tier 2 services throughout second grade. Robert continued with the core instruction in the classroom and was included in an extra reading remediation group. His progress was to be monitored weekly and the case was reviewed by a grade-level RTI team three times over the course of the school year. Figure 8.6 illustrates Robert's response to two different Tier 2 interventions and, finally, to a Tier 3 intervention.

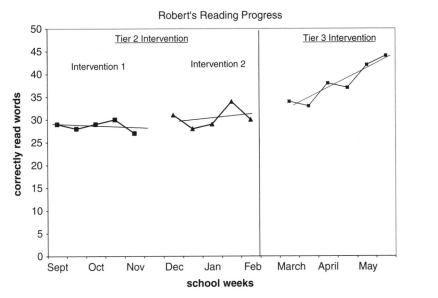

Figure 8.6

Robert's Reading Progress

At each the first two RTI meetings (November and February) Robert's performance level and rate of progress (weekly slope estimate) was compared to the third-grade norms in Tables 1 and 2. Each time he was found to be dually discrepant as compared to other third-grade students in that his performance and slope was below the discrepancy

(continued)

(continued)

scores for his grade. At the February meeting the team agreed to have him served in a special education resource room setting one hour per day, five days a week with a group size of three students to one teacher. His response to this Tier 3 resource room service was evaluated from March through May. Robert went from slopes of −.17 and .4 in November and February to 2.17 at the end of May. Based on his response to this Tier 3 intervention Robert was deemed to have an instructional need that was special education in nature. This, in addition to the dual discrepancy assessed while he received Tier 2 services, formed the rationale for the team's decision to refer Robert for a comprehensive, multiple methods, special education evaluation.

SUMMARY

In this chapter we reviewed a process for conducting special education eligibility determinations within an RTI model. Highlighting the importance of adequately developed Tier 1 and 2 supports we offer readers a Tier 3 worksheet in the Resources CD that may be used by school teams to determine whether they are ready for Tier 3 activities including eligibility determinations. The model proposed here incorporates the dual discrepancy and instructional need components consistent with eligibility standards developed in Iowa. Further, we have included a comprehensive evaluation component based on concerns raised by Fuchs and others. In addition to the description and case examples offered here, we have also included a Special Education Decision-Making Flowchart on the Resources CD to assist educational teams with making these often difficult and complex decisions.

IEP Goal Development

I T IS OFTEN stated and has even been written within this book that it is essential for RTI models to be viewed as a school-wide initiative as opposed to a special education initiative. Although this claim is absolutely true, there are several reasons why the changes that will result from the implementation of RTI in a school might be attributed to special education teachers and school psychologists. First, special education teachers and school psychologists are likely to serve in leadership roles in the implementation of RTI given the emphasis it places on procedures that are already part of their daily routines, such as varying levels of instructional intensity, evaluating individual student needs, and providing explicit instruction. Second, the assessment of a student receiving Tier 2 instruction is likely to look a great deal like a well-conducted assessment of a student receiving resource services. Third, unlike psychoeducational reports written as part of an IQ-achievement discrepancy model assessment, RTI reports should consist of information that is beneficial in the development of IEP goals and instruction to match those goals. Data within RTI reports should provide teachers with information that will assist them in knowing what to do with a child the first day that the student begins receiving special education services. In fact, the services that a student receives once qualified for special education might differ little from that which he/she was being provided prior to the eligibility determination. A final reason that RTI might understandably be viewed as a special education initiative is the extent to which it will facilitate the writing of quality IEPs.

An issue of the *Journal of Special Education* was dedicated to the question of what is special about special education (Cook & Schirmer, 2003). One answer to this question is that

9

Chapter

special education is individualized and thus how it is special for a student is dependent on the individual needs of the student (Hallahan & Kauffman, 2000). Special education services tend to provide students with additional resources, time, and more intense instruction. Whether these services in fact improve a student's functioning is in large part dependent upon the relevance of the data collected to aid in the development of the statement of a student's present level of academic achievement and functional performance. Within an RTI model, the data collected should provide IEP teams with information concerning (1) the student's skill sets, (2) the level and type of services that the student will need in order to make meaningful gains, and (3) an estimate of the level of growth the student might achieve when provided with the services. Not only should these data assist IEP teams in developing improved statements of present level of academic achievement and functional performance, but it should also assist teams in developing improved annual goals. Annual goals indicate the anticipated amount of progress that the student will make in one school year and help in the determination of whether special education is effective for the student. If developed correctly, data collected for the purpose of monitoring a student's progress toward his/her annual goals should assist parents and teachers in determining whether the special educational program is effective or if modifications are needed. Although goals must be written so that they are attainable, they should also be ambitious and result in meaningful improvements (Yell, 2009). Evaluation of a student's progress toward his/her special education goals provides data regarding just how special, special education is for that student.

The focus of this chapter is on how to develop effective IEP goals within schools implementing an RTI model. A primary component of most RTI models is the collection of meaningful data to ensure that all students are receiving high-quality instruction and making maximum rates of growth. Since special education students are regular education students first, RTI data should be useful in making sure they too are receiving high-quality instruction. Given that the purpose of annual IEP goals should be to make sure that a specific student is benefiting from instruction, it should be beneficial to regular and special education teachers if IEP goals are adapted to make use of those data collected through the RTI process. The current chapter will focus on those data that might be employed to improve annual IEP goals. For details regarding the components needed for a quality meaningful and legally sound IEPs see Yell (2009). For more information regarding the basics to developing complete objectives see Alberto and Troutman (2009). The chapter will first describe why short-term goals should be monitored, followed by steps on how to monitor and develop these goals in an RTI framework. In the second section of the chapter we review the importance of monitoring long-term goals, developing these goals within an RTI framework, and selecting appropriate measurement instruments for monitoring long-term growth.

SHORT-TERM GOALS

The instruments employed to monitor long-term goals, which measure global achievement in a specified area, are frequently not sensitive to the small changes in student performance that may occur across two- to three-week periods. For example, the monitoring of student progress using Reading-CBM probes involves the monitoring of global reading achievement, as these probes are not typically drawn from a student/school's curriculum. Research-based norms suggest that students should make between 1.5 to 2.5 words read correctly in a minute gained per week or approximately 4 words gain per month (Deno, Fuchs, Marston, & Shin, 2001). Given that the expected gains are relatively small and because for various reasons students' reading fluency differs across passages regardless of learning (i.e., error), more than two months of Reading-CBM data must be collected before decisions regarding intervention effectiveness can be made (Christ, 2006; Christ & Coolong-Chaffin, 2007; Christ & Hintze, 2007). The implementation of an ineffective intervention for more than two months translates to the loss/misuse of instructional time and a student who is likely further behind peers than he/she was two months earlier. When ineffective interventions are implemented, rates of gain must be accelerated to an even greater extent than initially determined if the student is to accomplish established long-term goals. Procedures must therefore be employed to assure that ineffective instruction is not implemented across extended periods of time. Monitoring students' attainment of short-term goals can decrease the probability of the long-term implementation of ineffective interventions.

Interventions that fail to improve a student's proficiency in the subskills that compose a long-term goal are likely to result in the student failing to achieve the related long-term goal. Students must not only be able to perform subskills independent of each other, but they must be proficient enough in each skill to perform the skills in combination with each other across multiple situations/settings (Ardoin, 2007). For instance, when we teach a child how to count money, the ultimate goal is not for the student to be able to count money for his/her teacher but for the student to be able to select the appropriate amount of money to give a cashier and know the amount of change to expect in return. In order to accomplish this long-term goal, the student must develop proficiency in many skills including recognizing the value of currency and counting to 100 in increments of 1, 5, 10, and 25. An inability to acquire or develop proficiency in any of these skills decreases the probability that the student will generalize the skill to other situations or combine the given skill with other more taxing skills (Binder, 1996). The greater a student's level of proficiency in each subskill that makes up a composite skill, the greater the likelihood that the student will achieve the established long-term goal. It is for this reason that short-term goals must be monitored.

Monitoring the impact of instruction on subskills allows for lack of instructional effects on student achievement to be recognized earlier than if only long-term goals are monitored (Ardoin, 2006). Haring and Eaton's Instructional Hierarchy (1978), described in detail within Chapter 5 of this book, provides an excellent heuristic for the development of both short- and long-term goals. According to the Instructional Hierarchy when developing a student's skills, it is important to first focus on developing accuracy, followed by the promotion of fluency, generalization, and finally adaptation. Short-term goals should be established that focus on the first two stages of the Instructional Hierarchy (accuracy and fluency). Monitoring of short-term goals should focus on a student's development of accuracy and fluency on the individual skills that are required to complete complex tasks and/or required to make progress on a global measure of academic achievement. Probes to monitor accuracy and fluency can be developed by creating pools of items that directly represent each of the specific skills being taught and randomly selecting problems from each of the pools to measure that specific skill. By giving students a specific period of time to complete the problems presented to him/her both accuracy and fluency can be assessed. In chorus with assessments of accuracy and fluency, generalization and adaptation can be evaluated through the measurement of composite (i.e., global) skills using procedures such as Reading-CBM (Ardoin & Christ, 2008; Ardoin et al., 2004). Probes used to monitor short-term goals differ from those used to monitor long-term goals in that the former consist of problems intended to measure gains made on a single skill and the latter measures gains across multiple skills.

There are two potential difficulties in evaluating short-term goals. Fortunately, each is facilitated with the implementation of an RTI model within a school. First, there is the difficulty of having to develop probes to measure each of the individual skills. Prior to RTI, special education teachers may have been the only individuals conducting ongoing monitoring of students' progress; with the implementation of RTI within a school, however, all individuals must become intimately involved in the monitoring of student progress. Regular and special education teacher efforts therefore can be combined to develop assessment materials. First-grade level curriculums can be dissected to evaluate the hierarchy of skills that are taught within and across academic years. The skills can then be divided amongst the teachers so that one teacher is not doing all of the work. Although for some skills it may be necessary for each school to develop its own probes, schools using the same curriculum within a district may choose to share the responsibilities. There are also various web-based sites, such as www.interventioncentral.com, that develop probes to assess specific reading and math skills. For instance, probes that this site will develop for you include, but are not limited to, quantity discrimination, missing number, number identification, letter name/sounds, and Dolch word lists.

A second difficulty of monitoring short-term goals is knowing what level of proficiency (accuracy and rate of performance) is desirable for each short-term goal. The implementation of RTI again simplifies this issue because, as stated previously, the entire school must be involved in data evaluation. While in the past such data may have only been used for special education teachers in their monitoring of students' IEP goals, now all teachers can make use of these data. There are two desirable types of data for developing short-term goals that should be easily obtainable in schools effectively implementing RTI. First, it is beneficial to know the level of accuracy and fluency on each short-term goal of those students who are already proficient in the long-term goal established for the student. For instance, if a student's long-term goal is to be fluent in completing word problems involving simple additions, it would be beneficial to know the fluency on prerequisite skills of students who are proficient in completing identical word problems. Probes might be administered that assess a students' accuracy and fluency in each of the following skills: (1) accuracy and fluency in reading the word problems, (2) identifying problem types, (3) completing basic math facts required to successfully complete the problems, and (4) recognizing superfluous information. These data would be critical for establishing criterion levels of performance for short-term goals and would be equally beneficial for determining the instructional needs of Tier 2 and 3 students (Hosp & Ardoin, 2008) as well as for establishing goals for Tier 2 students (see Chapter 9 of this book).

A second beneficial source of data that can be obtained in schools implementing RTI are estimates of the rates of gain that students should make on each short-term goal. Although research-based norms might be available for some measures used to evaluate student progress toward long-term goals (e.g., CBM), rates of gain are not typically available for the progress monitoring of individual skills. In schools implementing RTI, however, there are two potential sources of these data. The first potential source of data would be rates of gain made by Tier 1 students receiving instruction in the specific skill. Teachers who realize the value of progress monitoring of long-term goals might easily see the benefits of monitoring their students' progress on the subskills that make up the long-term goals. A second potential source for these rates of gain is from Tier 2 students who are learning the same skills with identical short-term goals and similar long-term goals.

When developing short-term goals based upon level and rates of gain made by Tier 1 students, consideration should be made regarding whether adjustments should be made to expected rates of gain. Multiple variables should be considered when determining whether rates of gain should be adjusted. First, when examining rates of gain consideration must be given to the amount of learning that occurs per instructional unit (time) during Tier 1 instruction (Cates et al., 2007). Tier 3 students might receive instruction on any given skill daily, whereas rates of gain made by Tier 1 students might be the results of instruction on the skill being provided only three times weekly. Thus, a Tier 3 student might get 300 minutes of instructional time on a skill weekly with 100 opportunities to practice the skill with feedback, whereas a Tier 1 student might receive only 90 minutes of instructional time with only 10 opportunities to practice the skill. When establishing desired rates of gain per week/month, consideration must therefore be given to a student's previous rates of learning as compared to peers and how increased instructional time might increase that rate of gain.

A second variable to consider in developing short-term goals is that Tier 3 students are Tier 3 students because they in fact demonstrated some difficulty responding to intervention. Fortunately, data regarding the rates of gain that a Tier 3 student made when provided with quality instruction should be available when writing the student's first IEP. It is important that when writing the initial IEP data collected during the assessment of a students' response to intervention be considered. Access to such data is a component of RTI models that distinguish it from test and place models. The students' rates of gain observed while receiving Tier 2 instruction should be considered in relation to other Tier 2 students who were receiving identical/similar intervention and to Tier 3 students who were receiving similar intervention. Consideration of the rate of gain made by the student in relation to the amount of services the student was being provided with should assist special education teachers in determining the number of instructional units a student needs per week and what rates of gain the student might be expected to make on short-term goals.

Examples of Probes for Monitoring

Short-Term Goals	Corresponding Long-Term Goal
Each probe measures performance on a single skill. After fluency is demonstrated on one skill, move to the next skill.	Probes consist of multiple skills

Math Example

Single Skilled Probes	Multiple Skilled Probe
- 1 digit by 1 digit addition problems	1 digit by 1 digit addition problems
- 2 digit by 1 digit addition problems	2 digit by 1 digit addition problems
- 2 digit by 2 digit addition problem	2 digit by 2 digit addition problem
- 1 digit by 1 digit subtraction	1 digit by 1 digit subtraction
- 2 digit by 1 digit subtraction	2 digit by 1 digit subtraction

Reading Example

Single Skilled Probes	Multiple Skilled Probe
- Letter sounds	First-grade CBM Oral Reading Fluency probes
- Nonsense word fluency	
- First-grade Dolch word list	

Example of Establishing a Short-Term Goal

When developing a short-term goal of skill X for Michael, his teacher knew that students performing the desired long-term goal at a mastery level were performing skill X at a rate of 25 correct per minute. Data from a regular education classroom suggested that with two hours of weekly instruction on skill X students' scores improved on average by 3. Looking back at Michael's rates of gain on similar skills indicated that when receiving Tier 2 instruction, which included two hours of practice on similar skills per week, his gains were approximately 60 percent of that being made by other Tier 2 students. Given that Michael was now going to receive three hours of one-on-one instruction per week, his teacher felt that Michael could make rates of gain equivalent to that of students receiving group-level instruction for two hours per week. Since his level of performance on the skills was currently at 12 correct per minute, it was expected that in four weeks his level of performance on this subskill would be near that of his peers (25 correct per minute). Michael's progress on skill X would be assessed four times per week. At the end of two weeks they would examine his progress and adjust the short-term goal if necessary. These data would also be used in establishing a desired rate of gain on the next subskill to be taught and progress monitored.

LONG-TERM GOALS

Measurement of long-term goals allows for the evaluation of the final two phases of Haring and Eaton's Instructional Hierarchy, generalization and adaptation (1978). For students to make use of the individual skills that they learn in the classroom, they need sufficient proficiency in the skills to allow them to generalize and adapt the individual skills to new situations. The use of measures that evaluate global skills allow for such evaluations. By monitoring students' global skills, a student's progress can be monitored across one or more academic years. If only short-term goals are monitored it is not possible to know whether students are retaining previously trained skills and/or whether they are able to combine and adapt individual skills to complete complex tasks. Mastery of subskills, monitored as part of the evaluation of short-term goals, might not be meaningful if they cannot be combined and applied to more complex tasks (i.e., long-term goals).

WHAT TO CONSIDER WHEN CHOOSING MEASURES

The development of long-term goals is of course facilitated by the implementation of RTI within a school. Between the implementation of RTI within a school and state-mandated testing, there should be numerous measures administered to all students within a school that will be appropriate for establishing long-term goals. One should not however just accept the measures that were chosen by a state/district/school as appropriate measures to be used in establishing a long-term goal.

When determining which measures should be used for establishing long-term goals, multiple considerations must be taken into account. First, only tests that are reliable and valid should be used in the assessment of long-term growth. Reliability is the degree to which a measure will provide an identical score if the student's skills/behavior has not changed. A common form of reliability reported for instruments is test-retest reliability, which involves the same test being administered with some time frame (e.g., one week) occurring between administrations. With this little time between two test administrations, students' performance, especially their performance relative to others, should not change.

Two other important types of reliability that should be considered for monitoring long-term goals include whether the different forms of a test are likely to produce equivalent scores (parallel-form reliability) and whether if administered by different individuals the test is likely to produce equivalent scores (inter-rater or inter-observer reliability). Validity, another important measure to consider when examining a test, is the degree to which a test measures what it suggests that it is measuring. For instance, a test that is meant to measure math achievement should measure just that and thus not rely heavily on a student's reading achievement. Individuals who regularly utilize the norm-referenced test should have a strong conceptual understanding of reliability and validity, and thus it may be valuable to seek their professional judgment when choosing measures.

After it has been determined that a test has adequate reliability and validity, consideration should be given to whether a test measures the skills that a student will be taught and the control that the school has over the administration and scoring of the test. For instance, although administrators, teachers, and parents may desire a child to achieve a passing score on a state-mandated test and thus select this as a goal, it is not always clear what skills these tests actually measure. Because these tests are typically group administered, they also tend to rely heavily on a student's reading skills and thus may not be an appropriate measure of a student's skills/knowledge in math/science/history. Schools also unfortunately do not generally control when/if changes are made to state-mandated tests or even when the tests are administered. A final drawback of state-mandated tests is that they cannot be immediately scored, and sometimes due to unforeseen complications scores are not returned to schools in a timely fashion.

A second factor to consider when choosing measures to assess long-term goals is the frequency at which the measure can be administered. Ideally, students can be assessed multiple times across an academic year to determine the probability of the student achieving the written goal. Although information regarding whether a student is achieving short-term goals can lend valuable information to whether the long-term goal will be achieved, it is beneficial to frequently assess a student's progress in generalizing and adapting the individual skills being taught. For a test to be administered multiple times across the academic year, there should be multiple forms of the measure or evidence that there will not be practice effects if administered multiple times and evidence that the multiple forms are equivalent in level of difficulty. If probes are not equivalent in level of difficulty, the change in student performance cannot be attributed to changes in a student's skills (Ardoin, 2008; Ardoin, 2005).

The sensitivity of measures is a third factor to consider when selecting measures for monitoring long-term goals. Even if a test can be administered multiple times across an academic year, if the test is not sensitive to small improvements in student performance there might be limited benefit to administering the test multiple times across the academic year. For instance, because many norm-referenced measures are intended to measure the gains of students across ages/grades, there are generally only a few items representing the multiple skills taught within a grade level (Deno, 1985) (Shriner, 2009). Substantial gains in a student's skill are therefore necessary before the gains are made apparent on test performance. Not only must consideration be given to whether the measure is sufficiently sensitive to changes in the skills being taught, consideration must be given to whether the measure is overly sensitive to factors other than changes in student achievement. For instance, data suggest that a student's performance on CBM probes might vary depending upon the instructions given to a student before he/she reads the probe (Colon & Kranzler, 2006; Eckert, Dunn, & Ardoin, 2006) as well as variation in the difficulty of the probes administered (Ardoin & Christ, 2008). It is therefore important that consistency can be maintained in administration procedures and the materials used across assessments (Ardoin, Roof, Klubnik, & Carfolite, 2008).

Universal Screening Data for Long-Term Goals

Strong consideration should be given to establishing long-term goals using the measurement device(s) being used by a student's school for conducting universal screenings across the academic year. Establishing long-term goals using a measure employed by the school for universal screening purposes has multiple advantages. First, regardless of whether the measure is used for establishing the student's long-term goal, the student will have to be assessed with the measure along with all other students. This assessment will therefore require minimal extra assessment time. Second, by using the same measure that is being used to measure other students as well as the general quality of instruction within a school, it helps to support the vision that the student is part of the larger student body as opposed to a separate entity of students.

A third potential benefit of utilizing a school's universal screening data to establish long-term goals is that due to the quick and easy nature of universal screening measures, students can be administered assessments across multiple grades. This allows for a student's level of achievement to be compared to Tier 1 students across multiple grades, which enables the determination of in what grade it might be appropriate for a student to receive instructional services within the regular education classroom. For example, we may assess a student in materials across grades 2 to 5 despite the student's grade equivalent work being third grade and age equivalent being sixth grade. This may help us to determine that the student was reading at a fluency rate in fourth-grade material near that of some of the struggling fourth-grade students. The identified student might then receive some instruction with one of these groups of students. A related fourth benefit is that these data can be used to establish the desired rate of growth for either catching a student up to peers at a specified time of year or maintaining a student's level of performance as compared to peers. For instance, if we wish Johnny to attend second-grade math classes in the winter of the following year we need to know at what level of performance second-grade students perform second-grade skills. By knowing Johnny's current level of performance on second-grade materials and knowing the average performance of second-grade students in the winter, we can determine the rate of growth that Johnny needs to achieve to participate in second-grade math class beginning next winter ([second-grade students' winter score—Johnny's current score]/number of instructional weeks between now and the desired time during the winter semester). Once Johnny begins receiving second-grade instruction within the regular education classroom, universal screening data from previous years can be used to predict the rate of gain he must maintain to not fall behind his peers. Through ongoing assessment of short- and long-term goals we can continually evaluate whether the level of resources, which would include instruction by the regular and special education teacher, is resulting in Johnny making sufficient response to instruction.

A fourth benefit of using universal screening data for establishing long-term goals is that it promotes continuity across years as well as between Tier 1, Tier 2, and Tier 3 instruction. Universal screening data will be collected on students regardless of their classification, and thus relevant data will be available on a student prior to, during, and even after services are discontinued if this should happen. Although it would be inappropriate to evaluate differences in an individual student's growth within or across years as a means of evaluating special education services for a student, evaluation of changes in a student's relative standing could be compared between periods of time. After receiving special education services one would hope that a student's level of performance relative to his/her peers would improve. However, depending on the level of services the student is receiving, it may no longer be possible to compare a student's performance on a class-wide test. Tests administered through universal screenings will/should however be administered in a consistent manner across students regardless of their disability. Universal screening data are therefore especially beneficial for the purpose of comparing a student's level and rate of growth to any group of peers receiving similar instruction within the same school/district.

A related and final benefit of using consistent measures for universal screening is that these data will have also been collected when the student was receiving Tier 2 services. Examining the rate of growth made by the student while receiving Tier 2 services can provide valuable information for estimating the rate of growth that the student will make when provided with Tier 3 services. Similar to the establishment of short-term goals, when developing long-term goals consideration should be given to an increase in the time and opportunities the student will have to respond/practice as compared to his/her previous circumstances (Tier 1/Tier 2). Having access to the rates of gains made by regular education peers will provide encouragement to parents and regular education teachers, when students who previously made less than half the rates of gains of their peers can now sustain their rate of growth near their peers.

CBM for Monitoring Long-Term Goals

Given the factors discussed above that should be considered in choosing a measure for establishing long-term goals, CBM is an ideal measurement tool. Beginning in the early 1980s Stan Deno and colleagues began the development and evaluation of curriculum-based measurement (CBM) for the purpose of assisting special education teachers in evaluating special education students' academic gains. It was hoped that special education teachers could use these quick and easy to administer objective measures as a means of evaluating a student's long-term goals (Deno, 1985; Deno, Marston, & Tindal, 1985; Deno, Mirkin, & Chiang, 1982). At the time of the CBM's initial development and evaluation, Stan Deno and colleagues could not have imagined the level of access to CBM data that special education teachers now have in schools implementing RTI. Access to universal screening data and the progress-monitoring data of Tier 2 students is a gold mine for special education teachers. In addition to data from the teachers' own schools, web-based resources such as AIMSweb and DIBELS can provide schools and special education teachers with information regarding the level and progress of general and special education students within and across districts.

With the implementation of RTI in schools and the widespread use of CBM for purposes of universal screening and progress monitoring of students receiving Tier 2 instruction, there is no reason special education teachers should not use CBM in the development of IEP goals. Extensive evidence exists demonstrating its reliability and validity (Ardoin et al., 2004; Hintze & Silberglitt, 2005): probes can be administered on a frequent basis, it has been shown to be sensitive to changes in student performance (Fuchs & Fuchs, 2002; Gansle et al., 2004; Shinn, Deno, & Espin, 2000), and it is widely used as part of universal screenings (Ardoin, Witt, Connel, & Koenig, 2005; VanDerHeyden, Witt, & Barnett, 2005). It is important, however, to realize that despite the ease of administering CBM, the number of studies supporting the use of CBM, and the number of schools using CBM as a primary variable in determining students' special education eligibility, CBM data should not be the only instrument used for monitoring a student's progress. Multiple sources of data should be collected regardless of the goal, and consideration must be given to the sensitivity of a measure to each goal specified.

Despite its wide use and the numerous studies supporting CBM, it does have its weaknesses—as do all measures. For instance, one of the greatest benefits of CBM is its sensitivity, but one of the biggest drawbacks of CBM is its sensitivity. CBM procedures are not only sensitive to student growth but also to other variables, some of which can be controlled and some of which cannot (Ardoin et al., 2008; Eckert et al., 2006). Student performance on CBM probes can be influenced by variation in the instructions used across assessment sessions. Research suggests that if students are told to read for accuracy versus reading for speed there are likely to be differences in students' accuracy and speed of reading (Eckert et al., 2006). Studies also suggested that students' fluency is likely to be affected by whether or not contingencies are established for their performance (Eckert, Ardoin, Daly, & Martens, 2002). Thus, at the onset of progress monitoring, decisions regarding whether or not goal setting will be employed for weekly monitoring, whether the student will graph his/her data, and/or whether rewards will be provided for exceeding an established score must be determined. Changes in these procedures are likely to have drastic effects on student performance and thus impact estimates of a student's rate of growth. Other sources of differences in student performance that can and should be controlled for when assessments are conducted include the location of the assessments, person conducting the assessments, and time of day that the assessments are conducted.

Unfortunately one source of variation in student performance that is hard to control is the variation in the difficulty of CBM probes within probe-sets (Ardoin, Suldo, Witt, Aldrich, & McDonald, 2005; Christ & Ardoin, in press). It is therefore important that when monitoring student progress, multiple data points be collected to account for variation in probe difficulty. Administering three probes per assessment occasion and recording a student's mean score can help to reduce this bounce and produce more reliable and accurate estimates of student growth.

Due to the variation in probe difficulty, it is also suggested that when conducting CBM tri-annual universal screenings that the same three probes are administered across each screening conducted in the academic year. Furthermore when comparing a student to peers as a means of evaluating relative standing, student performance should only be compared across the same probes. The only way to assure that passages are in fact exactly equal is to make comparisons using student performance on the same probes (Ardoin & Christ, 2008). Variation in probe difficulty could result in a student correctly reading 12 to 15 words more or less than other students in a minute. If the probes that a student is administered are much more difficult than those administered to peers, it may seem that the student's achievement relative to peers is much lower when in fact it is at the same level as average peers.

Although it is important to consider these factors when using CBM, the measure remains one of the friendliest, cost-effective, reliable, valid, and well-researched measures for establishing and monitoring long-term goals. Many of the above-stated concerns are also true with other assessment measures. It is always important to maintain consistency and ensure that if multiple forms/ probes exist, regardless of the type of measure, that all forms are equivalent. CBM is simply unlike most other measures in that other measures do not allow for such frequent measurement, thus they generally prohibit the amount of ongoing progress monitoring that is allowed through CBM (Deno, 1985; Deno et al., 1985; Shinn, 1998).

CRITERION REFERENCED TEST

Another useful form of measurement for developing long-term goals is criterion referenced tests. These tests are often times developed by states, school districts, and publishers of curriculums. Unfortunately, it may be difficult to come by criterion referenced measures that provide you with multiple probes for ongoing progress monitoring or that provide evidence of reliability and validity. These tests also are not necessarily developed for the purpose of monitoring progress or for comparing students to each other (Shriner, 2009). They are beneficial, however, in that if developed to match a specific curriculum the prerequisite skills necessary for students to meet the criterion established by the specific test should be made clear by the developer. The criterion established by the publisher for passing is useful for establishing a meaningful goal for the identified student. Finally, although normative data allowing for relative comparison may not be available from a publisher, if the criterion referenced test is used within the school/district, relative comparison can be made using data collected. Just as with the use of CBM, it is important to consider variables such as who administers the test, where the test is administered, and what types of directions and support are provided to students. These are all considerations that should be stated with the IEP.

SUMMARY

Although some students may succeed in spite of ineffective instruction, when effective instruction is provided all students will benefit to some degree and academic achievement will be maximized. It is with this in mind that those in support of RTI emphasize that RTI must be a school-wide initiative. Data collected as part of an RTI model are not only beneficial for evaluating Tier 1 instruction, but also for identifying students in need of supplemental instruction or for evaluating a student's response to Tier 2 instruction. These data are also beneficial in multiple ways once students have been identified as needing special education services. First, universal screening data can aid IEP teams in selecting meaningful goals as they provide clear evidence of the level of performance made by regular education students. Second, the data continue to provide a metric by which students in special education can be compared to their regular education grade- and age-equivalent peers. Third, the data can be used to evaluate an identified student's progress prior to and after being identified for special education. Fourth, for those identified students who continue to receive Tier 1 instruction, universal screening data provides some evidence that even outside of the special education the services being provided to the student are effective.

Listed above are only a few examples of how RTI can benefit IEP teams. However, these benefits are only likely to be recognized if RTI is accepted as a school-wide initiative and IEP teams treat the RTI model as such. Well-trained special education teachers and IEP team members should help in organizing, evaluating, and shaping the RTI models used in their schools. Moving towards a system where there is little difference between IEPs and plans developed for students identified as needing Tier 2 instruction will help regular education teachers to understand that special education students are regular education students first. Once students are identified, special education teachers should not necessarily be the only people responsible for collecting data and should definitely not be the only individuals who make use of the data. Establishing meaningful goals that are clearly related and linked to the assessments used with all students will further establish RTI as a school-wide initiative. Responsibility of providing effective instruction to a student must become and remain a shared responsibility between the regular and special education teachers.

When starting any new initiative it is important to remain cautious. This is true in regards to the implementation of RTI within a school. It is likely that various sources of data will be used when making important decisions that will impact the education provided. Data are however only as good as the device used to collect it and the fidelity with which the instrument is administered. Regardless of the decision being made it is important to use reliable and valid sources of data. When information is not available regarding the reliability and validity of a measure, it becomes even more important that multiple sources of data be collected and used. It is also important to remember that just because a measurement device is reliable and valid for making one decision, it is not necessarily reliable and valid for making all decisions. Just as a measure with evidence of reliability and validity for measuring students' writing skills is not adequate for measuring their reading achievement, a measurement with adequate reliability and validity for measuring long-term gains is not necessarily adequate for measuring short-term gains.

IEP teams must carefully choose the instruments selected for evaluating progress towards a long-term goal. Strong consideration should be given to evaluating progress toward a student mastering the prerequisite skills that make up a long-term goal. Although lack of change on a measure of global gain should not be ignored, one should not expect substantial progress within short periods of time. Lack of growth over short periods of time (e.g., 15 weeks) is, however, difficult to overcome when attempting to achieve a long-term goal. Thus, it is our advice that IEP teams develop short- and long-term goals for students with consideration to their current level of skills, observed rates of growth, and difference in the level of instruction (i.e., opportunities to respond) they have and will receive.

Example 1

Peter was a second-grade student who was first identified as needing supplemental instruction in the winter of his first-grade year. During the winter of first grade he was provided with intervention services in a group of five individuals three times weekly for 12 weeks. Data indicated that while the other four students made substantial gains during this period of time, Peter's level of achievement did not improve relative to the other four peers receiving instruction or relative to his classmates. Not only were his improvements less than these comparison groups, but he simply made little noticeable gains as compared to the initial assessments of his skills. Intervention intensity was therefore increased to five times a week and the group size was reduced to a total of three participants. This intervention was continued throughout the spring semester and commenced again immediately when the school was reconvened in the fall and Peter was in second grade. Even with modifications to instruction and increased levels of intensity, multiple sources of data indicated that Peter was not making the same rates of gain as either his classmates or other students receiving supplemental instruction. Peter's level and rate of gain on CBM measures were significantly below his peers as was his performance on the standardized norm-referenced assessment administered by his teacher. Furthermore, despite the assistance being provided, he continued to make failing grades.

After providing Peter with multiple levels of intervention intensity it was determined based upon multiple sources of data that Peter was in need of special education services. An IEP was drawn up for Peter that included two long-term goals. The first long-term goal was that Peter would be able to read second-grade AIMSweb oral reading fluency probes at a rate of 70 words correct per minute by May 15 of the academic year. This would require Peter to make a gain of 1.7 words gain per week. Given that Peter would now be receiving twice the amount of supplemental instruction time through special education services and that he was previously making a rate of gain of .9 words per week, it was believed that this goal would be achievable. Ongoing progress monitoring of this goal would occur twice monthly, during which time three AIMSweb CBM probes would be administered and the median score would be plotted. These data would be plotted and shared with Peter and his parents each time the assessment occurred.

The second goal established was that in May Peter would achieve a standard score of 85 in language arts on the same computerized standardized assessment that he

(*continued*)

(continued)

achieved a score of 70 on in the May of his first-grade year. This test would be administered to Peter as well as all other students in the building in January and again in May of the given year. Previous students receiving similar services to those designed for Peter in his IEP had made a 15-point increase in their standardized test scores. Although data from the January test would be examined, a goal had not been established for this time point since it was not believed that there were a sufficient number of instructional weeks to sufficiently impact performance between the development of the IEP and the January assessment.

A hierarchy of prerequisite skills was developed that were believed necessary for Peter to achieve this goal. These prerequisite skills included but were not limited to (1) fluency rate on nonsense words; (2) fluency rate on a second-grade word lists associated with the student's curriculum; (3) story oral retell rate; and (4) 70 percent accuracy in responding to who, what, and when questions related to paragraphs within the school's second-grade reading curriculum. These were all identified as prerequisite skills to achieving the identified long-term goals, skills in which the student had poor accuracy/fluency, and skills that could be easily assessed on a weekly basis. A schedule was established so that on a monthly basis the student would be assessed on all of the prerequisite skills and that when receiving instruction on a particular prerequisite skill the student would be assessed on a weekly basis A schedule was established to ensure that by early April the student would have achieved all of the short-term goals, thus allowing for time in case the student did not achieve goals at the specified rate and to allow for time to provide intense review of the prerequisite skills prior to testing.

HANDOUT

Critical data for developing a quality long-term goal:

- Universal screening data collected on identified student.
  - Provides estimate of student's level and rate of growth on general outcome measures.
  - Can be used directly for establishing long-term goals.
- Assessment data that provides an indication of the identified student's skill sets.
  - These data should be specific enough so that team can be made aware of what prerequisite skills the student has and has not mastered.
- Information regarding what prerequisite skills are needed to achieve long-term goals
- Information regarding previous level of support provided to identified student.

- Information regarding the student's previously observed rates of gain when provided with supplemental support.
  - Helps in determining if established goal is ambitious and reasonable.
  - When considered with previous level of support can be useful in determining whether the student will be able to achieve stated rate of growth.
- Universal screening data that provides estimates of the level and rates of growth made by all students in the school across grades.
  - These data may be useful in determining what students are achieving at a level commensurate with the identified student.
  - These data can be used to determine what level of achievement the identified student needs to achieve to be commensurate with an identified peer group.

FACTORS TO CONSIDER WHEN DEVELOPING LONG-TERM GOAL:

- Use school-based data to identify a goal(s) that will allow the student to achieve at a level commensurate with desired peer group.
- Will the goal result in meaningful changes in the student's skills, academic achievement, and/or behavior?
- Is the goal ambitious and reasonable given the student's current level of achievement?
- Is the goal ambitious and reasonable considering the student's previously demonstrated rates of progress? When answering this question, consider the student's previous level of support and the level of support that he/she will be receiving under the described IEP.
- The student's rate of progress will be a function of the quality and amount of instruction provided to him/her. If there is not an increase in one or both, the rate of gain observed in student performance will not change.

FACTORS TO CONSIDER WHEN SELECTING MEASURES TO MONITOR LONG-TERM GOALS:

- Is there evidence that the instrument being used to measure progress actually measures those skills that will be taught during instruction?

- If the student makes small changes/improvements, will the measure be sensitive to these improvements?
- How much improvement in the student's skills is necessary before there is noticeable improvement on the measure?
- Are there multiple forms of the measure to allow for multiple administrations of the measure across the academic year?
- Is there evidence that the multiple forms are equivalent in level of difficulty?
- Has a universal screening measure been selected so that goals can be established relative to the performance of other students in the building?
- Have multiple measures been identified? A single goal should be measured using multiple instruments.

STEPS TO DEVELOPING SHORT-TERM GOALS

- Determine what prerequisite skills are needed to achieve the long-term goal?
- Determine the identified student's level of performance on each of the prerequisite skills.
- Examine pre-existing data or administer assessments to determine the level at which students who have already achieved the long-term goal perform each of the prerequisite skills.
- Use data regarding the identified student's current performance on prerequisite skills and data regarding level of performance on these same skills by students who have already achieved the long-term goal to establish each short-term goal.
- For each prerequisite skill that the student has not achieved the necessary level of performance, develop a short-term goal.
- Develop a time frame for when each short-term goal should be achieved. When developing the time frame for each short-term goal consideration should be given to the student's current level of performance on the goal, desired level of performance, and amount of instruction that will be dedicated to that skill each week.
- Develop a weekly/biweekly progress-monitoring schedule for monitoring of the prerequisite skill the student is currently receiving instruction in.
- Develop a schedule to assess student's level of performance on each of the prerequisite skills at least once monthly. These data will

provide information regarding whether the student is retaining previously taught skills, if instruction in one skill is leading to improvements in previously untaught skills, and whether with the current level of instruction the student will achieve the established long-term goal.

- Develop a schedule for assessing the student's progress on the skill(s) the student is receiving instruction on. When classroom instruction is being provided on a specific skill, that skill should be monitored regularly (weekly, biweekly) until the student has mastered the skill.

Considering Reintegration and Special Education Exit Decisions within an RTI Service Delivery Model

KELLY A. POWELL-SMITH, PH.D.

10
Chapter

INTRODUCTION

Within an effective RTI service delivery system, reintegration and exit from special education should become regular occurrences. In this chapter, the knowledge and practices that will facilitate exit decisions within an RTI model are presented and discussed. First, a brief history and rationale for exit decision making are presented. Then, what it means to fade special education services responsibly is discussed, including facilitators and barriers to exit. Next, a step-wise model for exit decisions and several tools useful for those decisions are presented. Finally, a case study illustrating the process is provided. The goal of this chapter is to present and illustrate practical information that will assist school psychologists and other school practitioners in planning and implementing reintegration and exit procedures in the schools and systems in which they work.

BRIEF HISTORY AND RATIONALE

Reintegration often is described as the process of returning to general education classrooms special education students who have been served in special education programs. Reintegration is historically tied to the Regular Education Initiative (REI). In the late 1980s, after Assistant Secretary of Education Madeline Will issued a white paper on the REI (Will, 1986), discussions of REI featured prominently in education. The white paper's central message was that too many special education students were receiving services outside of their general education classes. In addition, the paper called for increased efforts to educate special education students in general education as well as greater collaboration between special and general educators. More recently, greater attention to outcomes and accountability for special education students has become a part of the Individuals with Disabilities Education Act (IDEIA, 2004). These changes have increased the focus on access to, and opportunities for success within, the general education curriculum. Subsequently, efforts with respect to reintegration and exit also have increased.

Importance of Reintegration and Exit

Two critical reasons reintegration and exit are important are (1) the continued growth of special education and its associated expenses, in the absence of solid data on exiting the system, and (2) the overwhelming legal support for it.

Growth of Special Education   According to the 26th Annual Report to Congress (USDE, 2006), about six million students were served in special education in the year preceding the report. Most of these children (75 percent) were those identified with mild disabilities (e.g., specific learning disability, speech and language impairment, and emotional disturbance) suggesting that large numbers of candidates for possible reintegration and exit exist. Additional data from Parrish (2006) indicate that the total percent of students receiving special education relative to all students enrolled in both public and private school has shown steady growth every year (e.g., from 1976 to 2004 it has increased from 7.5 percent to 12.2 percent).

Along with increased numbers come increased costs. As a case in point, consider fiscal year 2004 in which $10.1 billion were appropriated for Part B of IDEIA. This figure is more than double the amount appropriated for 1999, indicating an approximate $1 billion increase per year (Parrish, 2006). Increased numbers and costs are of even greater concern considering that only scant information about the number of students exiting special education can be found. Historical data suggest that only a very small percentage of students exit special education (Lytle & Penn, 1986; Shinn, 1986). Furthermore, despite the increased focus on accountability in the last decade, very little contemporary data on exiting exist other than data with respect to graduation and dropout (Powell-Smith & Ball, 2008).

Legal Support for Reintegration and Exit   Consistent legal support for exiting students from special education exists. First, the LRE clause of IDEIA tells us that students should be educated in general education environments to the *maximum extent appropriate.* Concepts within the LRE that are central to the notion of re-integration and exit are *benefit* and *satisfactory achievement.* Over time, these concepts have been both operationalized and clarified by several court cases, beginning with a hallmark Supreme Court case, *Hendrick Hudson District Board of Education v. Rowley* (1982). According to Rowley, benefit was defined as satisfactory achieve-ment in general education, and satisfactory achievement was defined in reference to the grading and achievement standards of general education. The ruling in the Rowley case identified one standard by which placements could be judged as meeting the LRE criteria. In addition to Rowley, several other circuit court cases have examined this issue. While a full discussion of these cases is beyond the scope of this chapter, many of the cases relevant to exit decisions and the standards used for decision making in each case are discussed in more detail by Powell-Smith and Ball (2008).

These court cases, along with the current educational milieu focusing on both greater access and greater accountability, suggest that the burden is on the school to gather data showing response to instruction (or lack thereof) indicating whether the child can achieve satisfactorily (i.e., make progress) with supplemental aids and ser-vices in general education. Without such evidence, more restrictive placement cannot be pursued or justified. No compelling argument exists for maintaining a student in special education in circum-stances where it is clear that the student can respond positively to instruction at a lower tier of support. Within a multitiered, school-wide service delivery system incorporating RTI, reintegration and exit become regular and naturally occurring outcomes.

WHAT IT MEANS TO FADE SERVICES RESPONSIBLY

Ensuring that services are faded responsibly in large part depends on following a process for exit decision making that is principle driven. In fact, the early work in the area of reintegration referred to the process as *Responsible Reintegration* (Fuchs, Fuchs, & Fernstrom, 1992) because it was founded on the notion that such decisions should be data based and individualized. In addition, part of a responsible approach to reintegration means attending to the LRE clause of IDEIA as well as case law related to reintegration decision making. The process described in this chapter is consistent with these ideals, beginning with case-by-case decision making.

A case-by-case decision-making framework means that exit decisions are not all-encompassing decisions for entire groups of students (i.e., full inclusion), but rather are made for individual students based upon each student's unique skills and necessary supports. Such an approach requires practitioners to be skilled in single-subject data collection and analysis as a means of monitoring outcomes. In addition, a case-by-case approach goes beyond assessment of the individual. Such an approach also includes gathering information about the classroom ecology and school climate variables likely to impact reintegration success, in essence more systems-based variables. While some of these variables may focus at the classroom system level (e.g., classroom organization, management, peer and teacher interactions, instruction), others may require analysis of the broader school-wide system of support (e.g., quality and success of instruction at Tier 1). When system-wide data are available, practitioners are encouraged to examine the overall success of instruction across all tiers of support. When Tier 1 instruction is not healthy (i.e., meeting the needs of approximately 80 percent of the student population; Tilly, 2008), then efforts to shore up Tier 1 are an important first step to ensuring success of reintegrated students.

Another aspect of fading services responsibly is that such decisions are made in a manner consistent with the reauthorization of IDEIA as well as important legal decisions. School practitioners need to be knowledgeable of these legal requirements as well as how to carry them out in practice. In most cases, this means that school-based personnel must be equipped to provide data indicating what the LRE is for a particular student as well as data that indicate the level of support necessary for the student to be successful and make progress within the general education curricula.

PROCEDURES FOR ENSURING SUCCESS

One way to help ensure success is to consider potential barriers and facilitators in advance of reintegration and exit efforts. Understanding barriers allows one to plan effectively how to handle those barriers when they present themselves. Knowing what might facilitate reintegration and exit efforts allows resources to be marshaled appropriately at each exit decision-making step. Barriers and facilitators likely will vary from one setting to another. As such, considering barriers and facilitators in this manner also is part of taking an ecological approach to reintegration and exit. Among the potential barriers and facilitators discussed here are stakeholder beliefs and concerns about reintegration efforts, the effectiveness of the overall instructional system, and the approach to decision making about student performance.

STAKEHOLDER BELIEFS AND CONCERNS

One of the most important places to examine facilitators and barriers to exit decision making is with respect to key stakeholders' beliefs and concerns. The model described in this chapter attends to the beliefs, needs, and concerns of key stakeholders in an ongoing fashion. However, before these concerns can be addressed, they must first be understood.

One of the issues with which schools contend is that we have yet to obtain philosophical consensus regarding exit decision making despite clear indications from court cases and advances in assessment technology as to the who, when, and how of reintegration. Generally speaking, exit decision making has relied heavily upon the volunteerism or goodwill (Fuchs et al., 1992) of teachers and parents. That is, these stakeholders must be willing to participate in and agree to the decision to return a special education student to the general education classroom. In a volunteerism approach, if any of the individuals disagrees with a change in placement, it is much less likely that the student will be reintegrated. Resistance to exiting may be a result of not attending to or addressing the beliefs, needs, and concerns of stakeholders. As such, it is worthwhile to consider the concerns of each stakeholder group with respect to reintegration and exit decision making.

Several key stakeholders' concerns or beliefs that may impact reintegration are delineated in Table 10.1. Of significant concern is that stakeholders do not have an expectation that reintegration will occur and, even if they do, it is rarely discussed at the time of initial eligibility. For example, Green and Shinn (1994) found that 71 percent of parents reported that exit criteria and ultimate goals of special education were not discussed at the time of initial special education placement. One way to address this problem is to ensure that exit and reintegration are discussed relative to the continuum of services when the initial Individual Educational Plan (IEP) is developed, as well as during annual and triannual reviews.

Addressing Stakeholder Needs   Given the concerns and beliefs listed in Table 10.1, points to emphasize when discussing reintegration and exit include:

- Reintegration and exit can result in positive outcomes of exit for *all* students, both special and general education students.
- Reintegration is a *collaborative* process, meaning that collaboration occurs between all key stakeholders to work toward a successful reintegration trial and eventual exit. A collaborative approach means that key stakeholders have the opportunity to provide feedback throughout the process and that these data are collected systematically and considered in decision making. Thus, in the model presented here assessment of key stakeholder opinions and attitudes is part of the process. These actions communicate a message that decision making is shared.

Table 10.1   Beliefs and Concerns of Stakeholders Regarding Reintegration and Exit

Belief/Concern	Person Typically Expressing the Concern or Belief				
	Administrator	SE Teacher	GE Teacher	Parent	Student
Exit from special education is not an expectation.	X	X	X	X	X
Exit is a means of reducing services needed to maximize student achievement.				X	
Reintegration removes the student from a nurturing environment.				X	
The student receives one-on-one instruction in SE.				X	
How will exit impact future eligibility for test accommodations in college?				X	X
How will exit impact future eligibility for vocational education services?				X	X
Additional skills and resources will be needed to address the reintegrated student's needs in GE.	X		X		
The impact of greater diversity in the classroom on test scores.	X		X		
SE programs may be reduced due to exiting students.	X	X			
How will program funding be impacted?	X				
Has the student made sufficient academic and behavioral progress to exit?		X	X	X	
How will the student perform once reintegrated; will he or she be successful?		X	X	X	

Note. SE, Special Education; GE, General Education

- The trial reintegration period is a *safety net*; data will be collected and changes made to the plan if needed.
- Training the student for success in general education prior to the reintegration trial can be part of the plan.
- *Continued supports* within general education will be available. For example, a number of naturally occurring supports are available in general education (e.g., 504 plans, building assistance teams, guidance services, and modifications during instruction like repeating directions, additional time for task completion, adjusting task length, frequent prompts and feedback, mass practice of skills, and individual or small-group instruction from teacher or paraprofessionals). Importantly, supports that occur naturally within general education will help the student generalize and maintain skills after the reintegration plan is faded.
- Reintegration is a part of our school-wide system (i.e., continuum) of support.

Parents and students need to know that reintegration is an intentional process designed to ensure success and to increase personal independence in both the short and long term. Parents need to understand that reintegration and exit are part of the school's overall system for addressing student needs (i.e., the continuum of services). Parents and students need to see the connection of the IEP to the notion of reintegration and exit. Again, such issues should be discussed at the time of initial IEP writing, reviewed at each annual IEP meeting, and again at triannual reviews.

Importantly, parents should feel like they are part of the planning and decision-making process, essentially, that they are part of the team. Thus, practitioners must communicate the critical role that parents play on the team that makes reintegration and exit decisions. Further, when concerns arise regarding future eligibility for services, they should be addressed directly. Should the exited student need services like test accommodations in college or vocational education later, it is possible that they may become eligible for such services again. However, it is important that stakeholders consider that the student may reduce his/her future need for these services as a result of being exited and more independent and self-sufficient, the ultimate goal of special education.

Some of the parental concerns may be mediated by special education teachers. For example, research by Ball (1997) suggests that special education teachers are in a position to influence parental views regarding their child's readiness for reintegration, even more persuasively than data indicating special education student skills are within the range of students in general education. Because parents may be less influenced by data indicating their child may be ready to exit, the special education teacher's views are critical. In addition, special education teachers are in a position to communicate the purpose and scope of special education services.

Given the important role of the special education teacher, any specific concerns they have must be addressed as well. Like the other stakeholders, special education teachers need to understand the long-term benefits to the student of becoming self-sufficient and more fully integrated. Special education teachers also need to understand the importance of special education student success in the general education curriculum. Changes in IDEIA now require greater attention to special education students' access to and progress in the general curriculum. Finally, special education teachers should understand that they can be a significant resource and consultant to the general education teacher in the process of reintegrating students.

Like special education teachers, general education teachers need to understand the importance of special education student success relative to the general education curriculum given the new requirements of IDEIA. However, sharing this information is only a starting place. General education teachers also need to understand that reintegrated students will not be vastly different than those they are already teaching. Data-driven decision making can help address this issue. For example, research by Rodden-Nord, Shinn, and Good (1992) as well as Shinn, Baker, Habedank, and Good (1993) found that general education teachers were more willing to reintegrate a student when they were given data showing that the student's skills were in the range of students in their classroom. Thus, general education teachers need to be part of the data-driven decision-making process and be part of the feedback loop during any reintegration attempts.

Beyond accepting the student into their classrooms, though, general education teachers need to feel supported with respect to implementing interventions the student may need during the process of reintegration. One way to address this potential concern is to ensure that general education teachers are given the opportunity to ask for consultative assistance and that those requests are honored. Finally, like parents and students, general education teachers need to understand the potential for students to obtain long-term benefits when they are reintegrated and exited, such as greater opportunities for further advancement both in school and later in life.

Regarding administrators, they need to understand that all students should be educated in general education to the maximum extent possible (i.e., understand the legal issues involved). They also need to understand that resources are available to help students succeed in general education; resources that are available to all general education students include tutoring, 504 plans, intervention plans, guidance services, and so on. School psychologists, given their background in assessment, are in an excellent position to refocus administrative attention from the fiscal nature of staffing decisions to greater attention on student outcomes. Understanding the long-term benefits to the students, such as when they are more independent and successful within the general education curriculum they are more likely to graduate and continue to be successful later in life, may help with these refocusing efforts.

EFFECTIVE INSTRUCTIONAL SYSTEM ACROSS TIERS

One of the best ways to ensure success of reintegration efforts is to take steps as a school system to work towards a healthy instructional support system across all instructional tiers. Details on effective academic support systems for all students (i.e., Tier 1) are described in Chapter 2 of this book. A healthy Tier 1 means that core instruction is resulting in about 80 percent of the student population is reaching benchmark goals (Tilly, 2008). Attending to a healthy Tier 1 is critical to the success of the reintegration process and exiting students from special education. Returning special education students to an environment that is ineffective likely will result in a lack of success, considerable frustration among stakeholders, and probable student return to special education in the future.

Similarly, attention to an effective supplemental or Tier 2 support system is important. Tier 2 support systems should be moving students toward benchmark (or typical classroom performance) expectations, rather than just maintaining the status quo. Effectively, this means that Tier 2 support results in accelerated rates of progress. Many students who are reintegrated and exited from special education will utilize Tier 2 supports. Thus, in a school with an effective Tier 2 system of supports, the likelihood of exiting students successfully is increased. Knowing that a healthy system of Tier 2 supports is available can ease stakeholder concerns as well. Details on intervention development for Tier 2, both individualized interventions developed through a problem-solving process as well as standard protocol interventions, are described in Chapter 5 of this book.

HYPOTHESIS TESTING AND DATA-BASED FORMATIVE EVALUATION

Another means of ensuring success of reintegration efforts is to approach reintegration as a hypothesis-testing process, where the effectiveness of reintegration efforts must be confirmed by outcomes (e.g., benefit and satisfactory achievement within general education). Hypothesis testing means that reintegration plans are not considered guarantees of success, but rather must be attempted and examined to determine success. It also means that changes are made to the student's reintegration plan when data suggest that the plan is not working. This approach also is consistent with previous research on reintegration (e.g., Shinn, Powell-Smith, Good, & Baker, 1997).

An essential component of any hypothesis-testing process is measuring relevant dimensions of student performance to determine the effectiveness of interventions. Critically, such measurement must be sensitive to small changes, hopefully improvements, in student performance. Unsatisfactory student performance or other issues of concern (i.e., the plan is not implemented with integrity) should prompt discussion among members of the reintegration team. This discussion may lead to necessary adjustments to the reintegration plan. The absence of such an approach means that ineffective plans, or those which are not being implemented with integrity, are allowed to continue unchecked resulting in unsuccessful reintegration and exit efforts. Therefore, one of the most critical factors for ensuring reintegration and exit success is collecting formative evaluation data during the reintegration process and then using those data to make decisions.

MAKING EXIT DECISIONS AND MONITORING SUCCESS

Exit decision making should follow a *systematic model* that begins with determining what is required for student success in the general education environment. Thus, the model includes the use of sensitive, relevant, ongoing measures of targeted skills for the student considered for exit as well as a relevant peer comparison group (i.e., those with skills within the range of general education peers performing at the lowest acceptable level), examining the environments in which special education students function and in which they will be expected to function, a trial out period for potential candidates, and then the ongoing monitoring of the reintegrated student and decision making relative to exit success.

The steps for making reintegration and exit decisions, including the process of monitoring student success, are detailed in Table 10.2. Along with each step of the model, the questions to be answered at each step, the data needed or activities to complete to answer the questions, and who is responsible for these activities are delineated. At each step of the decision-making process, teams made up of school personnel, teachers, parents, and the student (when appropriate) make the decisions. Much of what is described in Table 10.2 and in the steps described in what follows is based upon the process for reintegration discussed in Powell-Smith and Ball (2008).

STEP ONE: CONSIDER STUDENT FOR EXIT

The process begins with a student being considered for reintegration and exit. A student may be identified as a candidate for reintegration by anyone with pertinent knowledge of the student's skills (e.g., parent, teacher, the student herself). Often, the timing of these decisions would occur at the natural decision-making points for student evaluation (quarterly grading period,

Table 10.2 Reintegration and Exit Steps, Questions to Answer, Activities, & Personnel Responsible

Step	Questions to Answer	Data Needed and/or Activities to Complete	Who Is Responsible
1. Consider Student for Exit	• Is the student making adequate progress relative to GE peers? • Is there a significant decrease in the needs that resulted in SE services? • Are the expectations in the SE environment significantly different from the GE environment? • Are the GE and SE classroom environments significantly different?	• Collect or review formative assessment data on student and peers for skill domains in question. • Collect summative performance data. • Collect interview data. • Survey stakeholders. • Conduct direct observations.	• SE Teacher • GE Teacher • Support personnel and/or related services personnel (i.e., school psychologist)
2. Plan for Reintegration	• When will reintegration occur? • Who will be involved? • What will be monitored? • What schedule will be used for monitoring? • Who will collect monitoring data? • How often will monitoring data be reviewed? • What accommodations and/or support will be provided? • What will be the length of the reintegration trial? • How & under what conditions will supports be faded? • How will monitoring be faded?	• Information on major school events/school calendar. • Determine available support personnel resources. • Determine available materials resources. • Review data collected at Step 1.	• Reintegration or IEP team including parents and student, if appropriate.

(Continued)

Table 10.2   (Continued)

Step	Questions to Answer	Data Needed and/or Activities to Complete	Who Is Responsible
3. Monitor Reintegration Success	• Is the student making satisfactory progress? • Is the plan implemented as designed? • Are there changes that need to be made to the plan?	• Academic and behavioral progress data. • Surveys/opinions about the process from stakeholders. • Data on integrity of plan implementation.	• Reintegration or IEP team, including parents and student, if appropriate.
4. Determine Reintegration Success	• Did the student make sufficient progress? • Can the student continue in GE without SE supports? • What within GE supports are needed and available? • Do relevant stakeholders support exit?	• Review progress data. • Review survey/opinion data. • Discuss data with relevant stakeholders. • Review potential GE supports (if deemed necessary).	• Reintegration or IEP team, including parents and student, if appropriate.
5. Special Education Exit in Goal or Domain Area	• Should the student be exited completely from SE?	• Team meets to make judgment about exit.	• Reintegration or IEP team, including parents and student, if appropriate.

Note. SE, Special Education; GE, General Education

annual review, triannual review), but they should occur in an ongoing manner for systems implementing an RTI service-delivery model wherein progress-monitoring data are examined regularly.

At this beginning step, formative assessment data regarding relevant domains of performance are needed that allow comparisons relative to general education peers and will also be *sensitive* to small changes in student skill. Peer comparisons should be students who meet the *lowest acceptable* performance expectations for the receiving classroom (i.e., relative to the grading and achievement standards). This comparison standard is not meant to suggest that expectations be lowered for special education students to warrant their reintegration into general education. Rather, this standard is used so as not to require a higher standard of performance for special education students to access the general education curriculum than the standard applied to their general education peers.

In addition to gathering assessment data to determine student appropriateness for reintegration, stakeholder opinions should be assessed with respect to reintegration at this step. For example, stakeholders may be asked what they believe is the most appropriate placement for the student. They may also be asked the likelihood of success in the general education classroom. This step presents an important opportunity to ask the general education teacher what supports may be needed to ensure student success. Finally, the step is a logical opportunity to gauge the teacher's desire for consultative assistance.

At the conclusion of Step One, decision outcomes might include (1) reintegrate for a trial period and monitor; (2) reintegrate and provide training, support, and monitoring; or (3) wait on reintegration and continue working with the student until their skills better match the demands of the environment. These first two potential outcomes would be addressed at steps two and three of the reintegration and exit process. The third possible outcome should result in a closer examination of the training and supports necessary to achieve reintegration and exit. Thus, this third decision represents a need for increased efforts to help the special education student acquire the skills needed to succeed in the general education curriculum and to address any environmental issues necessary to make reintegration a reality. Such efforts may require working with general education teachers to improve classroom management. They may also mean working with special education teachers to make the special education classroom more like the general education classroom (i.e., assisting with generalization). Regardless of what is included in these efforts, they likely will result in greater collaboration and communication between the involved stakeholders.

Step Two: Plan for Reintegration

In this step of the process, the data gathered and reviewed during Step One are used to formulate a plan for reintegration. The decisions at Step Two are made by reintegration and exit planning teams. These teams include those who will be working with the target student during the reintegration and exit process as well as those who have relevant knowledge of the student's skills. These teams should include the parents of the student, the special education teacher, the receiving general education teacher(s), and the student (when appropriate). These teams also may include paraprofessionals, administrators, and support staff (e.g., school psychologist). Outside agency personnel (e.g., physician, social worker) should be included if the student is involved with such parties and they have information pertinent to educational planning for the student.

One of the most important decisions at this step is in regard to the supports the student will be provided and how those supports will eventually be faded. Many supports will mirror those available to all students in general education (e.g., naturally occurring Tier 1 and Tier 2 supports). Other supports may need to be faded systematically. As is shown in Table 10.2, many of the decisions include important logistical considerations. For example, scheduling a transition like a reintegration trial too close to regular school breaks and statewide testing is best avoided. In addition, teams might consider whether reintegration should occur fully or for a portion of the general education class with increased time based upon success. How long a reintegration trial will occur before some decision is made about exit also will be decided. The research on reintegration in reading suggests that a minimum of 8 to 12 weeks of data be collected (Powell-Smith & Stewart, 1998). However, the length of a "trial out" period may be dictated by state or local administrative rules. For example, Iowa special education regulations state that "prior to transfer from a special education program or service, an eligible individual may be provided a trial placement in the general education setting of not more than 45 school days. A trial placement shall be incorporated into this individual's IEP" (Iowa Administrative Code, 281—41.116 [256B, 34CFR300]).

Finally, the progress-monitoring schedule also is determined during this planning step including who is responsible for such monitoring. The monitoring schedule should include specific review periods (e.g., every four weeks) at which time student performance data can be reviewed and alterations made to the reintegration plan if needed. These review times also are when stakeholder beliefs and concerns are reexamined and addressed if needed.

STEP THREE: MONITOR REINTEGRATION SUCCESS

Several types of data are collected at Step Three (see Table 10.2), all of which are designed to examine and support the ongoing success of the reintegrated student. Thus, both direct and indirect measures of success are used. Direct measures include things like formative assessment data on student performance. These data are collected on the reintegrated student as well as a sample of appropriate comparison peers. Indirect measures include assessment of stakeholder opinions about the reintegration process. Most typically, formative assessments will be conducted weekly or biweekly. More or less frequent assessment and observation may be conducted depending on the measurement tools used and the level of concern about student success. Regardless of how frequently the data are collected, they will need to be summarized (i.e., progress monitoring graph) regularly (i.e., every four weeks) so ongoing decisions about whether the student is making satisfactory progress can be made.

Stakeholder assessment typically is conducted after formative assessment data have been summarized. These summarized data are then provided to stakeholders to help inform their responses to opinion surveys. Reintegration models described in the literature (Powell-Smith & Steward, 1998; Powell-Smith, & Ball, 2008) suggest these data summaries and stakeholder opinion surveys be conducted once per month. Stakeholder opinions surveys serve as indirect evidence of success. Once again, the intention is to provide feedback frequently enough to make adjustments to the plan if things are not going well.

Another element of monitoring success includes regularly checking in to see if the plan developed at Step Two has been implemented as designed. Assessing the integrity of the plan is an essential step not to be overlooked. If the student is not doing well during the reintegration trial, it is important to know if previously agreed upon interventions are not being implemented or are no longer considered feasible. Specific procedures for examining and ensuring fidelity of plan implementation are discussed in Chapter 6.

Step Four: Determine Reintegration Success

At Step Four, one of the most important activities is reviewing all of the progress-monitoring data. This activity is important because these data provide both formative and summative information about the impact of the reintegration trial on students' skills. An important issue to explore is whether the reintegrated student's progress is commensurate with general education peer comparisons. A central question is whether the student can continue in general education without special education supports. The opinion survey data from stakeholder groups about the reintegration trial also is important to consider as a means of keeping stakeholders involved in the decision-making process and preventing potential barriers to successful exit.

If a question is raised about the student's readiness for exit, then the team will need to return to steps two and three (Planning and Monitoring) to review the plan, determine if plans were implemented as designed, and re-examine the data collected. Maybe, the student continues to need support. If so, the team will need to make the necessary modifications to the original plan and begin the monitoring process again. Greater attention to the process of fading supports may be needed. On the other hand, the student may need to have access to supports available to other general education students on a continuing basis. These supports might include things like a 504 plan or access to guidance services. Supports might also include instructional accommodations or modifications like repeating directions, additional time for task completion, adjusting task length, providing more frequent prompts and feedback, providing additional skills practice, or providing individual or small-group instruction with the teacher or paraprofessional. Considering supports that occur naturally within general education will help the student generalize and maintain skills after the reintegration plan is faded.

STEP FIVE: EXITING IN GOAL OR DOMAIN

This final step is the time when special education exit occurs with respect to IEP goals or domain area(s). The team meeting to make this decision and the actions that follow are the culminating events for this process. The student who exits will no longer have an IEP with respect to the area in which they have been reintegrated and exited. Given the significance of the decision, it should be considered very carefully and be based upon the preponderance of the data collected throughout the reintegration process.

TOOLS AND CONSIDERATIONS

In this section, tools useful for reintegration decision making are presented for the most common domains of functioning in which reintegration and exit might be considered. However, the process described generalizes to other domains of functioning. First, assessing the classroom environment is discussed, as it is relevant regardless of the skill area considered for reintegration. Second, academic skill areas are discussed. Third, social, behavioral, and emotional skills are discussed. Finally, indexing stakeholder opinions is discussed.

Assessment of the Receiving Environment   When considering students for exit, one of the first questions to ask is: "What are the possible receiving environments?" It may be that a particular class is considered, but it might be useful to consider all classes within a grade level as a means of finding the best fit between the reintegration candidate's current skills and skill levels addressed in the general education environment. This decision impacts who is selected as appropriate peer comparisons.

Conducting an analysis, or ecological inventory, of the possible general education environments into which the special education student might be reintegrated is an important aspect of the reintegration and exit process. Specific classroom environment variables to consider include (1) classroom organization and routines, (2) instructional arrangements, (3) classroom physical arrangement, (4) number and length of transitions, and (5) the involvement of others (e.g., paraprofessionals, support specialists) in the classroom.

In addition, educators might want to consider how aligned various task dimensions (e.g., history, response form, modality, complexity, schedule, variation) are with reinforcement in the classroom (Kame'enui & Darch, 2004). For example, this assessment might help answer such questions as whether complex tasks result in greater and more frequent reinforcement? Importantly, this kind of assessment can help determine what the differences are between how these dimensions are aligned with re-inforcement in one environment versus another (i.e., special education classroom when compared to the general education classroom).

In addition, variables that are teacher related are important to assess as well. For example, tolerance for student misbehavior, the manner in which teacher attention is used, preferred motivational procedures, and classroom management practices are important variables to index in particular as they may vary widely between special education and general education environments. These variables may be best assessed via teacher interview and by reviewing existing instructional plans, though some may be best captured via direct observation. School personnel can create their own tools for this purpose or use available published tools. Two sample tools for obtaining these ecological data are the Classroom Ecological Inventory (CEI) classroom observation and the CEI teacher interview (Fuchs et al., 1994). Two additional interview formats to consider are the Teacher Interview Form for Academic Problems (Shapiro, 2004a) and the Instructional Planning Form Interview (Powell-Smith & Stewart, 1998). These examples should not be considered exhaustive, but may prove useful to school personnel as they pursue reintegration efforts.

Academic Skills   Throughout each of the reintegration steps, data are examined to make decisions. Formative assessment data on student performance are needed as a means of both comparing reintegrated student skills to those of comparison peers and as a way to monitor the impact of reintegration in an ongoing manner. Thus, these formative assessment tools in particular are of greatest use for reintegration decision making. Within RTI service delivery systems, these data are collected and likely are readily available. Examples of formative assessment data useful for reintegration decisions and which may be routinely collected in RTI systems include Curriculum-Based Measures (CBM; Deno, 1985; Shinn, 1989, 2008) and Dynamic Indicators of Basic Early Literacy Skills (DIBELS; Kaminski & Good, 1996, 1998; Kaminski, Cummings, Powell-Smith, & Good, 2008). These sets of tools are discussed in detail in Chapter 3 of this book. In addition to these data, classroom work samples, portfolios, and other available test data may be considered.

In addition to data on academic skill levels and progress, school personnel likely will need to consider other skills critical for academic success in the general education classroom. For example, rates of academic engagement along with study, organizational, test-taking, self-help, and self-management skills can make the difference between a successful reintegration and exit process and an unsuccessful one. Therefore, indexing these skills is also important. Means of assessing these sets of skills are rating scales (e.g., Academic Competence Evaluation Scale, ACES; Diperna & Elliott, 2000), direct observation, and teacher interview. Observations of reintegration candidate and comparison peers can be conducted using systematic observation procedures or observation checklists. Interviewing the special education teacher is another way to obtain information on engagement rates, work completion, accuracy and self-management. Finally, it is helpful to understand the general education teacher's expectations regarding these behaviors in the general education classroom so that those expectations may be compared to those in the special education classroom.

Behavioral, Social, and Emotional Skills   The tools used to determine levels of acceptable behavior can be those that are typically used to address normative functioning in those domains. Existing data useful for this purpose might include discipline referrals or teacher checklists of student behavior. However, it is likely that additional, more direct data will be needed. Key behaviors

that may be examined are follows directions, accepts consequences, listens, works independently, uses materials appropriately, makes need for assistance known, controls anger, and
cooperates with others.

One way to collect more direct data is via classroom observations. Classroom observations may be conducted using systematic
observation protocols. Two examples of such tools are the Behavioral Observation of Students in Schools (BOSS; Shapiro, 2004b)
and the Student Interaction in Specific Settings (SISS; Cushing &
Horner, 2003). However, school personnel may find it is most
useful to construct their own observation protocol for target
behaviors relevant to the specific reintegration candidate and
circumstances. An excellent reference regarding conducting systematic behavioral observations, including both the dimensions to
consider if developing your own observation protocol as well as a
review of characteristics of available codes, is Hintze, Volpe, and
Shapiro (2008). Finally, in addition to direct observation, conducting interviews with the student, parent, and/or teacher, as well as
reviewing the student's records can provide a good picture of
relevant target behaviors.

Indexing Stakeholder Opinions   As indicated previously, one of
the ways to facilitate successful reintegration and exit is to be
sure to address the concerns of stakeholders in such decisions.
One way to accomplish this goal is to survey stakeholder opinions
regarding the reintegration candidate's likelihood of success and
necessary supports to achieve successful reintegration and exit. For
example, initial opinion surveys might ask about the likelihood of
success if the special education student is reintegrated, what the
most appropriate placement is for the special education student,
and areas in which the student may need additional support in
order to be successful in general education. These surveys are also a
way for general education teachers to indicate areas in which they
would like consultative support to achieve reintegration success.
Similar surveys can be used to check in with stakeholders throughout the reintegration process. Those opinion surveys might ask
some of the same questions as initial ones, as well as add questions
about how successful the reintegrated student is across a number of
dimensions in the general education environment (e.g., homework

completion, behavior during instruction, quality and number of assignments completed, etc.). Specific examples of these surveys used in previous reintegration research are found in Powell-Smith and Stewart (1998).

CASE STUDY

Background Information

Brent initially was referred in first grade due to academic concerns in reading and written expression in addition to behavioral concerns such as attention problems, anger outbursts, and social skills difficulties (e.g., hitting, name-calling, difficulty working cooperatively). Several academic and behavioral interventions were attempted within the classroom (Tier 1 and Tier 2 support), but his response to those interventions was not sufficient and thus special education support services were pursued. Subsequently, Brent was determined to be eligible for special education services in reading and writing, as well as services designed to support his emotional/behavioral difficulties.

In second grade, Brent responded well to intensive reading intervention and by winter was reading on a first-grade level, according to his DIBELS progress-monitoring data. CBM data indicated that his writing skills were now above first-grade level and confirmed that his math skills continued to be on grade level. Teacher interviews indicated that Brent's classroom behavior also had improved. Brent's academic performance in reading and writing continued to improve in third grade. He received reading instruction on the second-grade level in the resource room, while his peers in the general education classroom were instructed in materials on the third-grade level. He continued to receive special education support for writing skills. According to his special education teacher, Brent's ability to generate story ideas and his use of detail was better than that of most students in his special education class. During Brent's third-grade IEP review meeting, the team decided to place Brent in the school's reintegration and exit process to determine whether Brent should be fully reintegrated into the general education class and exited completely from special education services.

Step One: Brent Is Considered for Reintegration and Exit

The school psychologist and Brent's teachers gathered and/or reviewed assessment data that covered a four-week prereintegration period. Most of these data were already existing progress-monitoring data. Brent's general education teacher was asked to select at least three peers from the general education classroom who were receiving Tier 2 support, but who were not candidates for special education (i.e., were achieving satisfactorily). Academic progress-monitoring data already were collected on these peers, and they were making good progress with the support provided. The process of comparing Brent's skills to appropriate comparison peers in that general education environment was facilitated by the pre-existence of these progress monitoring data that were part of the school's multitiered prevention-oriented service delivery model.

During *Step One*, the following assessment data were collected and/or examined:

1. DIBELS Oral Reading Fluency progress monitoring (weekly).
2. CBM Written Expression probes (weekly).
3. Classroom observations twice per week, once in general education class and once in special education class, using the Behavioral Observation of Students in Schools (BOSS; Shapiro, 2004b). These observations were conducted using four comparison peers. Data from the four peers formed a composite for graphing and comparison purposes.
4. Classroom Ecological Inventory (CEI; Fuchs et al., 1994) data (Interview & Observation).
5. Stakeholder survey data from teachers, parents, and Brent.

The DIBELS ORF and CBM Written Expression data are shown in Figures 10.1 and 10.2 respectively. As can be seen by examining the first four weeks of data in Figure 10.1, Brent's reading progress during pre-reintegration is within the range of the three comparison peers. In addition, Brent's reading trajectory, or path of his reading progress, is accelerating. If he were to remain on this trajectory, it is likely his reading skills will be

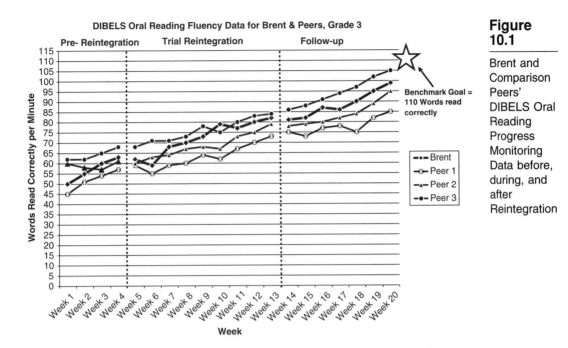

Figure 10.1

Brent and Comparison Peers' DIBELS Oral Reading Progress Monitoring Data before, during, and after Reintegration

near, or possibly at, the third-grade benchmark of 110 words read correct. Similar to his reading progress during the prereintegration period represented on the graph, Brent's progress in written expression during the prereintegration period is within the range of the three peers selected by the teacher (see Figure 10.2).

The classroom observation data collected are shown in Figures 10.3 and 10.4. Academic engagement data are displayed in Figure 10.3, and off-task behavior data are shown in Figure 10.4. A review of the prereintegration data indicates that Brent's rates of academic engagement are similar to, and in some cases better than, the selected peers (see Figure 10.3). Likewise, the data for off-task behaviors during the prereintegration time period suggests that Brent engaged in off-task behaviors generally no more frequently than his general education peers (see Figure 10.4).

Teacher interviews and informal observations in both the special education classroom and the general education classroom were conducted during the prereintegration period. According to these data, anger outbursts had been reduced to only one occurrence in the past six months, and Brent's social skills showed continued improvement across both special and general education

Figure 10.2

Brent and Comparison Peers' CBM Written Expression Progress Monitoring Data before, during, and after Reintegration

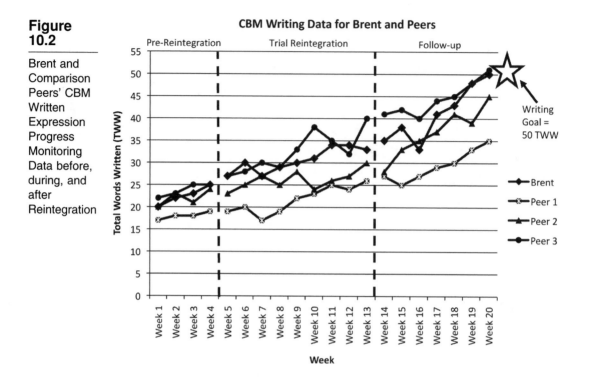

CBM Writing Data for Brent and Peers

Figure 10.3

Brent and Comparison Peers' Estimates of Academic Engaged Time before, during, and after Reintegration

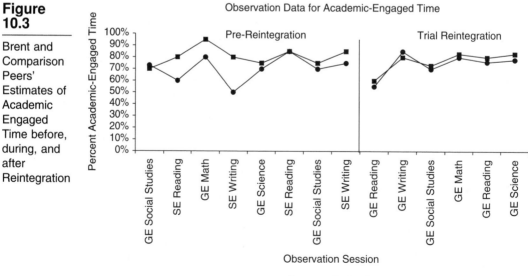

Observation Data for Academic-Engaged Time

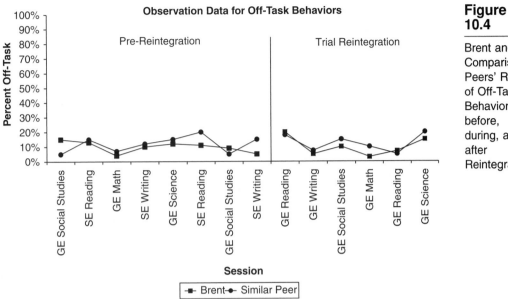

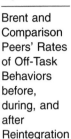

Figure 10.4

Brent and Comparison Peers' Rates of Off-Task Behaviors before, during, and after Reintegration

settings. However, several notable differences between the two classroom environments were noted. In the resource room, Brent's desk was located near the teacher's desk, and no more than 10 students were in the classroom at any time while Brent was present. The teacher in the special education classroom provided Brent with a ratio of positive to negative or directive remarks of 3:1. The special education teacher worked with Brent and the rest of the students in small groups and individually. Homework was given daily for reading and writing in different forms and amounts for each student. Brent's homework was at a third-grade level and averaged 45 minutes per night. Reading comprehension tests were not timed. Class assignments were sent home if not finished in class.

In contrast, Brent's desk was located near the back of the room and there were 30 students in the general education classroom. Brent's general education teacher provided him with a ratio of positive to negative or directive remarks of 1:1. The mode of instruction for reading and writing was primarily teacher-directed lecture conducted in a large group. The same homework was given in reading and writing for all students and averaged 45 minutes per night. All homework was on a third-grade level.

Reading comprehension tests were timed. Class assignments not completed in class were not sent home with students to be completed. Instead, students either lost points or could opt to complete those assignments during recess or free time.

Stakeholder attitude data also were collected via a survey process. Special education and general education teachers indicated that the general education classroom was the most appropriate placement for Brent for both reading and writing instruction. Parents indicated that the general education class was most appropriate if consultative support was provided by the special education teacher. Brent stated that he thought he could do the reading and writing work and that general education is where he belonged for instruction. All stakeholders believed that Brent would be successful in general education in both reading and writing and were confident that he would make progress commensurate with comparison peers. Similarly, teachers and parents were fairly confident that Brent's behavior would remain on track. However, the general education teacher requested consultative assistance for developing a behavior management plan for Brent that could be implemented during reading and writing instruction. In particular, the general education teacher sought information on how to address Brent's specific needs while maintaining much of the teacher's already existing classroom management plan.

STEP TWO: PLANNING BRENT'S REINTEGRATION

Based upon the data collected at *Step One*, a reintegration and exit plan was agreed upon by the IEP team including Brent and his parents. Reintegration would occur immediately, according to the plan. The plan included a 45-day trial out period (nine weeks). As part of the plan, the school psychologist agreed to work with the teacher on adjusting the classroom management plan. Progress monitoring for Brent and his peers was to continue on a weekly basis in reading and written expression. During the trial reintegration period, BOSS observations were to be conducted every two weeks in Brent's regular classroom. These data were to be summarized and provided to parents and teachers, as well as discussed with Brent. Each of these stakeholders would then have the opportunity to provide feedback about the process. It was agreed upon that following this nine-week period, if things were going well, then additional supports would be faded, and Brent would be exited from special education.

STEP THREE: BRENT IS REINTEGRATED AND MONITORED

The reintegration plan was implemented as designed. Progress-monitoring data on reading and written expression were collected weekly and summarized every four weeks. Survey data were collected from stakeholders on a monthly basis to ensure satisfaction and ongoing input to the process. The supports provided to Brent included the consultative services that the teacher had requested. Brent also was allowed to take home any unfinished work from class to be completed as homework. The classroom management procedures in Brent's class were reviewed and revised such that Brent received increased positive reinforcement for appropriate academic engagement, problem solving, and positive peer interactions.

STEPS FOUR AND FIVE: BRENT IS REINTEGRATED AND EXITED

Upon conclusion of the 45-day reintegration trial, a team meeting was held and all the data were reviewed and discussed. Upon reviewing all of the data, the decision to exit Brent from special education was made. Additional supports Brent had been provided (i.e., specialized behavior management plan) were faded. Although follow-up monitoring continued for an additional seven weeks until the end of the year, the long-term plan was to fade the monitoring such that it would be no more frequent than other peers in his class (e.g., three to four times per year).

Data from the reintegration trial period (nine weeks) and the follow-up period (seven weeks) are presented in Figures 10.1 through 10.4. Figure 10.1 shows Brent's reading data relative to peers. Throughout the reintegration trial and during the seven-week follow-up Brent maintained performance commensurate with his peers with respect to reading. In addition, at the end of the follow-up period, Brent's reading performance was near the third-grade benchmark goal. A similar pattern of performance is noted for written expression (Figure 10.2). In terms of academic engagement, Brent's behavior remained consistent with peers during the reintegration trial. Brent and his peers' academic engagement are show in Figure 10.3. Brent displayed some lower rates of engagement initially when reintegrated, but over time his rates of engagement improved to rates that were similar to those during prereintegration. Data for off-task behaviors are shown in Figure 10.4. Brent showed generally low rates of off-task behaviors that were similar to peers and similar to his previously low rates of off-task behavior in special education.

Survey data collected from stakeholders at the end of the nine-week trial period indicated that special education and general education teachers continued to rate the general education classroom as the most appropriate placement for Brent for both reading and writing. Parents also rated the general education class as most appropriate. Brent stated that he was confident he could do the general education reading and writing work and that general education was where he belonged. All stakeholders believed that Brent's success would continue in general education and were confident that he would continue to make progress commensurate with comparison peers. Similarly, teachers and parents were very confident that Brent's behavior would remain on track. The general education teacher did not request any additional consultative assistance and indicated that she was pleased with the outcomes she was seeing. Brent was completing assignments and getting along well with peers. Occasionally, Brent needed to take an assignment home to complete.

RESEARCH SUPPORT FOR REINTEGRATION AND EXIT PROCESS

The procedures described in this chapter are not only well-aligned with an RTI service delivery model, they also are research based. A *responsible reintegration* approach, like the one described in this chapter, may identify numerous students who are appropriate candidates for reintegration and exit. For example, in two studies reported by Shinn, Habedank, Rodden-Nord, and Knutson (1993) reintegration candidates were determined by administering three CBM oral reading fluency passages (using median) and one CBM maze passage. The results indicated that 36 percent to 48 percent of students who served part time in special education for reading had reading skills within the range of the general education comparison peers.

In addition, the research indicates that general education teachers respond favorably to the academic performance data (e.g., CBM) provided to them about reintegration candidates (Rodden-Nord, Shinn, & Good, 1992; Shinn, Baker, et al., 1993). General education teacher attitudes toward having one these reintegration candidates placed back in their classroom for instruction became more positive upon seeing CBM reading data indicating that the student had skills within the range already being instructed. Notably, the CBM data played a greater role in changing the teacher's opinion than other published nationally norm-referenced test scores.

Perhaps most importantly, research suggests positive student outcomes can result from reintegration and exit. For example, data reported by Shinn, Powell-Smith, Good, and Baker (1997) indicate that students who are reintegrated can, on average, make gains commensurate with their general education peers reading within the lowest acceptable level in the general education classroom. Further, reintegrated students with reading skills within the range of these comparison peers were more likely to be successful than reintegrated students with skills below the range of these comparison peers (Shinn, Powell-Smith, & Good, 1996).

CONCLUSION

Continuing research has yet to establish what reintegration and exit numbers will look like within school systems implementing a multi-tiered RTI approach to service delivery. As more schools move in the direction of a prevention-oriented service delivery model, including the use of universal screening and progress monitoring, multiple tiers of support, and examining response to intervention, greater opportunities for observing successful reintegration are expected. Within these systems, outcomes for all students, including those exited from special education, are likely to be improved.

ORGANIZATIONAL CONSIDERATIONS AND CONCLUSIONS

V

PART

RTI and Systems Change

11

Chapter

RESPONSE TO INTERVENTION is an effective model for delivering timely and targeted assistance to struggling students. However, there are many components to RTI, making this a complex initiative to introduce within a school setting. To implement RTI at the building level, for example, the school must ensure that its core curriculum and standard classroom teaching strategies at Tier 1 are consistent with best evidence-based practices in instruction and behavior management. Additionally, the school must build the capacity to deliver interventions at Tier 2 through small-group instruction as an economical method to match numbers of struggling students to effective treatments. The school should also have a problem-solving team at Tier 3 that can assemble individualized intervention plans as needed. And the school has an obligation under RTI to screen the student population for possible academic or behavioral needs and to monitor the short-term progress of any student receiving small-group or individualized intervention services.

While the components described above are only a partial listing of essential elements of RTI, they demonstrate that rolling out RTI at the building and district level is a complicated undertaking. In fact, RTI represents nothing less than a comprehensive overhaul of instruction, behavior management, resource allocation, assessment, professional development, and decision making throughout a school system. But the challenges of RTI implementation do not end with the initial rollout of the model. Schools must also be prepared to monitor new developments in RTI research and strategically apply those research findings to continually improve their own RTI models. Furthermore, schools must track and be responsive to changes in state and federal regulations that inevitably will shape the structure of their RTI services and decision rules. And, finally, schools must make an ongoing effort to promote an understanding of, and support for, RTI among their stakeholders, including teachers, support staff, administrators, and parents.

RTI: GETTING STARTED

As with any comprehensive reform effort, RTI requires that schools proactively create the structures and processes necessary to achieve and sustain systems-level change. The remainder of this chapter will detail five essential steps to help schools to move RTI from a new initiative to an institutionalized part of their culture. Those steps include (1) establishing a district-level RTI Steering Group, (2) sharing information about RTI with school stakeholders and enlisting their support for the model, (3) developing and updating a multiyear plan for RTI implementation, (4) inventorying and organizing resources available to support RTI, and (5) building the capacity for the district's RTI model to evolve over time to incorporate advances in RTI research and changes in state and federal regulations.

Step 1: Establish an RTI Steering Group

Given the comprehensive nature of the RTI model, its implementation in a school district is best overseen by a committee that possesses the authority and controls the resources necessary to make RTI a success. Ideally, this RTI Steering Group serves as the command and control center of RTI for the district. The group has the responsibility for writing and regularly updating a multiyear district plan to implement RTI. It also supervises the implementation of that plan over time to maintain consistency in RTI practices across each of its school buildings and ensures that the district's RTI plan remains consistent both with emerging research on effective RTI practices and with state and federal RTI guidelines.

Because the RTI Steering Committee has the task of creating a detailed blueprint of how the RTI model is to be put into practice in the school district, it must be able effectively to coordinate significant changes in operations and procedures across grade levels, school buildings, and departments. Therefore, this committee should include influential members who represent key stakeholder groups and who control resources needed for the success of RTI. By recruiting a diverse range of members, the RTI Steering Group counters the tendency of school systems to partition resources into separate silos (Ervin & Schaughency, 2008). The Steering Group should include people in district-level positions with authority over personnel, resources, and/or policies of importance to RTI (e.g., administrators responsible for funding staff development, implementing the core curriculum, or supervising reading teachers). It is also suggested that the RTI Steering Group include representatives from school buildings who can provide the group with accurate first-hand information about the challenges of establishing RTI in applied settings—and also allow for the rapid dissemination of information from the centralized Steering Group to each campus. (In smaller school districts, every school may have a representative on the Steering Group, while in larger districts representatives from a sampling of schools might be recruited.) The RTI Steering Group should meet at least monthly to ensure good communication among group members and allow the Steering Group to identify any problems with RTI implementation at an early stage and intervene quickly to remedy them.

One useful initial exercise for the RTI Steering Group is to assess the current capacity of its school system to adopt the RTI model. Interested readers are directed to the document *RTI school readiness survey* on the accompanying CD as an example of such a survey. As staff turnover occurs at the district and building level, the membership of the Steering Group should be updated regularly to reflect those personnel changes. If members request to cycle off of the Steering Group, the district should make an effort to recruit replacements that will bring the same or similar experience, influence, and resources to the Steering Group. (For a more complete description of how to set up a district RTI Steering Group, review the document *Guidelines for establishing an RTI steering group* on the accompanying CD.)

Step 2: Promote Stakeholder Understanding and Support

The staff of every school is linked by a series of interlocking relationships, shared beliefs, and professional expectations that can be defined as that building's work culture. When RTI is first introduced into a school setting, planners might encounter some resistance among staff toward the RTI model. Because implementation of the RTI model requires significant change, a certain amount of resistance is to be expected. Indeed, initial resistance of staff to a new initiative can sometimes serve a positive function by alerting the school to potential concerns that might otherwise have been overlooked (Wickstrom & Witt, 1993). For example, some teachers in a building may embrace the idea of early intervention that RTI represents but be reluctant to put their support behind the initiative because they believe (perhaps rightly) that the school has allocated too few resources to be successful with the RTI model.

A necessary early step when introducing RTI to a building is to map out the school culture to note whether, and to what degree, that culture is ready to support RTI. (For a listing of specific competencies that the RTI model expects of teachers, building administrators, and district administrators, readers are directed to the document *Implementing RTI: Top 10 expectations for teachers, building administrators, and school districts* on the accompanying CD.) The school then develops a plan to provide staff with information about RTI, to enlist their participation in developing aspects of the model, and to build support for RTI within the school culture. The importance of promoting the buy-in and support of school stakeholders for RTI cannot be overemphasized. When the school staff understands RTI and realizes its potential to assist them to better support struggling students, this grassroots support can serve as an important force multiplier that makes the RTI model stronger and more resilient. If, however, the staff has not been actively recruited to support RTI but instead perceives that the model has been imposed on them from above, their potential resistance can serve as a debilitating drag—possibly sapping the momentum of RTI or even undermining any chance of success.

Inform Stakeholders about the RTI Model   A school staff that is knowledgeable about the RTI model is more likely to support it. When planning to share information about RTI with staff, however, schools should avoid the temptation to offer a single compressed group presentation about RTI (for example, at a one-hour faculty meeting), as such one-time workshops may feel rushed and not permit staff sufficient time to absorb the information or ask questions. Instead, the school should consider dividing the body of essential RTI information for staff into a series of shorter presentations to be offered over time. Planners can also be creative in selecting venues or methods for presenting these mini-lessons in RTI. For example, a school may select a monthly faculty meeting as the forum to provide all staff with an initial shared overview of the RTI model, then follow up at grade-level or department meetings with a more detailed presentation of issues relating to Tier 1 RTI classroom interventions. Additionally, the school may choose to distribute supplemental RTI-related readings to teachers or provide them with links to online RTI resources to expand their understanding of the model.

Solicit Staff Feedback   Once the staff has been informed about the RTI model, the school should seek to get feedback from them about what they view as potential benefits of RTI, as well as concerns or questions that they may still have about the model. When soliciting staff feedback, of course, the school makes clear that it has already decided to move forward in adopting the RTI model and that the purpose of staff input is simply to help the school to tailor its RTI plan to best meet the needs of teachers and support staff. RTI planners may want to use several methods to solicit staff feedback, such as reserving time at the end of introductory RTI presentations for informal question-and-answer sessions and distributing questionnaires to allow staff to anonymously share their views about RTI. (An example of a staff RTI feedback questionnaire, *Response to Intervention (RTI): staff feedback form*, is included in the CD accompanying this book.) One particularly useful yes/no question to ask stakeholders on an anonymous survey is whether the respondent supports implementing RTI in the school at the present time. If the school finds that fewer than 80 percent of respondents express support the adoption of an RTI model, it is likely that significant pockets of resistance to RTI exist among staff. In such a case, planners should consider their first priority with RTI to be creating additional staff support.

Develop a Plan to Build Staff Support   By pooling information from anonymous teacher questionnaires, question-answer sessions, and other sources, planners will be able to assess the degree to which teaching and support staff favored the RTI initiative. If the school discovers a lack of support among staff for RTI, it should identify the likely reason(s) for that low level of support and then develop a plan in response. (A listing of possible causes of teacher resistance appears in Table 11.1, along with ideas to address them.) While every school has its unique characteristics, most schools share some broad similarities in their culture that can provide insights into possible staff objections to RTI. As Walker (2004) notes, for example, teachers tend to be more supportive of instructional and behavior management strategies if they are adapted for use with groups, rather than with individual children, and if they "involve a standard dosage that is easy to deliver" (Walker, 2004, p. 401). There are also a range of reasons that individual instructors may not support RTI. General education teachers may believe, for example, that they lack the skills to address the instructional or behavioral needs of struggling learn-ers (Gerber, 2003); that their job is to teach content, not serve as interventionists in such areas as literacy instruction (Kamil et al., 2008); that unmotivated students do not deserve more intensive intervention support than is available to "more deserving" stu-dents (Walker, 2004); or that only special education can adequately meet the needs of struggling students (Martens, 1993).

Even if a school finds that its staff is accepting of the RTI model, planners should put substantial effort into helping teachers to refashion their instruction to conform to the expectations of RTI. First, the school can increase support by helping teachers to see that they can better attain their instructional goals through RTI. Most teachers are unlikely to be convinced to substantially alter their classroom practices to conform to RTI based solely on the promise of long-term benefits such as improved student gradua-tion rates (Ervin & Schaughency, 2008). Teachers should instead be shown that RTI can assist them to address their more immedi-ate concerns, such as improving student literacy skills in the class, boosting student performance on state tests, and so on.

Second, the school should explain the kinds of changes that RTI will require in teacher practice. Under RTI, for example, classroom teachers are expected to implement and document a series of evidence-based Tier 1 interventions for struggling

Table 11.1 Potential Sources of Teacher Resistance to RTI

	Possible Solutions
Teachers believe that they lack the skills to implement specific instructional or behavior management strategies. (Fisher, 2007; Gerber, 2003; Kamil et al., 2008).	• Provide teachers with training, coaching, and follow-up support to effectively use whole-group or individual instructional and behavior management techniques.
Teachers feel that they don't have adequate time to implement individualized intervention strategies in the classroom.(Kamil et al., 2008; Walker, 2004).	• Provide training in instructional time management to increase available teaching time. • Identify whole-group instructional and behavior management strategies that are time efficient and also support struggling learners.
Teachers believe that their role is to provide content-area instruction—and does not extend to more global goals such as teaching reading-related skills or managing behaviors (e.g., Kamil et al., 2008). Or they are not convinced that there will be an adequate instructional pay-off in their content area if they implement specific intervention strategies in the classroom (Kamil et al., 2008).	• Demonstrate to teachers that improvements in student reading skills increase those students' grasp of course content, while improvements in student behaviors reduce classroom disruptions.
Teachers are reluctant to put extra effort into implementing interventions for students who appear unmotivated (Walker, 2004) when there are other, more deserving students who would benefit from teacher attention.	• Highlight success stories of teachers who have succeeded with seemingly unmotivated students. Present those stories at faculty meetings. • Collect and share instructional ideas to engage reluctant, unmotivated learners. • Develop a school mission statement and shared commitment among staff to identify and support all struggling learners.
Teachers are afraid that if they adopt a wide range of instructional strategies to promote student learning (e.g., extended discussion, etc.) they may have difficulty managing classroom behaviors (Kamil et al., 2008).	• Provide teachers with training, coaching, and follow-up support in the use of innovative instructional methods that elicit student engagement. Be sure to include behavior management training as part of this professional development.
Teachers believe that special education is magic (Martens, 2003). This belief implies that general education interventions will be insufficient to meet the student's needs and that the student will benefit only if he or she receives special education services.	• Identify effective components of classroom instruction. Share these components with general-education teachers to demonstrate that the "magic" of good instruction follows universal laws of learning that any teacher can replicate. • Have special education teachers serve as coaches, trainers, and/or consultants, giving away their best strategies to general-education educators.

Source: Adapted from Wright, J. (2008). *Engaging the reluctant teacher: Seven reasons why instructors may resist implementing classroom RTI interventions.* Retrieved on November 15, 2008, from http://www. interventioncentral.org/index.php.

students before considering those students for referral to higher tiers of intervention. With staff participation, the school should identify a core set of effective Tier 1 interventions in common areas of student concern (e.g., reading fluency, content-area vocabulary, study and organizational skills) and train teachers in their use—while also providing specific guidelines on how teachers are to document and measure student response to those strategies.

Finally, the school should organize its existing resources to provide additional support to assist teachers in changing their classroom practices. For example, RTI planners can strategically use professional development opportunities such as conference days to offer teacher workshops in Tier 1 academic and behavioral interventions, student assessment, and other relevant RTI topics. Educators whose job description includes providing teacher training can serve as RTI mentors or coaches for staff—for example, by showing teachers how to use specific intervention strategies and giving those teachers performance feedback. Teachers may be encouraged to use common planning times to discuss with their colleagues innovative instructional and intervention techniques. Schools might consider allowing instructional staff release time to visit other classrooms in their school or to travel to other schools to observe good RTI classroom practices. Or if the school already pays staff for curriculum development activities, it might direct participating teachers to create additional instructional, intervention, and assessment materials to support RTI goals.

Step 3: Create and Update a Multi-Year RTI Implementation Plan

RTI is an exacting, resource-intensive model, yet the reality is that most schools will probably have to depend almost entirely on existing resources to implement RTI. And in addition to limited resources, there are other constraints on the speed with which RTI can be put into practice in any school: For example, stakeholders must be allowed adequate time to absorb information about the RTI model and to learn new professional skills. The reality is that any district must be prepared to set aside several years for full implementation of RTI.

To facilitate an orderly and complete implementation of the RTI model over time, the RTI Steering Group should draft an initial multi-year RTI plan that stages the rollout process at a rate that is feasible using currently available resources. The RTI rollout plan will be successful if it both sets a high expectation for bringing change to schools and also recognizes that the RTI process must be sustainable with existing resources and personnel. In particular, the plan should allocate time in the early stages of RTI implementation to build awareness and support at each school for the RTI model.

Remember also that implementing RTI is an inexact science. Therefore, the multi-year rollout plan will need to be reviewed and revised at least annually to take into account fluctuations in district resources, possible changes in state and federal guidelines, and new RTI research findings. Additionally, the RTI Implementation Plan should acknowledge the four stages of scaling up required to make RTI fully institutionalized in a school system (Ervin & Schaughency, 2008). Those stages include (1) creating readiness for RTI as a new initiative; (2) initially implementing RTI; (3) institutionalizing RTI as a part of routine school and district practices; and (4) changing the RTI model over time to match changing conditions, such as revisions in state and federal guidelines and new findings in RTI research. (The accompanying CD contains the *RTI implementation planning sheet*, a form that can be useful in organizing the RTI plan according the scaling-up framework.)

The RTI plan for the district should incorporate program evaluation as a central element. Program evaluation information can tell RTI planners whether they are attaining those goals that they identify as most important. A multiple-year program evaluation of the RTI process implemented by Minneapolis Public Schools, for example, found that under the RTI model the number of children being identified for special education services in that district did not increase—even though the district experienced substantial growth in the volume of students referred to RTI building problem-solving teams (Marston, Muyskens, &, Lau, 2003). It is beyond the scope of this chapter to engage in a detailed discussion of program evaluation techniques. However, each stage of the RTI scaling-up process dictates its own relevant program evaluation questions. When a district is first creating readiness for RTI, for instance, implementation activities are focused primarily on promoting building staff understanding of RTI and support for the model. Logical program evaluation questions at this stage might include items such as "What is the current level of support among staff for bringing the RTI model to the school?" and "What are the most common concerns voiced by staff about the RTI model?" A portfolio of information would be assembled—derived from different sources and using different assessment methods—to answer each program evaluation question. To assess the level of staff support for RTI, for example, a school may conduct faculty focus groups, carry out structured individual interviews with influential staff members, and ask all teachers and support staff to complete anonymous questionnaires.

STEP 4: INVENTORY EXISTING RESOURCES TO SUPPORT IMPLEMENTATION OF RTI

As has been mentioned elsewhere in this chapter, most districts will largely have to make do with existing resources when implementing RTI. Before launching the RTI model, then, districts should thoroughly map out resources that they currently have available that could be channeled to support RTI. Table 11.2 offers several ideas for identifying a district's RTI resources. In particular, schools should inventory blocks of time when instructional and non-instructional personnel might be available to participate in RTI activities, specific staff who possess formal training/expertise in RTI-relevant topics (e.g., in academic and behavioral interventions), and any research-based commercial and teacher-made materials (including software) that can support core instruction or be used for supplemental interventions. It can also be a very useful exercise for planners to review their district's current RTI Implementation Plan, decide how those inventoried resources can be used most effectively to support the plan, and also note what additional resources will be needed to successfully implement RTI.

STEP 5: BUILD CAPACITY IN THE DISTRICT RTI MODEL TO EVOLVE AS CONDITIONS CHANGE

It is not sufficient that an RTI model in any school district be technically adequate or even that it prove effective for the moment. Additionally, the successful RTI model is one that has the capacity to adapt over time to new conditions. This quality of adaptability is

Table 11.2 Potential RTI Building and District Resources

Potential RTI Building and District Resources	Ideas for Inventorying
Staff Expertise: Staff with formal training/ expertise in RTI-relevant topics (e.g., academic and behavioral interventions, progress-monitoring, data collection and interpretation) to serve as consultants, trainers, and/or coaches.	• List all personnel whose job descriptions include providing consultation, training, coaching activities. • List any additional staff members with specialized training (e.g., in specialized reading interventions) that might be valuable to RTI.
Staff Time: Direct time that instructional and non-instructional personnel can devote to RTI activities such as intervention planning and implementation, student assessment, progress-monitoring, and so on.	• Review staff schedules to determine which personnel have pockets of time that can be allocated to RTI. • Review staff job descriptions to determine staff members who can redefine professional roles to allocate time to RTI. • Consider training non-instructional personnel, such as adult volunteers or student teachers, to engage in RTI activities such as tutoring with appropriate school supervision.
Instructional/Intervention Materials: Commercial and teacher-made materials (including software) that are research-based and support core instruction or can be used for supplemental interventions.	• Survey teachers about classroom curriculum and intervention materials that they can make available for RTI use. • Survey building principals and district administrators about available curriculum and intervention materials that may be suitable for RTI. • Identify district budgets used to purchase instructional materials and determine what part of these funds can be used to obtain RTI instructional and intervention materials.

not acquired by chance. Rather, districts can take explicit steps to build adaptability into the RTI model to increase the odds that the model will continue to be viable even in the face of new developments in RTI research and revisions to state and federal RTI regulations. Additionally, districts have the potential to improve the quality of their RTI efforts by networking with other school systems in their region to share their best practices.

Select Knowledge Brokers   Because interest in RTI is so high in schools across the country, the number of publications providing research findings and guidance on the RTI process is likely to increase dramatically over the next few years. School districts must have the capacity to keep abreast of important RTI research and recommendations and to modify their RTI model as appropriate in light of this new information. Because RTI is a model still in development (Barnett, Daly, Jones, & Lentz, 2004), universities, school districts, national organizations, and government agencies can be expected to contribute to the burgeoning RTI literature, raising the possibility that the sheer volume of new material might overwhelm practitioners. One economical district strategy to manage the growing flood of RTI technical information is to appoint *knowledge brokers* (Ervin & Schaughency, 2008) whose role is to stay current on specific RTI topics. RTI planners first partition the RTI model into manageable topic areas (e.g., reading fluency, basic reading comprehension, classroom management, and so on). Next, planners select district or school staff members to serve as knowledge brokers in each topic area based on those individuals' specific training, experience, and/or interest. Knowledge brokers are expected to stay up to date on emerging RTI research findings by regularly reviewing educational research journals and other publications from reputable organizations or government agencies. Knowledge brokers are invited periodically to report their most recent findings to the RTI Steering Group, which then modifies its RTI Implementation Plan and RTI practices as needed to conform to the updated information.

Monitor Changes in State and Federal RTI Regulations   While the RTI research literature can provide guidance on best practices in RTI, it is equally important that schools stay attuned to changing state and federal regulations that dictate how they are to implement the RTI process. While federal regulations set broad parameters for RTI, the US Department of Education has given states significant latitude in how they define specific details of the RTI model (US Department of Education, 2006). For this reason, districts should monitor closely changes and updates in RTI regulations issued by their state, and should also make use of any technical assistance or guidance documents that their state education department makes available.

Proactive districts may even seek to identify those education department personnel at the state level responsible for RTI compliance and contact them directly with questions or concerns. The district RTI Steering Group should also make a point at least annually to review state and federal regulations relating to RTI to ensure that their RTI Implementation Plan remains in compliance with these guidelines.

Network with Other School Districts on Effective RTI Practices   Thousands of school systems across the nation are actively implementing the RTI model. In effect, each district serves as a systems-level applied RTI experiment. With large numbers of schools moving forward with RTI, it is inevitable that staff in different districts will discover their own ingenious and economical ways to put various elements of the model into practice. A final recommendation for districts attempting to scale up RTI to meet the needs of all struggling students, then, is that they join informal or formal networks to identify and share their best RTI strategies and ideas with other school systems. In districts organized at the county level, communication across schools can be facilitated directly through the district central office. States that have multiple school districts per county frequently have county-level education agencies whose task is to disseminate state education department information to schools. Such agencies are often ideal vehicles for creating RTI networks that span the county or even larger regions. RTI networks can foster information sharing in a number of ways: through meetings at which schools present ideas for RTI implementation, via face-to-face or online technical assistance workshops to address common school RTI training needs, and by means of visits by network members to other schools to observe best RTI practices in action.

RTI AS ORGANIZATIONAL CHANGE: A CASE EXAMPLE

In this section, we present a case example to illustrate how a school system might get started in implementing the RTI model district wide. The subject of the case example, Baylor Schools, is a composite based on actual school systems with whom the fourth author has consulted on the implementation of RTI. The case example is limited to events that unfolded during the first year of this district's RTI implementation.

Located in the Northeastern United States, Baylor Schools is a suburban school district with a student population of about 6,000 students. The district has literacy and mathematics test scores that are about average when compared with districts throughout the state that have resources and student populations similar to Baylor's. The district has five elementary schools (grades K to 4), one middle school (grades 5 and 6), one junior high school (grades 7 and 8) and one high school. At the time that Baylor Schools began the process of implementing RTI, its school superintendent, Ann Douglas, had served in her current position for three years. She was knowledgeable about RTI and had established as a priority the goal of instituting an RTI process in her school district.

Step 1: Establish an RTI Steering Group

To oversee the RTI process across the district's schools, the superintendent established an RTI steering group that was known within the district as the RTI Leadership Team. Team membership was selected to ensure the involvement of key decision makers who controlled access to significant resources that could assist RTI and also had substantial authority to shape district policies relevant to RTI, including instructional practices, student assessment, and documentation required for special education referrals. Building-based staff members served on the team to provide a school-based perspective and also to facilitate the regular communication of information to the faculty of each school about the district's RTI plan.

The superintendent recruited a number of senior administrators to serve on the team, including the assistant superintendent of curriculum and instruction and the director of pupil services. The team also included the principals of each of Baylor's eight schools. Additionally, two building-based elementary reading specialists, a middle school guidance counselor, and two school psychologists with multiple building assignments spanning elementary and middle school grades were assigned to the team. For the first six months of its existence, the RTI Leadership Team did not include the special education director. This administrator's initial absence from the team was intentional, as both the super-intendent and the special education director wanted to convey the message that RTI is primarily a general education initiative in Baylor Schools. (After the first six months, when the RTI process had acquired momentum and was gaining acceptance among school staff across the district, the special education director quietly began to attend team meetings.) The team agreed to meet at least once per month during the first year as it plotted the initial steps of RTI implementation.

Step 2: Promote Stakeholder Understanding and Support

The team was well aware that it could not be successful with RTI unless it first enlisted the support of staff members. Therefore, the team set as priorities building an understanding of RTI among staff, soliciting feedback from building personnel about their questions and concerns regarding RTI, and developing positive staff attitudes toward RTI.

Inform Stakeholders about the RTI Model   The RTI Leadership Team moved quickly to build understanding among school staff about the RTI model. First, the team defined the core RTI concepts that they believed were most important for teachers to learn about. To convey some of this information, the team designed a uniform PowerPoint providing a general description of RTI that all build-ing principals would present at the first faculty meeting of the school year. This first whole-faculty RTI presentation was delib-erately kept short, to about 15 minutes. Each principal then developed an individualized plan in his or her school to deliver additional core RTI information to teachers, using grade-level teacher meeting times, for example, or scheduling additional short workshops during conference days.

Solicit Staff Feedback   The RTI Leadership Team was also very interested in assessing the degree of staff support for RTI in each of its schools, particularly at the elementary level. It acquired this information in several ways. First, after staff received introductory training in key RTI concepts, principals in each of the schools distributed anonymous questionnaires to faculty asking them to share their opinions about the building's readiness to move ahead with RTI. (Of course, principals also made clear to their staff that their feedback was being collected not to decide *whether* to implement RTI but rather to help the school to do a *better* job of RTI implementation.) Each principal also was asked to identify up to 10 most influential staff members in their schools, especially teachers, whose opinions were likely to carry significant weight with other faculty. Principals met individually with these high-influence staff members to gauge their support for RTI and brought their findings back to the RTI Leadership Team. After pooling information from teacher surveys, face-to-face staff interviews, and their own knowledge of each school, the Leadership Team compiled school profiles that indicated which buildings would probably require additional effort to build staff support of RTI.

Develop a Plan to Build Staff Support   In response to feedback about building attitudes toward the new initiative, each principal developed a plan to strengthen their faculty's support of RTI and shared that plan with the RTI Leadership Team. Before creating their plans, principals first met to brainstorm about those problems that teachers faced every day in their classrooms and asked themselves how the RTI model might assist teachers to better manage those challenges. For example, teachers in one elementary school often expressed anxiety about the prospect of marginal students performing poorly on state tests and concern over misbehaving students who disrupted instruction. In that school, therefore, the point was made to staff that RTI would allow teachers proactively to refer struggling students for more intensive academic interventions and that this additional academic support was likely to result in improved student test scores. Furthermore, teachers were assured that the building's RTI problem-solving team could assist them to reduce classroom disruptions with evidence-based strategies to manage problem student behaviors.

Next, each school conveyed clearly to teachers how classroom practices would change under RTI and how those changes were intended ultimately to result in improved student outcomes. At one elementary school, for example, a consulting team made up of the principal, school psychologist, and reading specialist met with each grade-level team during that team's common planning time for several sessions across four weeks. At those meetings, teachers were surveyed about whole-group and individual strategies that they currently used to instruct students with academic delays and to manage behaviors. The consulting team listed these strategies and, just as important, helped teachers to locate the educational research supporting their use. The product of this series of meetings at each grade level was a menu of Tier 1 instructional and intervention ideas that teachers in that school *were already using*. Listings of classroom strategies from each grade level were consolidated into a school-wide "intervention menu" that was shared with all staff. This exercise had a number of positive outcomes: teachers came to realize that RTI required that they refine—not replace—their current instructional practices: they received valuable additional intervention ideas from their colleagues; and they now had a firm understanding of the kinds of instructional and intervention ideas that were feasible and appropriate for Tier 1.

Finally, schools reorganized their existing resources to build teacher capacity to carry out classroom interventions and assessment. For example, each building created an RTI consultant list of those staff whose job descriptions included consultation, mentoring, or peer coaching. At the elementary level, reading specialists, math specialists, school psychologists, and social workers were among those selected as RTI consultants. Schools then identified those instructional or behavior management areas in which each consultant was qualified to provide support. Schools also defined the services that these RTI consultants could offer to teachers to include training, demonstration and modeling of interventions in classroom settings, and coaching of teachers in using those intervention strategies. Teachers were then given each building's list of RTI consultants with an explanation of their services, and they were encouraged to use these consultants when needed to assist them with additional Tier 1 strategies.

Step 3: Create and Update a Multi-Year RTI Implementation Plan

The RTI Leadership Team realized that the process of bringing RTI to Baylor Schools would be so complex that it would require a written implementation plan that would span at least three years.

One of the early decisions of the RTI Leadership Team was to roll out its RTI model in stages. The team agreed that it would concentrate on reading interventions alone in year one of RTI implementation, and then it would expand to mathematics and behavioral interventions in year two. The team also decided to limit the scope of RTI in years one and two to the elementary schools, in part because the education department in that state had notified school districts that, within several years, they must develop an RTI process to diagnose reading disabilities in grades K through 4. However, secondary school personnel continued to participate on the RTI Leadership Team with the expectation that by year three of the model, RTI would advance to the middle and high schools.

Before starting the RTI Implementation Plan, the team divided the RTI model into more manageable components, including promoting staff understanding and support for RTI; reading interventions for all tiers; math interventions for all tiers, class-wide and individual student behavioral interventions and assessments; RTI problem-solving teams, methods of academic progress monitoring, and the development of a formal RTI process and decision rules for identifying students with reading disabilities. The team created work groups to investigate each of these RTI components to identify the best available practices in the research literature. Each work group drafted a report envisioning how Baylor Schools would implement that RTI component over the next three years, using the scaling-up framework (Ervin & Schaughency, 2008) to include (1) creating readiness in the school system for the RTI component, (2) the initial implementation of the component, (3) institutionalizing the RTI component as a part of routine school and district practices, and (4) ideas for ensuring that the RTI component stayed current with changing revisions in state and federal guidelines and emerging findings in RTI research. The draft reports of all the workgroups were then reviewed and modified as needed by the entire RTI Leadership Team before being combined into a single comprehensive RTI Implementation Plan.

Step 4: Inventory Existing Resources to Support Implementation of RTI

It was apparent to the RTI Leadership Team that, for at least the first three years, Baylor Schools would probably have to rely entirely on its existing resources to implement RTI. However, the team also realized that although the district was not wealthy it did have considerable resources that could be reallocated to support RTI. Before the district could efficiently access those resources, though, the team would first need to inventory and organize them.

To assist with its systematic inventory, the team identified networks of people throughout the school system with knowledge of various resources that might be useful to RTI. Those networks included senior administrators, building administrators, Title 1 reading and math teachers, and school psychologists. The team next developed a listing of potential resource categories to guide its inventory efforts. A top item on the resource category list was funding, specifically any district or building monies that RTI planners might be able to access to purchase curriculum and intervention materials; training and consultation services; and computer hardware, software, and web services. Other RTI resource categories included personnel at the district and building level whose specialized training could make them valuable RTI consultants; noninstructional personnel (e.g., adult volunteer tutors, paraprofessionals) who might have time available to assist with interventions or other RTI activities; and all staff training time available on the school calendar (e.g., conference days, early release days, and summer training days).

The RTI Leadership Team asked each network assisting with the inventory to use these categories as a guide to identify as many district and building RTI resources as possible. The team then combined the resource lists from the networks into a master inventory of RTI resources. Through this comprehensive resource inventory effort, the team discovered that it had located a large percentage of the resources it would need to carry out its ambitious RTI Implementation Plan. In fact, the team found the district RTI resource inventory to be so helpful that it decided to update that inventory annually.

STEP 5: BUILD CAPACITY IN THE DISTRICT RTI MODEL TO EVOLVE AS CONDITIONS CHANGE

As the RTI Leadership Team grew more knowledgeable about RTI, members realized that the RTI model is still in development and that they needed to build in mechanisms that would allow the team to adapt over time to new RTI circumstances. The team decided to monitor emerging trends in RTI research, track changes in state and federal RTI regulations, and network with other school systems in their region that were implementing RTI models of their own.

Select Knowledge Brokers   To stay current on the large number of research developments in RTI, the RTI Leadership Team appointed individuals to serve as knowledge brokers. As a preparatory step, the team generated a list of 15 RTI topics for which recommended best practices seemed likely to change rapidly in response to new research. A sampling of topic areas defined by the team included interventions and progress monitoring for phonemic awareness/alphabetics, interventions and progress monitoring for reading fluency, and RTI decision rules for LD. For each key RTI topic area, the team then selected at least two people from the district with expertise and knowledge of the topic to serve as knowledge brokers. Staff appointed as knowledge brokers were expected to monitor existing best practices and new research findings on their RTI topic area by reading research articles, monitoring important websites, and attending workshops. The team allocated modest funds to allow knowledge brokers to purchase books on their topics as well as to cover workshop and webinar registration fees. The team also earmarked funding to pay knowledge brokers to meet for two days each summer to discuss their research findings. Knowledge brokers were expected to present status reports to the RTI Leadership Team at least annually on research developments in their topic area.

Monitor Changes in State and Federal RTI Regulations   The Baylor School District's RTI model needed to remain consistent with future changes in state and federal RTI regulations. To monitor the district's congruence with RTI government guidelines, three members of the RTI Leadership Team—the assistant superintendent for curriculum and instruction, the director of special education, and a school psychologist—volunteered to serve as a workgroup. The group kept abreast of updates in state and federal RTI regulations and communicated any significant regulation changes to the RTI

Leadership Team. Additionally, the group established a connection with the state education department's RTI coordinator, receiving ongoing information from that person about RTI grants and helpful advance notice about proposed changes to state RTI regulations.

Network with Other School Districts on Effective RTI Practices   The special education agency in the county in which Baylor Schools is located set up a regional RTI school network that met monthly, and Baylor Schools was among the first districts to join. The network allowed schools to share their current RTI practices with one another, to attend workshops on challenging RTI topics (e.g., developing staff support for RTI; effective classroom interventions in mathematics), and, through the county agency network facilitator, to communicate their RTI needs and concerns to the state education department.

Conclusions

A S ARTICULATED IN the opening chapter of our book, this text was not developed to be the complete works on RTI procedures or implementation. We are fully aware that the RTI model and its implementation are still in the infancy stage and many unanswered questions remain. This awareness, however, is tempered by our conviction that traditional models of LD assessment and instruction as widely implemented in the schools are too often ineffective, unreliable, invalid, potentially harmful, and ultimately in need of revision. We welcome an era of education, where assessment is not solely focused on the identification of select students that meet eligibility criteria for special education, but rather on ensuring the success of all students. We embrace the opportunity to implement empirically valid assessments of student academic performance and growth with techniques that have strong relevance to effective intervention. The legislative requirements and supports for the implementation of RTI models have provided the necessary impetus for school-based professionals to seriously consider these procedures and begin to engage in the lengthy process of organizational reform required to implement them with the students they serve. In this, the last chapter of our book, we highlight the promise that we believe RTI procedures hold for educators, review the limitations of RTI procedures and what remains unknown in this field, and end with what we believe are the next steps in the evolutionary development of this large-scale initiative.

THE PROMISE OF RTI PROCEDURES

As discussed in the first chapter, perhaps the most promising aspect of implementing large-scale models of RTI is the potential to focus educator energy toward ensuring the academic success for all students, rather than on special education referral and eligibility activities. Large-scale implementations of both prereferral intervention teams and field-based RTI implementations have generally reported increases in student academic and behavioral performance and decreases in rates of students referred to special education (e.g., Marsten, Muyskens, Lau, & Canter, 2003; McDougal, Moody-Clonan, & Martens, 2000). Research on large-scale RTI implementations has also noted improved student scores on state proficiency exams and decreases in grade retentions. In addition, student participation in RTI has been associated with improvements in students' reading skills, adaptive behavior, time-on-task, and task completion rates. Furthermore, positive results were also demonstrated for those students ultimately placed in special education, including earlier and more intense intervention services that were more directly linked to specific student needs (see Burns & Ysseldyke, 2005, for review of this research).

At a conceptual level, systematic implementation of three-tier RTI models, including screening and progress-monitoring procedures, have the promise to overcome some of the difficulties inherent in even contemporary models of prereferral intervention and instructional support teams. Preventative and proactive screening avoids the need for students to evidence significant histories of failure and reliance on teacher referrals that are typically idiosyncratic in nature. Preventative services offered early (prior to grade 3) are most effective and hold the promise of overcoming the wait-to-fail approach that predominated special education for over 30 years. Additionally, school/district-wide RTI procedures hold the promise of increased efficiency in intervention delivery. Efficiency is increased by rechanneling educator energy toward increasing the quality of classroom instruction, systematic application of scientifically supported intervention programs, and developing an intensity of service to meet student needs instead of designing an individualized intervention for each student referred by the teacher or completing psychological testing.

Two main components for RTI implementation include (1) empirically validated instructional procedures and (2) valid and reliable assessment practices with high relevance to intervention and instruction. In terms of scientifically based instruction, much progress has been made recently in outlining effective practices, especially in the area of early literacy development. The vast array of instructional materials available at the Florida Center for Reading Research (http://www.fcrr.org/), for instance, serves as an example of the availability of these resources. In addition, many commercially published literacy series have been evaluated in terms of the existence of scientifically based instructional components, with a good listing available on the *Big 5 ideas in beginning reading* website http://reading.uoregon.edu/. With continued emphasis on scientifically based instructional practices comes the promise of validation of practices in areas beyond early literacy, both in terms of teaching in other subjects and in the application of effective procedures in the intermediate and secondary levels.

Indeed, some of this work is now underway, as evidenced by reports issued by the National High School Center of the American Institutes for Research as well as the Center on Instruction focusing on implementing tiers models of intervention and effective reading remediation at the secondary-school level. In addition, both the National Center on Learning Disabilities and the National Center on Response to Intervention offer information and resources for implementing RTI at the secondary level and in math and content areas. More research in these areas is needed, but the availability of RTI-related material for subject areas beyond reading and for secondary level implementation is growing.

In addition to the routine use of effective instructional practices, perhaps the most promising feature of RTI model implementation is the systematic application of brief direct assessments of academic skill development. These instructional and curriculum-based assessments have clear implications for instructional intervention and have demonstrated validity and reliability for student screening and progress monitoring. Thus, in addition to the promise of increased use of scientifically based instruction comes the promise of educators routinely using data to determine which students are responding to the instruction and the timely identification of those who are not. Application of CBM procedures by teachers to monitor student response to instruction has been shown to be an effective form of treatment yielding average effect sizes around .7 (Fuchs & Fuchs, 1986). This significant treatment effect would appear to be related simply to teachers having frequent feedback related to student progress and then the timely opportunity to revise instruction based on this weekly data. While currently available methods for assessing within student processing deficits have been critiqued as inadequate and lacking in their relationship to effective treatment, CBM and other direct instructional assessments do appear to have sufficient technical adequacy for monitoring students' response to instruction on a continual basis. Thus, the pairing of empirically based direct assessments of student progress with scientifically based instruction holds the promise of increasing educator effectiveness as demonstrated by increases in student progress and performance. Further, these techniques also hold the promise of increased educator efficiency by limiting the use of ineffective instructional procedures and allowing educators to address student skill gaps in a timely manner.

In terms of procedures for the identification of students with learning disabilities (LD), the RTI model holds the promise of overcoming shortcomings inherent in severe discrepancy methods. Reschley's (2003) summary of the current evidence suggests that severe discrepancy criteria are:

> (a) unreliable (particularly in the sense of stability), (b) invalid (poor readers with higher IQs do not differ on relevant variables from those with IQs commensurate with reading levels), (c) easily undermined in practice by giving multiple tests, finding a score that is discrepant, and ignoring disconfirming evidence, and (d) harmful because the severe discrepancy delays treatment from kindergarten or first grade when the symptoms of reading disability are first manifested to 3rd or 4th grade when reading problems are more severe, intervention more complex, and the school curriculum shifts to "reading to learn (p. 6)."

While a variety of identification approaches within the RTI model have been examined (e.g., Burns & Senesac, 2005), in general these approaches require that student performance and progress or response to increasingly intense and individualized intervention is significantly lower than peers or a normative group. This approach avoids the previously highlighted shortcomings of severe discrepancy criteria in that assessments are conducted across time so temporal stability is less of a problem, neither IQ nor differences between measures is considered prior to service provision, and treatments can be administered as early as kindergarten and certainly by the first grade. While we are not advocating an identification approach that relies solely on student progress monitoring results, these assessments over time would serve as an important piece of the multiple method individualized assessment. Field-based implementations of RTI identification procedures have generally demonstrated improvements in screening and early intervention, proportionate representation of minorities in special education, relevance of IEP goals, and the effectiveness of special education, programming overall (e.g., Grimes, 2002; Marston, 2002). For students in special education, the RTI component that requires peer comparison of student performance and progress over time allows for (1) the setting of realistic IEP goals and exit criteria for special education students, and (2) the opportunity for more relevant reviews of student progress (e.g., Reschly, 2003).

In summary, the promise of RTI includes the opportunity to systematically assess the academic performance and progress of all students with brief and repeatable assessments that are valid and reliable for progress monitoring. Results of these assessments may be used to ensure that the core curriculum and instruction is effective for the majority of the students who receive it. Further, those students behind peers in terms of performance and/or rates of progress may be identified early such that more intense and perhaps individualized instructional intervention can be provided in a preventative fashion. As the research base in this field grows, so too does the list of scientifically based interventions that might be effectively applied. The promise realized in several field applications is that many of the students intervened with in a similar fashion are remediated with grade-appropriate learning trajectories or supported instructionally in the general education environment. Those students who are eventually referred to special education have evidenced a history of failing to respond to increasingly intense instruction that has been demonstrated to be effective for other students at that setting. Therefore, the RTI process has provided for significant documentation that a lack of appropriate instruction is not a determining factor in the special education referral. RTI documentation has identified the student as requiring a more in-depth and individualized multimethod assessment, though the time-consuming and irrelevant search for an IQ-achievement discrepancy is not required. Further, the learning goals the student had prior to referral would also guide IEP goals for those who eventually do receive special education services. Those services too would be assessed in terms of their positive effect on the student.

LIMITATIONS OF RTI AND WHAT IS CURRENTLY UNKNOWN

While the promise of wide-scale RTI implementation is intriguing, numerous limitations and barriers to implementation have also been cited in the literature. Perhaps the largest limitation or barrier relates to the immense organizational reform that is required to implement this type of initiative. Large-scale educational reform will require top-level administrative support and understanding, sustained efforts to phase in three-tier implementation over the course of several years, and attitudinal shifts in educator practice and expectation. Organizational reform will require substantial amounts of professional development and continuing education as educators develop skills with scientifically based instruction, progress-monitoring assessments, data-based decision-making procedures, and structured teaming procedures. Further, at the level of higher education, significant commitment must be made in schools of education across the country to train preservice individuals in these procedures such that they arrive at schools ready to perform. This large-scale implementation will require considerable and sustained effort which historically has been quite difficult to orchestrate in the realm of public education.

Given the required organizational reform discussed previously, we believe that the top five unanswered questions with respect to RTI are as follows.

1. Where does the educational responsibility for RTI implementation lie? While much of the legislative requirements

for RTI are based on special education law (IDEIA, 2004), much of the actual implementation with respect to scientifically based instruction and universal screening is conducted in the realm of general education. While the No Child Left Behind Act (NCLB) requires that additional support be provided for all struggling students, it is currently unclear how these mandates will meld in practice to support RTI implementation across both general and special education.

2. What level of staff development and educator role revision will be required to effectively implement RTI? The staff development requirements of RTI have been a widely cited obstacle for implementation (i.e., Vaughn & Fuchs, 2003). This initiative will require broad training of administrators, general and special education teachers, and other professions in the schools (school psychologist, speech/language specialists, etc.). Training will be required in terms of the RTI model, effective instructional approaches, universal screening techniques, progress monitoring and formative assessment techniques, data-based decision making, and effective teaming procedures. It is currently unclear exactly the level of staff development required for effective RTI implementation nor the extent to which the training will require educators to revise their professional roles in the schools.

3. How do we define "nonresponders"? This question is generally posed around three dimensions: cut-off scores, interventions, and length of time. With respect to cut-off scores there is no clear consensus for what constitutes low performance or a lack of progress. Common cut-off levels discussed in the literature include performance/rates of progress below one standard deviation or below the 25th, 16th, and/or 10th percentile. There is also no clear consensus as to the comparison group—is it classmates, grade-level peers in the building or district, state or national norms, or predefined benchmark levels? Additional considerations related to designating nonresponders relate to the interventions received—type, intensity, frequency, and duration as well as the length of time the intervention

process has been in place. The types of interventions implemented in each tier require greater clarification as does the typical group size, meeting frequency and duration, as well as the specific procedures to be implemented. Lastly, the length of time a student should receive an intervention before being deemed a nonresponder requires greater elaboration.

4. How will fidelity be assessed? The RTI process relies on fidelity both in terms of implementing the model and in terms of the specific instructional interventions being provided to students. The large-scale implementations of RTI reviewed by Burns and Ysseldyke (2005) highlighted both intervention and model fidelity as key obstacles to overcome for educators. RTI models can be rendered ineffective by educational teams not following a prescribed data-based problem-solving process or by teachers not following validated instructional/intervention protocols. Currently there is consensus that fidelity of the model and the interventions must be maintained but little consensus as to how it should be assessed.

5. What type of leadership is required to make RTI effective? Many questions related to leadership remain unanswered. At the state level is RTI to be required and supported by the Department of Education, Special Education, or by local districts? At the district level, is effective implementation based on leadership from the superintendent or assistant superintendent level, the director of curriculum and instruction, or the director of special education? Lastly, at the school level, what is the role of administration support, scheduling, and teacher evaluation, or core membership on the teams implementing RTI?

Other areas in need of greater elaboration include the implementation of RTI at the secondary level and in subject areas beyond math and reading, the role of parents in the process, and when to consider students as entitled to due process provisions consistent with special education regulations. See Burns and Ysseldyke, 2005, and Fuchs, 2003, for more detailed discussion of unanswered questions in RTI.

We pose these questions not to inhibit RTI implementation but to assist educators in entering into the implementation process with eyes wide open and cognizant of the questions that will likely have to be answered at the local level. Our experience with RTI implementation is that it can look quite differently across sites and yet demonstrate similar effectiveness. These questions are among those that would likely need to be answered by a district-level steering group described in Chapter 11 in order to successfully engage in this comprehensive reform process. Toward this end the next section reviews some *next steps* in RTI and offers general advice to those working to implement the process.

NEXT STEPS IN RTI

As districts across the country engage in the RTI implementation process, many of the questions posed earlier will be addressed by educators. Taking the next steps in RTI will require districts to implement the process and reflect on their outcomes in addition to the work of researchers continuing to identify promising practices. In this section we end with a brief summary of some next steps that will be required to facilitate the institutionalization of the RTI model within contemporary educational practices in the United States.

For the RTI model to become even more widely diffused, legislation across the realms of special and general education will have to be better aligned. Given the supportive revisions of IDEIA 2004 it is our hope that the revised NCLB will be even more explicit in supporting RTI as the model most likely to truly ensure that no child is left behind. In addition to legislative support more explicit information related to the phased-in implementation of the RTI model would be helpful to districts initially engaging in this process. Identification of a sequence of required professional development offerings, multiple-year timelines for implementation activities, and implementation evaluation materials would give greater structure for educators engaging in this process. This information should become more readily available based on the increases in implementations noted across the country.

As RTI implementation progresses it is also our hope that some consensus is obtained with respect to indicators of success for this model. In addition to special education rates, perhaps performance on state accountability tests, rates of grade retention, attendance, other indicators of academic and behavioral functioning, and even student progress within special education programming could be performance indicators. Some consistency in these indicators would facilitate program evaluation efforts for each site and allow for comparisons across multiple implementations.

As districts continue implementation and provide important information on those efforts, researchers have a continued role to play. As previously mentioned there is much work to be done in terms of validating effective treatments for areas other than math and reading. In addition, the research on progress monitoring for reading comprehension and skill obtainment in content-area classes is incomplete. Further, all aspects of RTI at the middle and high school levels are under-researched and unclear. More work in these important areas will be required in the future for RTI to fulfill its true potential. Lastly, we believe that researchers should assist educators in deciding the appropriate place for cognitive assessments and also in identifying additional assessments beyond RTI that should be required for a multiple measure comprehensive evaluation.

CONCLUSION

It is our desire that the information and materials in this book assist educators in understanding and implementing the RTI model in schools. In this last chapter of our text we have attempted to identify the promise of RTI practices, highlight the limitations of the model and the unknowns, and offer a brief summary of what we consider some next steps for the evolution of RTI. The real test of course will be in the schools—in the application of the information and materials presented here toward actual improvements in student performance. Supporting educators in this mission of increased student performance was the rationale for the development of the "Practitioners' Guide to RTI: Implementation and Applications." We are hopeful that the future will demonstrate that by implementing what we know with respect to screening, progress monitoring, tiered intervention, and data-based decisions we were successful in improving educational outcomes for all students.

References

A. W. v. Northwest R-1 School District, 813 F.2d 158 (8th Cir. 1987).

Adams, M. (1990). *Begining to read: Thinking and learning about print.* Cambridge, MA: MIT Press.

Alberto, P. A., & Troutman, A. C. (2009). *Applied behavior analysis for teachers* (8th ed.). Upper Saddle River, NJ: Pearson Education.

Al Otaiba, S., & Torgesen, J. (2007). Effects from intensive standardized kindergarten and first-grade interventions for the prevention of reading difficulties. In S. R. Jimerson, M. K. Burns, & A. M.VanDerHeyden (Eds.), *Response to intervention: The science and practice of assessment and intervention* (pp. 212–222).

Amato, P. R. (2001). Children of divorce in the 1990s: An update of the Amato and Keith (1991) *Meta-Analysis. Journal of Family Psychology, 15*(3), 355–370.

Ardoin, S. P. (2006). The response in response to intervention: Evaluating the utility of assessing maintenance of intervention effects. *Psychology in the Schools, 43*(6), 713–725.

Ardoin, S. P., & Christ, T. J. (2008). Evaluating curriculum-based measurement slope estimates using data from tri-annual universal screenings. *School Psychology Review, 37*, 109–125.

Ardoin, S. P., & Christ, T. J. (submitted). Curriculum-based measurement of oral reading: Estimates of standard error when monitoring progress using alternate passage sets.

Ardoin, S. P., Eckert, T. L., & Pender, C. A. S. (2008). Promoting generalization of reading: A comparison of two fluency-based interventions for improving general education student's oral reading rate. *Journal of Behavioral Education, 17*, 237–252.

Ardoin, S. P., Roof, C. M., Klubnik, C., & Carfolite, J. (2008). Evaluating curriculum-based measurement from a behavioral assessment perspective. *The Behavior Analyst Today, 9*, 36–48.

Ardoin, S. P., Suldo, S. M., Witt, J. C., Aldrich, S., & McDonald, E. (2005). Accuracy of readability estimates' predictions of CBM performance. *School Psychology Quarterly, 20*(1), 1–22.

Ardoin, S. P., Witt, J. C., Connel, J. E., & Koenig, J. (2005). Application of a three-tiered response to intervention model for instructional planning, decision making, and the identification of children in need of services. *Journal of Psychoeducational Assessment*, *23*(4), 362–380.

Ardoin, S. P., Witt, J. C., Suldo, S. M., Connel, J. E., Koenig, J. L., Resetar, J. L., et al. (2004). Examining the incremental benefits of administering a maze and three versus one curriculum-based measurement reading probe when conducting universal screening. *School Psychology Review*, *33*, 218–233.

Ball, P. L. (1997). The effects of classroom reading data and teacher recommendations on parents' attitudes about reintegration. Unpublished doctoral dissertation, University of Oregon, Eugene.

Barnett, D. W., Daly, E. J., Jones, K. M., & Lentz, F. E. (2004). Response to intervention: Empirically based special service decisions from single-case designs of increasing and decreasing intensity. *Journal of Special Education*, *38*, 66–79.

Barnett, D. W., Elliott, N., Wolsing, L., Bunger, C. E., Haski, H., McKissick, C., et al. (2006). Response to intervention for young children with extremely challenging behaviors: What it might look like. *School Psychology Review*, *35*(4), 568–582.

Beaver, J. (2001). *Technical manual for the developmental reading assessment*. Pearson Learning Group.

Bergan, J. R. (1995). Evolution of a problem-solving model of consultation. *Journal of Educational and Psychological Consultation*, *6*(2), 111–123.

Binder, C. (1996). Behavioral fluency: Evolution of a new paradigm. *The Behavior Analyst*, *19*, 163–197.

Bos, C. S., Mather, N., Narr, R. F., & Babur, N. (1999). Interactive, collaborative professional development in early literacy instruction: Supporting the balancing act. *Learning Disabilities Research & Practice*, *14*, 227–238.

Bradley, R., Danielson, L., & Doolittle, J. (2003). Response to intervention. *Journal of Learning Disabilities*, *38*(6), 485–486.

Brown-Chidsey, R., & Steege, M. W. (2005). *Response to intervention: Principles and strategies for effective practice*. New York: Guilford Press.

Burns, M. K. (2004). Empirical analysis of drill ratio research: Defining the instructional level for drill tasks. *Remedial and Special Education*, *25*, 167–175.

Burns, M. K., Appleton, J. J., & Stehouwer, J. D. (2005). Meta-analytic review of responsiveness-to-intervention research: Examining field-based and research-implemented models. *Journal of Psychoeducational Assessment*, *23*(4), 381–394.

Burns, M. K. & Senesac, B. V. (2005). Comparison of dual discrepancy criteria to assess response to intervention. *Journal of School Psychology, 43*, 393–406.

Burns, M. K., VanDerHeyden, A. M., & Boice, C. H. (2008). Best practices in intensive academic interventions. In A. Thomas & J. Grimes (Eds.), *Best practices in school psychology V* (pp. 1151–1162). Bethesda, MD: National Association of School Psychologists.

Burns, M. K., VanDerHeyden, A. M., & Jiban, C. (2006). Assessing the instructional level for mathematics: A comparison of methods. *School Psychology Review, 35*, 401–418.

Burns, M. K., & Wagner, D. (2008). Determining an effective intervention within a brief experimental analysis for reading: A meta-analytic review. *School Psychology Review, 37*, 126–136.

Burns, M. K., & Ysseldyke, J. E. (2005). Comparison of existing response to intervention models to identify and answer implementation questions. *The California School Psychologist, 10*, 9–20.

Carnine, D. (1994). Diverse learners and prevailing, emerging and research-based educational approaches and their tools. *School Psychology Review, 23*, 341–350.

Carnine, D., Silbert, S., & Kame'enui, E. J. (1990). *Direct instruction reading* (2nd ed.). New York: Prentice Hall.

Cates, G. L., Dunne, M., Erkfritz, K. N., Kivisto, A., Lee, N., & Wierzbicki, J. (2007). Differential effects of two spelling procedures on acquisition, maintenance and adaption to reading. *Journal of Behavioral Education, 16* (1), 71–82.

Chafouleas, S., Riley-Tillman, T. C., & Sugai, G. (2007). *School-based behavioral assessment: Informing intervention and instruction.* New York: Guilford Press.

Chalfant, J. C., Pysh, M. V., & Moultrie, R. (1979). Teacher assistance teams: A model for within-building problem solving. *Learning Disability Quarterly, (2) 3*, 85–96.

Chamberlin, J. (2005, November). A learning disability dialogue. *Monitor on Psychology, 36*(10). Retrieved August 9, 2008, from APA Online.

Christ, T. J. (2006). Short term estimates of growth using curriculum-based measurement of oral reading fluency: Estimates of standard error of the slope to construct confidence intervals. *School Psychology Review, 35*, 128–133.

Christ, T. J., & Ardoin, S. P. (in press). Curriculum-based measurement of reading: Passage equivalence and selection. *Journal of School Psychology.*

Christ, T. J., & Coolong-Chaffin, M. (2007). Interpretations of curriculum-based measurement outcomes: Standard error and confidence intervals. *School Psychology Forum: Research in Practice, 1*(2), 75–86.

Christ, T. J., & Hintze, J. M. (2007). Psychometric considerations when evaluating response to intervention. In S. R. Jimmerson & A. M. VanDerHeyden (Eds.), *Handbook of response to intervention: The science and practice of assessment and intervention* (pp. 93–105). New York: Springer.

Colon, E. P., & Kranzler, J. H. (2006). Effect of instructions on curriculum-based measurement of reading. *Journal of Psychoeducational Assessment, 24*(4), 318–328.

Compton, D. L., Fuchs, D., Fuchs, L. S., & Bryant, J. D. (2006). Selecting at-risk readers in first grade for early intervention: A two-year longitudinal study of decision rules and procedures. *Journal of Educational Psychology, 2,* 394–409.

Cook, B. G., & Schirmer, B. R. (2003). What is special about special education? Overview and analysis. *Journal of Special Education, 37*(3), 200–205.

Crawford, L., Tindal, G., & Steiber, S. (2001). Using oral reading rate to predict student performance on statewide achievement tests. *Educational Assessment, 7,* 303–323.

Cushing, L. S., & Horner, R. (2003). Student interaction in specific settings (SISS) measure, coding procedures, and definitions. Unpublished coding manual. (Available from Peabody College at Vanderbilt University, Box 328, Nashville, TN 37203.

Daly, E. J., Martens, B. K., Barnett, D., Witt, J. C., & Olson, S. C. (2007). Varying intervention delivery in response to intervention: Confronting and resolving challenges with measurement, instruction, and intensity. *School Psychology Review, 36,* 562–581.

Daly, E. J., Murdoch, A., Lillenstein, L., Webber, L., & Lentz, F. E. (2002). An examination of methods for testing treatments: Conducting brief experimental analyses of the effects of instructional components on oral reading fluency. *Education and Treatment of Children, 25,* 288–316.

Daniel, R. R. v. State Board of Education, 874 F.2d 1036, (5th Cir. 1989).

Darch, C. B., & Kame'enui, E. J. (2004). *Instructional classroom management: A proactive approach to behavior management* (2nd ed.). Upper Saddle River, NJ: Pearson.

Deno, S. L. (1985). Curriculum-based measurement: The emerging alternative. *Exceptional Children, 52,* 219–232.

Deno, S. L. (2003). Developments in curriculum-based measurement. *Remedial and Special Education, 37,* 184–192.

Deno, S. L., Fuchs, L. S., Marston, D., & Shin, J. (2001). Using curriculum-based measurement to establish growth standards for students with learning disabilities. *School Psychology Review, 30*, 507–524.

Deno, S. L., Marston, D., & Tindal, G. (1985). Direct and frequent curriculum-based measurement: An alternative for educational decision making. *Special Services in the Schools, 2*(2), 5–27.

Deno, S. L., & Mirkin, P. K. (1977). *Data-based program modification: A manual.* Reston, VA: Council for Exceptional Children.

Deno, S. L., Mirkin, P. K., & Chiang, B. (1982). Identifying valid measures of reading. *Exceptional Children, 49*, 36–45.

Deno, S. L., Reschly, A. L., Lembke, E. S., Magnusson, D., Callender, S. A., Windram, H., et al. (2009). Developing a school-wide progress-monitoring system. *Psychology in the Schools, 46*, 44–55.

DiPerna, J. C., & Elliott, S. N. (2000). *Academic Competence Evaluation Scales (ACES).* San Antonio, TX: Harcourt.

Dohrn, E., Volpiansky, P. Kratochwill, T. R., & Sanetti, L. H. (2007). *Progress monitoring toolkit: Responsive education for all children.* Retrieved July 24, 2008, from Wisconsin Department of Public Instruction: http://www.reachwi.com/index.php?option=com_docman&task= cat_view&gid=49&Itemid=28.

Donovan, M. S., & Cross, C. T. (2002). *Minority students in special and gifted education.* Washington, DC: National Academy Press.

Durkin, D. (1993). *Teaching them to read* (6th ed.). Boston, MA: Allyn & Bacon.

Eckert, T. L., Ardoin, S. P., Daly, E. J., III, & Martens, B. K. (2002). Improving oral reading fluency: A brief experimental analysis of combining an antecedent intervention with consequences. *Journal of Applied Behavior Analysis, 35*, 271–281.

Eckert, T. L., Dunn, E. K., & Ardoin, S. P. (2006). The effects of alternate forms of performance feedback on elementary-aged students' oral reading fluency. *Journal of Behavioral Education, 15*(3), 148–161.

Ellis, E., Worthington, L., & Larkin, M. (1994). *Executive summary of the research synthesis on effective teaching principles and the design of quality tools for educators.* Retrieved December 3, 2007, from University of Oregon: http://idea.uoregon.edu/~ncite/documents/techrep/tech06.html.

Ervin, R. A., & Schaughency, E. (2008). Best practices in accessing the systems change literature. In A. Thomas & J. Grimes (Eds.), *Best practices in school psychology V* (pp. 853–873). Bethesda, MD: National Association of School Psychologists.

Fairbanks, S., Sugai, G., Guardino, S., & Lathrop, M. (2007). Response to intervention: Examining classroom behavior support in second grade. *Exceptional Children, 73*, 288–310.

Fass, S., & Cauthen, N. K. (2007, November). *Who are America's poor children? The official story*. Retrieved July 1, 2008, from National Center for Children in Poverty: http://www.nccp.org/publications/pub_684.html.

Fisher, C. W., & Berliner, D. C. (Eds.) (1985). *Perspectives on instructional time*. New York: Longman.

Fletcher, J. M., Denton, C. & Francis, D. J. (2005). Validity of alternative approaches for the identification of learning disabilities. *Journal of Learning Disabilities, 38*, 545–552.

Fletcher, J. M., Shaywitz, S. E., Shankweiler, D. P., Katz, L., Liberman, I. Y., Stuebing, K. K., Francis, D. J., Fowler, A. E., & Shaywitz, B. A. (1994). Cognitive profiles of reading disability: Comparisons of discrepancy and low achievement definitions. *Journal of Educational Psychology, 86*, 6–23.

Florian, L. (1998). Inclusive practice: What, why, and how? In C. Tilstone, L. Florian, & R. Rose (Eds.), *Promoting inclusive practice* (pp. 13–26). London: Routledge.

Florida Center for Reading Research. (n.d.). The Florida Center for Reading Research. Retrieved from http://www.fcrr.org/. Accessed January 20, 2009.

Flugum, K. R., & Reschly, D. J. (1994). Prereferral interventions: Quality indices and outcomes. *Journal of School Psychology, 32*, 1–14.

Foorman, B. R., Francis, D. J., Fletcher, J. M., Schatschneider, C., & Mehta, P. (1998). The role of instruction in learning to read: Preventing reading disabilities in at-risk children. *Journal of Educational Psychology, 90*, 37–55.

Foorman, B. R., & Torgesen, J. (2001). Critical elements of classroom and small-group instruction promote reading success in all children. *Learning Disabilities Research and Practice, 16*(4), 203–212.

Francis, D. J., Fletcher, J. M., & Morris, R. D. (2003). *Response to intervention: A conceptually and statistically superior alternative to discrepancy*. Paper presented at the National Research Center on Learning Disabilities Responsiveness-to-Intervention Symposium, Kansas City, MO.

Francis, D. J., Fletcher, J. M., Stuebing, K. K., Lyon, G. R., Shaywitz, B. A., & Shaywitz, S. E. (2005). Psychometric approaches to the identification of LD: IQ and achievement scores are not sufficient. *Journal of Learning Disabilities, 38*, 98–108.

Francis, D. J., Santi, K. L., Barr, C., Fletcher, J. M., Varisco, A., & Foorman, B. R. (2008). Form effects on the estimation of students' oral reading fluency using DIBELS. *Journal of School Psychology, 46*, 315–342.

Francis, D. J., Shaywitz, S. E., Stuebing, K. K., Shaywitz, B. A., & Fletcher, J. M. (1996). Developmental lag versus deficit models of reading disability: A longitudinal, individual growth curves analysis. *Journal of Educational Psychology, 88,* 3–17.

Frankenberger, W., & Franzalglio, K. (1991). A review of states' criteria and procedures for identifying children with learning disabilities. *Journal of Learning Disabilities, 24*(8), 495–500.

Fuchs, D., & Deshler, D. D. (2007). What we need to know about responsiveness to intervention (and shouldn't be afraid to ask). *Learning Disabilities Research & Practice, 22*(2), 129–136.

Fuchs, D., Fernstrom, P., Scott, S., Fuchs, L., & Vandermeer, L. (1994). Classroom ecological inventory: A process for mainstreaming. *Teaching Exceptional Children, 26*(4), 11–15.

Fuchs, D., & Fuchs, L. S. (2001, September/October). Responsiveness-to-intervention: A blueprint for practitioners, policy makers, and parents. *Teaching Exceptional Children, 38,* 57–61.

Fuchs, D., & Fuchs, L. S. (2006). Introduction to response to intervention: What, why, and how valid is it? *Reading Research Quarterly, 41*(1), 93–99.

Fuchs, D., Fuchs, L. S., & Burish, P. (2000). Peer-assisted learning strategies: An evidenced-based practice to promote reading achievement. *Learning Disabilities Research & Practice, 15*(2), 85–91.

Fuchs, D., Fuchs, L. S., & Fernstrom, P. (1992). Case-by-case reintegration of students with learning disabilities. *Elementary School Journal, 92,* 261–281.

Fuchs, D., Fuchs, L. S., Harris, A. H., & Roberts, H. (1996). Bridging the research-to-practice gap with mainstream assistance teams: A cautionary tale. *School Psychology Quarterly, 11*(3), 244–266.

Fuchs, D., Fuchs, L. S., Thompson, A., Svenson, E., Yen, L., Otaiba, S. A., et al. (2001). Peer-assisted learning strategies in reading: Extensions for kindergarten, first grade, and high school. *Remedial and Special Education, 22,* 15–21.

Fuchs, D., Mock, D., Morgan, P. L., & Young, C. L. (2003). Responsiveness-to-intervention: Definitions, evidence, and implications for the learning disabilities construct. *Learning Disabilities Research & Practice, 18*(3), 157–171.

Fuchs, L. S. (2003). Assessing intervention responsiveness: Conceptual and technical issues. *Learning Disabilities Research & Practice, 18,* 172–186.

Fuchs, L. S. (2004). Determining adequate yearly progress from kindergarten through grade 6 with curriculum-based measurement. *Assessment for Effective Intervention, 29,* 25–37.

Fuchs, L. S., Deno, S. L., & Mirkin, P. K. (1984). The effects of frequent curriculum-based measurement and evaluation on student achievement, pedagogy, and student awareness of learning. *American Educational Research Journal, 21*, 449–460.

Fuchs, L. S., & Fuchs, D. (1986a). Curriculum-based assessment of progress toward long-term and short-term goals. *Journal of Special Education, 20*(1), 69–82.

Fuchs, L. S., & Fuchs, D. (1986b). Effects of systematic formative evaluation: A meta-analysis. *Exceptional Children, 53*(3), 199–208.

Fuchs, L. S., & Fuchs, D. (2002). Curriculum-based measurement: Describing competence, enhancing outcomes, evaluating treatment effects, and identifying treatment nonresponders. *Peabody Journal of Education, 77*(2), 64–84.

Fuchs, L. S., Fuchs, D., & Compton, D. L. (2004). Monitoring early reading development in first grade: Word identification fluency versus nonsense word fluency. *Exceptional Children, 71*, 7–21.

Fuchs, L. S., Fuchs, D., & Deno, S. L. (1982). Reliability and validity of curriculum-based informal reading inventories. *Reading Research Quarterly, 18*, 6–26.

Fuchs, L. S., Fuchs, D., Hamlett, C. L., Walz, L., & Germann, G. (1993). Formative evaluation of academic progress: How much growth can we expect? *School Psychology Review, 22*, 27–48.

Fuchs, L. S., Fuchs, D., Hosp, M. K., & Jenkins, J. R. (2001). Oral reading fluency as an indicator of reading competence: A theoretical, empirical, and historical analysis. *Scientific Studies of Reading, 5*(3), 239–256.

Fuchs, L. S., Fuchs, D., & Maxwell, L. (1988). The validity of informal reading comprehension measures. *Remedial and Special Education, 9*(2), 20–28.

Fuchs, L. S., & Shinn, M. R. (1989). Writing CBM IEP objectives. In M. R. Shinn (Ed.), *Curriculum-based measurement: Assessing special children.* New York: Guilford.

Gansle, K. A., & Noell, G. H. (2007). The fundamental role of intervention implementation in assessing response to intervention. In S. R. Jimerson, M. K. Burns, & A. M. VanDerHeyden (Eds.), *Response to intervention: The science and practice of assessment and intervention* (pp. 244–251).

Gansle, K. A., Noell, G. H., Vanderheyden, A. M., Slider, N. J., Hoffpauir, L. D., Whitmarsh, E. L., et al. (2004). An examination of the criterion validity and sensitivity to brief intervention of alternate curriculum-based measures of writing skill. *Psychology in the Schools, 41*(3), 291–300.

Gerber, M. M. (2003). *Teachers are still the test: Limitations of response to instruction strategies for identifying children with learning disabilities.* Paper presented at the National Research Center on Learning

Disabilities Responsiveness-to-Intervention Symposium, Kansas City, MO.

Gettinger, M., & Seibert, J. K. (2002). Best practices in increasing academic learning time. In A. Thomas (Ed.), *Best practices in school psychology IV*. (4th ed.) (pp. 773–787). Bethesda, MD: National Association of School Psychologists.

Glover, T. A., & DiPerna, J. C. (2007). Service delivery for response to intervention: Core components and directions for future research. *School Psychology Review, 36*, 526–540.

Good, R. H., & Kaminski, R. A. (Eds.) (2002). *Dynamic indicators of basic early literacy skills* (6th ed.). Eugene, OR: Institute for the Development of Educational Achievement. Available from http://dibels.uoregon.edu/.

Good, R. H., Kaminski, R. A., Smith, S., Simmons, D., Kame'enui, E., & Wallin, J. (In press). Reviewing outcomes: Using DIBELS to evaluate a school's core curriculum and system of additional intervention in kindergarten. In S. R. Vaughn & K. L. Briggs (Eds.), *Reading in the classroom: Systems for observing teaching and learning*. Baltimore: Paul H. Brookes.

Good, R. H., III, Simmons, D., & Kame'enui, E. (2001). The importance and decision-making utility of a continuum of fluency-based indicators of foundational reading skills for third-grade high-stakes outcomes. *Scientific Studies of Reading, 5*, 257–288.

Good, R. H., III, Simmons, D., Kame'enui, E., Kaminski, R. A., & Wallin, J. (2002). Summary of decision rules for intensive, strategic, and benchmark instructional recommendations in kindergarten through third grade (Technical Report No. 11). Eugene, OR: University of Oregon.

Graden, J. L., Casey, A., & Bonstrom, O. (1985). Implementing a prereferral intervention System: II. The data. *Exceptional Children, 51*(6), 487–496.

Green, S., & Shinn, M. R. (1994). Parent attitudes about special education and reintegration: What is the role of student outcomes? *Exceptional Children, 61*(3), 269–281.

Gresham, F. M. (1989). Assessment of treatment integrity in school consultation & prereferral intervention. *School Psychology Review, 18*, 27–50.

Gresham, F. M. (2002). Responsiveness to intervention: An alternative approach to the identification of learning disabilities In R. Bradley, L. Danielson, & D. L. Hallahan (Eds.), *Identification of learning disabilities: Research to practice* (pp. 467–519). Mahwah, NJ: Erlbaum.

Gresham, F. M., Gansle, K. A., & Noell, G. H. (1993). Treatment integrity in applied behavior analysis with children. *Journal of Applied Behavior Analysis, 26*(2), 257–263.

Grimes, J. (2002). Responsiveness to interventions: The next step in special education identification, service, and exiting decision making. In R. Bradley, L. Danielson, & D. P. Hallahan (Eds.), *Identification of learning disabilities: Research to practice* (pp. 531–547). Mahwah, NJ: Lawrence Erlbaum.

Habedank, L. (1995). Best practices in developing local norms for problem solving in the schools. In A. Thomas & J. Grimes (Eds.), *Best practices in school psychology III* (pp. 701–715). Washington, DC: National Association of School Psychologists.

Hallahan, D. P., & Kauffman, J. K. (2000). *Exceptional learners: Introduction to special education* (8th ed.). Boston: Allyn & Bacon.

Hallahan, D. P., Kauffman, J. M., & Lloyd, J. W. (1999). *Introduction to learning disabilities.* Boston, MA: Allyn & Bacon.

Haring, N. G., & Eaton, M. D. (1978). Systematic procedures: An instructional hierarchy. In N. G. Haring, T. C. Lovitt, M. D. Eaton, & C. L. Hansen (Eds.), *The fourth R: Research in the classroom.* Columbus, OH: Charles E. Merrill Publishing Co.

Haring, N. G., Lovitt, T. C., Eaton, M. D., & Hansen, C. L. (Eds.), (1978). *The fourth R: Research in the classroom.* Columbus, OH: Charles E. Merrill Publishing Co.

Hartman, W. T., & Fay, T. A. (1996). *Cost effectiveness of instructional support teams in Pennsylvania.* The Center for Special Education Finance, Policy Paper 9, Palo Alto, CA: American Institutes for Education.

Hartmann v. Loudoun County Board of Education, 118 R.3rd 996 (1997).

Hasbrouck, J., & Tindal, G. A. (2006) Oral reading fluency norms: A valuable assessment tool for reading teachers. *The Reading Teacher, 59* (7), 636–644.

Hendrick Hudson District Board of Education v. Rowley, 458 U.S. 176, 102 S. Ct. 3034, 73, L. Ed. 2d 690, 5 Ed. Law Rep. 34, 1982.

Heward, W. L. (1996). Three low-tech strategies for increasing the frequency of active student response during group instruction. In R. Gardner, D. M. Sainato, J. O. Cooper, T. E. Heron, W. L. Heward, J. W. Eshleman, & T. A. Grossi (Eds.), *Behavior analysis in education: Focus on measurably superior instruction* (pp. 283–320). Pacific Grove, CA: Brooks/Cole.

Heward, W. L. (2003). Ten faulty notions about teaching and learning that hinder the effectiveness of special education. *Journal of Special Education, 36*(4), 186–205.

Hintze, J. M., Ryan, A. L., & Stoner, G. (2003). Concurrent validity and diagnostic accuracy of the dynamic indicators of basic early literacy skills and the comprehensive test of phonological processing. *School Psychology Review, 32,* 541–556.

Hintze, J. M., Shapiro, E. S., & Lutz, J. G. (1994). The effects of curriculum on the sensitivity of curriculum-based measurement in reading. *Journal of Special Education, 28,* 188–202.

Hintze, J. M., & Silberglitt, B. (2005). A longitudinal examination of the diagnostic accuracy and predictive validity of R-CBM and high-stakes testing. *School Psychology Review, 34*(3), 372–386.

Hintze, J. M., Volpe, R. J., & Shapiro, E. S. (2008). Best practices in the systematic direct observation of student behavior. In A. Thomas & J. Grimes (Eds.), *Best Practices in School Psychology V* (pp. 319–336). Bethesda, MD: National Association of School Psychologists.

Hoskyn, M., & Swanson, L. H. (2000). Cognitive processing of low achievers and children with reading disabilities: A selective meta-analytic review of the published literature. *School Psychology Review, 29,* 102–109.

Hosp, J. L., & Ardoin, S. P. (2008). Assessment for instructional planning. *Assessment for Effective Intervention, 33*(2), 69–77.

Howell, K., & Nolet, V. (2000). *Curriculum-based evaluation: Teaching and decision-making* (3rd ed.). Belmont, CA: Wadsworth.

Ikeda, M. J., & Gustafson, J. K., (2002). *Heartland AEA 11's problem solving process: Impact on issues related to special education.* Research report no. 2002–01. Johnston, IA: Heartland Area Education Agency 11.

Individuals with Disabilities Education Improvement Act, U.S.C. H.R. 1350 (2004).

Individuals with Disabilities Education Improvement Act (IDEIA) of 2004, PL 108-446, 20 USC §§ 1400 et seq.

Iowa Administrative Code. Education Department [281]. Chapter 41 SPECIAL EDUCATION. 281—41.116 (256B,34CFR300) Placements. Retrieved May 1, 2009, from http://search.legis.state.ia.us/NXT/gateway.dll?f=templates&fn=default.htm.

Iowa Department of Education. (2006, January). *Special education eligibility standards.* Des Moines, IA: State of Iowa, Department of Education.

Kame'enui, E. J., & Simmons, D. C. (1990). *Designing instructional strategies: The prevention of academic learning problems.* Columbus, OH: Merrill Publishing Company.

Kamil, M. L., Borman, G. D., Dole, J., Kral, C. C., Salinger, T., & Torgesen, J. (2008). *Improving adolescent literacy: Effective classroom and intervention practices: A practice guide* (NCEE #2008-4027). Washington, DC: National Center for Education Evaluation and Regional Assistance,

Institute of Education Sciences, U.S. Department of Education. Retrieved from http://ies.ed.gov/ncee/wwc.

Kaminski, R. A., Cummings, K. D., Powell-Smith, K. A., & Good, R. H., III. (2008). Best practices in using dynamic indicators of basic early literacy skills (DIBELS) for formative assessment and evaluation. In A. Thomas & J. Grimes (Eds.), *Best practices in school psychology V* (pp. 1181–1204). Bethesda, MD: National Association of School Psychologists.

Kazdin, A. E. (1989). *Behavior modification in applied settings* (4th ed.). Pacific Grove, CA: Brooks/Cole Publishing.

Kirk, S. (1962). *Educating exceptional children.* Boston: Houghton Mifflin.

Kirschner, P. A., Sweller, J., & Clark, R. E. (2006). Why minimal guidance during instruction does not work: An analysis of the failure of constructivist, discovery, problem-based, experiential, and inquiry-based teaching. *Educational Psychologist, 41*(2), 75–86.

Kosanovich, M., Ladinsky, K., Nelson, L., & Torgesen, J. (n.d.). Differentiated reading instruction: Small group alternative lesson structures for all students. Florida Center for Reading Research. Retrieved on November 5, 2008, from http://www.fcrr.org/assessment/pdf/smallGroupAlternativeLessonStructures.pdf.

Kovaleski, J. F., Gickling, E. E., Morrow, H., & Swank. (1999). High versus low implementation of instructional support teams: A case for maintaining program fidelity. *Remedial and Special Education, 20*(3), 170–183.

Kratochwill, T. R., & Shernoff, E. S. (2004). Evidence-based practice: Promoting evidence based interventions in school psychology. *School Psychology Review, 33,* 34–48.

LaBerge, D., & Samuels, S. J. (1974). Toward a theory of automatic information processing in reading. *Cognitive Psychology, 6,* 293–323.

Lee, J., Grigg, W., and Dion, G. (2007). *The nation's report card: Mathematics 2007* (NCES 2007-494). National Center for Education Statistics, Institute of Education Sciences, U.S. Department of Education, Washington, D.C.

Lee, J., Grigg, W., & Donahue, P. (2007). *The nation's report card: Reading 2007* (NCES 2007-496). National Center for Education Statistics, Institute of Education Sciences, U.S. Department of Education, Washington, D.C.

Lentz, F. E., & Shapiro, E. S. (1986). Functional assessment of the academic environment. *School Psychology Review, 15,* 346–357.

Linan-Thompson, S., Vaughn, S., Hickman-Davis, P., & Kousekanani, K. (2003). Effectiveness of supplemental reading instruction for second grade English language learners with reading difficulties. *Elementary School Journal, 18*(3), 221–238.

Lytle, J., & Penn, W. (1986). *Special education: Views from America's cities.* Philadelphia: Research for Better Schools.

MacQuarrie, L. L., Tucker, J. A., Burns, M. K., & Hartman, B. (2002). Comparison of retention rates using traditional, drill sandwich, and incremental rehearsal flash card methods. *School Psychology Review, 31,* 584–595.

Marston, D. (2005). Tiers of intervention in responsiveness to intervention: Prevention outcomes and learning disabilities identification patterns. *Journal of Learning Disabilities, 38*(6), 539–544.

Marston, D., Muyskens, P., Lau, M. Y., & Canter, A. (2003). Problem-solving model for decision making with high-incidence disabilities: The Minneapolis experience. *Learning Disabilities Research & Practice, 18*(3), 187–200.

Martens, B. K. (1993). A case against magical thinking in school-based intervention. *Journal of Educational and Psychological Consultation, 4*(2), 185–189.

Martens, B. K., & Witt, J. C. (2004). Competence, persistence, and success: The positive psychology of behavioral skill instruction. *Psychology in the Schools, 41*(1), 19–30.

Marzano, R., & Pickering, D. P. (2001). *Classroom instruction that works: Research-based strategies for increasing student Achievement.* Association for Supervision & Curriculum Development.

McCurdy, M., Daly, E., Gortmaker, V., & Bonfiglio, C. (2006). Use of brief instructional trials to identify small group reading strategies: A two experiment study. *Journal of Behavioral Education, 16,* 7–26.

McDougal, J. L., Moody, Clonan, S., & Martens, B. K. (2000). Using organizational change procedures to promote the acceptability of prereferral intervention services: The school based intervention team project. *School Psychology Quarterly, 15*(2), 149–171.

McGlinchey, M. T., & Hixson, M. D. (2004). Using curriculum-based measurement to predict performance on state assessments in reading. *School Psychology Review, 33,* 193–203.

McMaster, K. L., Fuchs, D., & Fuchs, L. S. (2006). Research on peer-assisted learning strategies: The promise and limitations of peer-mediated instruction. *Reading & Writing Quarterly, 22,* 5–25.

Mercer, C. D., Jordan, L., & Allopp, D. H. (1996). Learning disabilities definitions and criteria used by state education departments. *Learning Disability Quarterly, 19*(4), 217–232.

Messick, S. (1995). Validity of psychological assessment: Validation of inferences from persons' responses and performances as scientific inquiry into score meaning. *American Psychologist, 50,* 741–749.

Moats, L. (2006). *Whole language high jinks: How to tell when "scientifically-based reading instruction" isn't.* Retrieved March 21, 2008, from http://www.sopriswest.com/pdfs/whole_language_high_jinks.pdf.

Muyskens, P., & Marston, D. B. (2002). *Predicting success on the Minnesota Basic Skills Test in reading using CBM.* Unpublished manuscript, Minneapolis Public Schools.

National Center on Student Progress Monitoring. (2006). *What are the benefits of progress monitoring?* Retrieved October 22, 2006, from http://www.studentprogress.org.

National Reading Panel. (2000). *Teaching children to read: An evidence-based assessment of the scientific research literature on reading and its implications for reading instruction.* Bethesda, MD: National Institute of Child Health & Human Development, National Institutes of Health.

No Child Left Behind Act of 2001, Pub. L. No. 107-110, 115 Stat. 1425 (2002).

Northwest Evaluation Association. (n.d.). *2008 measures of academic progress.* Retrieved March, 14, 2008, from http://www.nwea.org/assessments/map.asp.

Oberti v. Board of Education of Clementon School District, 995 F.2d 1204 (3rd Cir. 1993).

Odom, S. L., Brantlinger, E., Gersten, R., Horner, R. H., Thompson, B., & Harris, K. R. (2005). Research in special education: Scientific methods and evidence-based practices. *Exceptional Children, 71*(2), 137–148.

Parrish, T. B. (2006, March). *National and state overview of special education funding.* Presentation given to Kansas Association of Special Education Administrators. Lawrence, KS. Retrieved online November 25, 2006, from http://www.csef-air.org/presentations/KS%20speciale-ducation%20presentation%203-1-06.pdf.

Powell-Smith, K. A., & Ball, P. (2008). Best practices in reintegration and special education exit decisions. In A. Thomas & J. Grimes (Eds.), *Best practices in school psychology V* (pp. 263–280). Bethesda, MD: National Association of School Psychologists.

Powell-Smith, K. A., & Stewart, L. H. (1998). The use of curriculum-based measurement in the reintegration of students with mild disabilities. In M. R. Shinn (Ed.), *Advanced applications of curriculum-based measurement* (pp. 254–307). New York: Guilford.

President's Commission on Excellence in Special Education. (2002). A new era: Revitalizing special education for children and their families.

Retrieved March 15, 2005, from http://www.ed.gov/inits/commissionboards/whspecialeducation/reportshtml.

Reschly, R. J. (2003). *What if LD identification changed to reflect research findings?* Paper presented at the National Research Center on Learning Disabilities Responsiveness-to-Intervention Symposium, Kansas City, MO.

Reynolds, M. C., & Birch, J. W. (1977). *Teaching exceptional children in all America's schools*. Reston, VA: Council for Exceptional Children.

Roach, A. T., & Elliott, S. N. (2008). Best practices in facilitating and evaluating intervention integrity. In A. Thomas & J. Grimes (Eds.), *Best practices in school psychology V* (pp. 195–208). Bethesda, MD: National Association of School Psychologists.

Rodden-Nord, K., Shinn, M. R., & Good, R. H. (1992). Effects of classroom performance data on general education teacher's attitudes toward reintegrating students with learning disabilities. *School Psychology Review, 21*(1), 138–154.

Ronker v. Walter, 700 F.2d 1058 (6th Cir.), cert. denied, 464 U.S. 864 (1983).

Rosenfield, S. (1992). Developing school-based consultation teams: A design for organizational change. *School Psychology Quarterly, 7*, 27–42.

Rutter, M., & Yule, W. (1975). The concept of specific reading retardation. *Journal of Child Psychology and Psychiatry, 16*, 181–197.

Sacramento Unified School District v. Rachel H., 14 F.3d 1398, 1404 (9th Cir.), cert. denied, 129 L. Ed 2d 813, 114 S. Ct. 2679 (1994).

Salahu-Din, D., Persky, H., & Miller, J. (2008). *The nation's report card: Writing 2007* (NCES 2008-468). National Center for Education Statistics, Institute of Education Sciences, U.S. Department of Education, Washington, D.C.

Schreiber, P. A. (1991). Understanding prosody's role in reading acquisition. *Theory into practice, 30*, 158–164.

Shapiro, E. S. (2004a). *Academic skills problems: Direct assessment and intervention* (3rd ed.). New York: Guilford.

Shapiro, E. S. (2004b). *Academic skills problems workbook* (Rev. ed.). New York: Guilford.

Shinn, J., Deno, S. D., & Espin, C. (2000). Technical adequacy of the maze task for curriculum-based measurement of reading growth. *Journal of Special Education, 34*, 164–172.

Shinn, M. R. (1986). Does anyone care what happens after the referral-test-placement process? The systematic evaluation of special education effectiveness. *School Psychology Review, 15*, 49–58.

Shinn, M. R. (Ed.). (1989). *Curriculum-based measurement: Assessing special children*. New York: Guilford.

Shinn, M. R. (Ed.). (1998). *Advanced applications of curriculum-based measurement*. New York: Guilford Press.

Shinn, M. R. (2008). Best practices in curriculum-based measurement and its use in a problem-solving model. In A. Thomas & J. Grimes (Eds.), *Best Practices in School Psychology V* (pp. 243–262). Bethesda, MD: National Association of School Psychologists.

Shinn, M. R., Baker, S., Habedank, L., & Good, R. H. (1993). The effects of classroom reading performance data on general education teachers' and parents' attitudes about reintegration. *Exceptionality, 4*(4), 205–228.

Shinn, M. R., Good, R. H., & Stein, S. (1989). Summarizing trend in student achievement: A comparison of methods. *School Psychology Review, 18*, 356–370.

Shinn, M. R., Habedank, L., Rodden-Nord, K., & Knutson, N. (1993). Using curriculum-based measurement to identify potential candidates for reintegration into general education. *Journal of Special Education, 27*(2), 202–221.

Shinn, M. R., Powell-Smith, K. A., & Good, R. H., III (1996). Evaluating the effects of responsible reintegration into general education for students with mild disabilities on a case-by-case basis. *School Psychology Review, 25*(4), 519–539.

Shinn, M. R., Powell-Smith, K. A., Good, R. H., III & Baker, S. (1997). The effects of reintegration into general education reading instruction for students with mild disabilities. *Exceptional Children, 64*(1), 59–78.

Siegel, L.S. (1989). Why we do not need intelligence test scores in the definition and analyses of learning disabilities. *Journal of Learning Disabilities, 22*(8), 514–518.

Silberglitt, B., Burns, M. K., Madyun, N. H., & Lail, K. (2006). Relationship or reading fluency assessment data with state accountability test scores: A longitudinal comparison of grade levels. *Psychology in the Schools, 43*, 527–535.

Simmons, D. C., Kame'enui, E., Coyne, M., & Chard, D. (2006). Effective strategies for teaching beginning reading. In Coyne, Kame'enui, & Carnine, *Effective teaching strategies that accommodate diverse learners*. Upper Saddle River, NJ: Pearson Prentice Hall.

Skinner, C. H., Pappas, D. N., & Davis, K. A. (2005). Providing opportunities for responding and influencing students to choose to respond. *Psychology in the Schools, 42*, 389–403.

Smith, C. R. (1998). *Learning disabilities: The interaction of learner, task, and setting*. Boston: Allyn & Bacon.

Stahl, S., & Fairbanks, M. (1986). The effects of vocabulary instruction: A model-based meta-analysis. *Review of Educational Research, 56*, 72–110.

Stanovich, K. E. (1989). Has the learning disabilities field lost its intelligence? *Journal of Learning Disabilities, 22*(8), 487–492.

Stanovich, K. E., & Siegel, L. S. (1994). Phenotypic performance of children with learning disabilites: A regression based test of the phonological-core-variable-difference model. *Journal of Educational Psychology, 85*, 24–53.

Stuebing, K. K., Fletcher, J. M., LeDoux, J. M., Lyon, G. R., Shaywitz, S. E., & Shaywitz, B. A. (2002). Validity of IQ-discrepancy classifications of reading disabilties: A meta-analysis. *American Educational Research Journal, 39*, 469–518.

Szadokierski, I., & Burns, M. K. (2008). Analogue evaluation of the effects of opportunities to respond and ratios of known items within drill rehearsal of Esperanto words. *Journal of School Psychology, 46*(5), 593–609.

Telzrow, C. F., McNamara, K., & Hollinger, C. L. (2000). Fidelity of problem solving implementation and relationship to student performance. *School Psychology Review, 29*(3), 443–461.

Tilly, W. D., III, (2008). School psychology as a problem solving enterprise. In A. Thomas & J. Grimes (Eds.), *Best practices in school psychology V* (pp. 17–36). Bethesda, MD: National Association of School Psychologists.

Tindal, G., Hasbrouck, J., & Jones, C. (2005). *Oral reading fluency: 90 years of measurement: Technical report #33*. Eugene, OR: Behavioral Research & Teaching. Retrieved January 5, 2009, from http://www.brtprojects. org/tech_reports.php.

Topping, K. (1987). Paired reading: A powerful technique for parent use. *Reading Teacher, 40*, 608–614.

Torgesen, J. K. (1998, Spring/Summer). Catch them before they fall. *American Educator*, 32–39.

Trent, S., Kea, D., & Oh, K. (2008). Preparing preservice educators for cultural diversity: How far have we come? *Exceptional Children, 14*(3), 328–350.

U.S. Office of Education (1977, December 29). Assistance to states for education of handicapped children: Procedures for evaluating specific learning disabilities. *Federal Register, 42*, 65082–65085. Washington, DC: U.S. Government Printing Office.

U.S. Department of Education. (2006, August 14). Assistance to states for the education of children with disabilities and preschool grants for children with disabilities: Final rule. *Federal Register, 71*, 34 CFR Parts 300 and 301.

U.S. Department of Education, Office of Special Education and Rehabilitative Services Office of Special Education Programs. (2006). Twenty-sixth annual (2004) report to Congress on the implementation of the Individuals with Disabilities Education Act (Vol. 1). Washington, D. C.: author.

VanDerHeyden, A. M., & Snyder, P. (2006). Integrating frameworks from early childhood intervention and school psychology to accelerate growth for all young children. *School Psychology Review*, *35*(4), 519–534.

VanDerHeyden, A. M., Witt, J. C., & Barnett, D. W. (2005). The emergence and possible futures of response to intervention. *Journal of Psychoeducational Assessment*, *23*(4), 339–361.

Vaughn, S. (2003). *How many tiers are needed for response to intervention to achieve acceptable prevention outcomes?* Paper presented at the National Research Center on Learning Disabilities Responsiveness-to-Intervention Symposium, Kansas City, MO.

Vaughn, S., & Fuchs, L. S. (2003). Redefining learning disabilities as inadequate response to instruction: The promise and potential problems. *Learning Disabilities Research & Practice*, *18*(3), 137–146.

Vellutino, F. R., Scanlon, D. M., & Lyon, G. R. (2000). Differentiating between difficult-to-remediate and readily remediated poor readers: More evidence against the IQ-achievement discrepancy definition of reading disability. *Journal of Learning Disabilties*, *33*, 223–238.

Vellutino, F. R., Scanlon, D. M., Small, S., & Fanuele, D. (2003, December). *Response to Intervention as a vehicle for distinguishing between reading disabled and non-reading disabled children: Evidence for the role of kindergarten and first grade intervention.* Paper presented at the National Research Center on Learning Disabilities Responsiveness-to-Intervention Symposium, Kansas City, MO.

Walker, H. M. (2004). Use of evidence-based interventions in schools: Where we've been, where we are, and where we need to go. *School Psychology Review*, *33*, 398–407.

Watson, V. Kingston City School District (2005). Retrieved November 30, 2006, from http://www.ca2.uscourts.gov/.

What Works Clearinghouse. (2008). WWC intervention report: Open court reading. Retrieved August 13, 2008, from http://ies.ed.gov/ncee/wwc/pdf/WWC_OpenCourt_081208.pdf.

What Works Clearinghouse. (n.d.). Retrieved from http://ies.ed.gov/ncee/wwc/.

Wickstrom, K. F., & Witt, J. C. (1993). Resistance within school-based consultation. In J. K. Zins, T. R. Kratochwill, & S. N. Elliott (Eds.). *Handbook of consultative services for children: Applications in educational and clinical settings*. San Francisco: Jossey-Bass.

Will, M. C. (1986). Educating children with learning problems: A shared responsibility. *Exceptional Children, 52*, 411–415.

Witt, J. C., Daly, E. J., III, & Noell, G. H. (2000). *Functional assessments: A step-by-step guide to solving academic and behavior problems.* Longmont, CO: Sopris West.

Wright, J. (2007). *The RTI toolkit: A practical guide for schools.* Port Chester, NY: National Professional Resources, Inc.

Wright, J. (in press). A survival guide to managing interventions under RTI: Six recommendations. *The School Psychologist.*

Yell, M. L. (2009). Developing educationally meaningful and legally sound individualized education programs. In M. L. Yell, N. B. Meadows, E. Drasgo, & J. Shriner (Eds.), *Evidence-based practice for educating students with emotional and behavioral disorders* (pp. 190–214). Upper Saddle River, NJ: Pearson Education.

Zins, J. K., Kratochwill, T. R., & Elliott, S. N. (Eds.). *Handbook of consultation services for children: Applications in educational and clinical settings.* San Francisco: Jossey-Bass.

Author Index

Adams, M, 34, 35
Al Otaiba, S., 99, 106, 107, 108, 115
Alberto, P. A., 199
Aldrich, S., 157, 211
Allsopp, D. H., 7
Amato, P. R., 25
Appleton, J. J., 156
Ardoin, S. P., 153, 156, 157, 161, 164, 166, 167, 168, 175, 176, 177, 200, 201, 202, 207, 210, 211, 212

Babur, N., 48
Baker, S., 229, 231, 251
Ball, P. L., 223, 229, 232, 237
Barnett, D. W., 98, 101, 107, 111, 112, 156, 157, 210, 266
Barr, C., 176
Bateman, Barbara, 3
Beaver, J., 60
Bergan, J. R., 99, 100, 117
Berliner, D. C., 30
Binder, C., 200
Birch, J. W., 33
Boice, C. H., 108, 112, 116, 117, 118
Bolt, 55, 56
Bonfiglio, C., 113
Bonstrom, O., 13
Borman, G. D., 260, 261
Bos, C. S., 48
Bradley, R., 20, 21
Brantlinger, E., 114
Brown-Chidsey, R., 156, 157
Bryant, J. D., 66
Bunger, C. H., 157

Burish, P., 173
Burns, M. K., 89, 98, 101, 106, 107, 108, 109, 112, 113, 116, 117, 118, 124, 133, 134, 156, 171, 278, 280, 284

Callender, S. A., 66
Canter, A., 17, 278
Carfolite, J., 207, 211
Carnine, D., 26, 28, 29, 39, 40, 118
Casey, A., 13
Cates, G. L., 203
Cauthen, N. K., 25
Chafouleas, S., 120
Chalfant, J. C., 12
Chamberlin, J., 192
Chiang, B., 210
Christ, T. J., 161, 164, 176, 177, 199, 201, 207, 211, 212
Clark, R. E., 28, 30
Colon, E. P., 207
Compton, D. L., 66, 136
Connel, J. E., 153, 156, 201, 210
Cook, B. G., 197
Coolong-Chaffin, M., 199
Crawford, L., 58
Cross, C. T., 107
Cummings, K. D., 241
Cushing, L. S., 242

Daly, E., 98, 101, 107, 111, 112, 113, 156, 159, 211, 266
Danielson, L., 20, 21
Darch, C. B., 240

Davis, K. A., 117, 118
Deno, Stan L., 66, 67, 87, 133, 134, 139, 143, 156, 164, 199, 207, 210, 212, 241
Denton, C., 9
Deshler, D. D., 97, 100, 103, 105
Dion, G., 25
DiPerna, J. C., 97, 98, 102, 115
Dohrn, E., 97
Dole, J., 260, 261
Donahue, P., 25
Donovan, M. S., 107
Doolittle, J., 20, 21
Dunn, E. K., 207, 211
Dunne, M., 203
Durkin, D., 39

Eaton, M. D., 108, 109, 200, 205
Eckert, T. L., 175, 207, 211
Elliott, N., 119, 120, 157, 241
Elliott, S. N., 241
Ellis, E., 26
Erkfritz, K. N., 203
Ervin, R. A., 257, 260, 263, 266, 272
Espin, C., 164, 210

Fairbanks, M., 39
Fairbanks, S., 102
Fanuele, D., 19
Fass, S., 25
Fay, T. A., 16
Fernstrom, P., 224, 225, 240, 244

Fisher, C. W., 30, 261
Fletcher, J. M., 9, 10, 37, 176
Florian, L., 25
Flugum, K. R., 13
Foorman, B. R., 28, 36, 37, 176
Fowler, A. E., 10
Francis, D. J., 9, 10, 37, 176
Frankenberger, W., 6
Franzalglio, K., 6
Fuchs, Doug, 6, 11, 13, 14, 16, 17, 18, 19, 37, 38, 66, 85, 86, 97, 99, 100, 103, 105, 123, 134, 136, 138, 139, 140, 144, 146, 148, 156, 168, 173, 181, 183, 191, 210, 224, 225, 240, 244, 280
Fuchs, Lynn S., 13, 19, 20, 37, 38, 66, 67, 85, 86, 91, 107, 115, 123, 134, 136, 138, 139, 140, 143, 144, 146, 148, 156, 157, 168, 173, 181, 191, 199, 210, 224, 225, 240, 244, 280, 283, 284

Gansle, K. A., 119, 120, 210
Gerber, M. M., 260, 261
Germann, G., 85, 138, 139, 140
Gersten, R., 114
Gettinger, M., 117
Gibbons, 98, 101, 106, 107, 109, 116, 124
Gickling, E. E., 16
Glover, T. A., 97, 98, 102, 115
Good, R. H., 58, 60, 81, 83, 87, 136, 141, 144, 147, 229, 231, 241, 251
Gortmaker, V., 113
Graden, J. L., 13
Green, S., 226
Gresham, F. M., 20, 119

Grigg, W., 25
Grimes, J., 281
Guardino, S., 102
Gustafson, J. K., 17

Habedank, L., 84, 229, 250, 251
Hallahan, D. P., 3, 198
Hamlett, C. L., 85, 138, 139, 140
Hansen, C. L., 108, 109
Haring, N. G., 108, 109, 200, 205
Harris, A. H., 13
Harris, K. R., 114
Hartman, B., 112
Hartman, W. T., 16
Hasbrouck, J., 123, 125, 133
Haski, H., 157
Heward, W. L., 118
Hickman-Davis, P., 19
Hintze, J. M., 61, 164, 199, 210, 242
Hixson, M. D., 87, 88
Hoffpauir, L. D., 210
Hollinger, C. L., 15
Horn, Wade, 11
Horner, R. H., 114, 242
Hoskyn, M., 10
Hosp, J. L., 166, 168, 175, 202
Hosp, M. K., 37
Howell, K., 27, 28

Ikeda, M. J., 17

Jenkins, J. R., 37
Jiban, C., 133
Jones, C., 101, 107, 123, 125, 156, 266
Jordan, L., 7

Kame'enui, E. J., 26, 31, 39, 40, 58, 60, 81, 83, 87, 141, 240
Kamil, M. L., 260, 261

Kaminski, R. A., 81, 83, 136, 141, 241
Katz, D. P., 10
Kauffman, J. K., 3, 198
Kaufman, Nadeen, 192
Kazdin, A. E., 120
Kea, D., 25, 29
Kirk, Samuel, 3
Kirschner, P. A., 28, 30
Kivisto, A., 203
Klubnik, C., 207, 211
Knutson, N., 250
Koenig, J., 153, 156, 201, 210
Kosanovich, M., 123
Kousekanani, K., 19
Kovaleski, J. F., 16
Kral, C. C., 260, 261
Kranzler, J. H., 207
Kratochwill, T. R., 97, 115, 116

LaBerge, D., 38
Ladinsky, K., 123
Lail, K., 89
Larkin, M., 26
Lathrop, M., 102
Lau, M. Y., 17, 263, 278
LeDoux, J. M., 10
Lee, J., 25
Lee, N., 203
Lembke, E. S., 66
Lentz, F. E., 101, 107, 112, 113, 156, 266
Liberman, L., 10
Lillenstein, L., 112, 113
Linan-Thompson, S., 19
Lloyd, J. W., 4
Lovitt, T. C., 108, 109
Lutz, J. G., 164
Lyon, G. R., 9, 10
Lytle, J., 223

MacQuarrie, L. L., 112
Madyun, N. H., 89
Magnusson, D., 66

Marston, D., 17, 87, 139, 156, 157, 199, 210, 212, 263, 278, 281
Martens, B. K., 13, 14, 98, 107, 111, 112, 117, 118, 211, 260, 261, 278
Marzano, R., 26
Mather, Nancy, 48, 192
Maxwell, L., 38
McCurdy, M., 113
McDonald, E., 157, 211
McDougal, J. L., 13, 14, 278
McGlinchey, M. T., 87, 88
McKissick, C., 157
McMaster, K. L., 123, 173
McNamara, K., 15
Mehta, P., 37
Mercer, C. D., 7
Messick, S., 55, 57
Miller, J., 25
Mirkin, P. K., 67, 133, 134, 143, 210
Moats, L., 36
Mock, D., 6, 11, 13, 14, 16, 17, 18, 19, 99, 100, 183
Moody-Clonan, S., 13, 14, 278
Morgan, P. L., 6, 11, 13, 14, 16, 17, 18, 19, 99, 100, 183
Morris, R. D., 9
Morrow, H., 16
Moultrie, R., 12
Murdoch, A., 112, 113
Muyskens, P., 17, 87, 263, 278

Narr, R. F., 48
Nelson, L., 123
Noell, G. H., 119, 120, 159, 210
Nolet, V., 27, 28

Odom, S. L., 114
Oh, K., 25, 29
Olson, S. C., 98, 111, 112

Pappas, D. N., 117, 118
Parrish, T. B., 222
Pender, C. A. S., 175
Penn, W., 223
Persky, H., 25
Pickering, D. P., 26
Pollock, 26
Powell-Smith, K. A., 221, 223, 231, 232, 236, 237, 240, 241, 243, 251
Pysh, M. V., 12

Reschly, A. L., 13, 66, 102, 106, 192
Reschly, R. J., 280, 281
Resetar, J. L., 153, 201, 210
Reynolds, M. C., 33
Riley-Tillman, T. C., 120
Roach, A. T., 119, 120
Roberts, H., 13
Rodden-Nord, K., 229, 250, 251
Roof, C. M., 207, 211
Rosenfield, S., 13
Rutter, M., 4
Ryan, A. L., 61

Salahu-Din, D., 25
Salinger, T., 260, 261
Salvia, 55, 56
Samuels, S. J., 38
Sanetti, L. H., 97
Santi, K. L., 176
Scanlon, D. M., 10, 19
Schatschneider, C., 37
Schaughency, E., 257, 260, 263, 266, 272
Schirmer, B. R., 197
Schreiber, P. A., 37
Scott, S., 240, 244
Seibert, J. K., 117
Senesac, B. V., 280
Shankweiler, D. P., 10
Shapiro, E. S., 101, 134, 164, 240, 242, 244

Shaywitz, B. A., 9, 10
Shaywitz, S. E., 9, 10
Shernoff, E. S., 97, 115, 116
Shinn, J., 129, 139, 144, 147, 156, 164, 192, 199, 210
Shinn, M. R., 212, 223, 226, 229, 231, 241, 250, 251
Shriner, J., 207, 212
Siegel, L. S., 8, 10
Silberglitt, B., 61, 89, 210
Silbert, S., 39, 40
Simmons, D., 26, 31, 40, 58, 60, 81, 83, 87, 141
Skinner, C. H., 117, 118
Slider, N. J., 210
Small, S., 19
Smith, C. R., 4
Smith, S., 81
Snyder, P., 156
Stahl, S., 39
Stanovich, K. E., 8, 10
Steege, M. W., 156, 157
Stehouwer, J. D., 156
Steiber, S., 58
Stein, S., 144, 147
Stewart, L. H., 236, 237, 240, 243
Stoner, G., 61
Stuebing, K. K., 9, 10
Sugai, G., 102, 120
Suldo, S. M., 153, 157, 201, 210, 211
Swank, 16
Swanson, L. H., 10
Sweller, J., 28, 30
Szadokierski, I., 171

Telzrow, C. F., 15
Thompson, A., 114
Thompson, B., 114
Tilly, W. D. III, 224, 230
Tindal, G. A., 58, 123, 125, 133, 210, 212
Topping, K., 112, 124

Torgesen, J., 28, 34, 35, 36,
    99, 106, 107, 108, 115, 123,
    260, 261
Trent, S., 25, 29
Troutman, A. C., 199
Tucker, J. A., 112

VanDerHeyden, A. M., 108,
    112, 116, 117, 118, 133,
    156, 210
Vandermeer, L., 240, 244
Varisco, A., 176
Vaughn, Sharon, 11, 19, 20,
    102, 115, 157, 283

Vellutino, F. R., 10, 18, 19
Volpe, R. J., 242
Volpiansky, P., 97

Wagner, D., 113
Walker, H. M., 115, 260, 261
Wallin, J., 81, 83
Walz, L., 85, 138, 139, 140
Webber, L., 112, 113
Whitmarsh, E. L., 210
Wickstrom, K. F., 258
Wierzbicki, J., 203
Will, Madeline C., 221
Windram, H., 66

Witt, J. C., 98, 111, 112, 117,
    118, 153, 156, 157, 159,
    201, 210, 211, 258
Wolsing, L., 157
Worthington, L., 26
Wright, J., 97, 102, 103, 111,
    119, 121, 261

Yell, M. L., 198
Young, C. L., 6, 11, 13, 14,
    16, 17, 18, 19, 99, 100, 183
Ysseldyke, J. E., 55, 56, 278,
    284
Yule, W., 4

Subject Index

Academic-engaged time, 246
Academic interventions, 116–118
Academic learning time (ALT), 30
Academic programs for all students, 25–52
  components of, 33–44
  effective instruction, general elements of, 26–32
  effective school programs, developing (case studies), 49–52
  mathematics, 41–44
  reading/literacy, 33–34
  Tier 1, 26, 44–49
Academic skills, reintegration and special education exit, 240–241
Acquisition stage, instructional hierarchy, 111
Actual achievement, discrepancy-based models, 8
Adequate Yearly Progress (AYP), 90–92
AIMSweb, 76, 132–133, 151
  long-term goals, monitoring, 210
Alphabetic principle, 35–37
ALT. See Academic learning time (ALT)
American Institutes for Research, National High School Center, 279
AYP. See Adequate Yearly Progress (AYP)

Bateman, Barbara, 3
Baylor Schools, 22, 267–275
BEA. See Brief experimental analysis (BEA)
Behavioral Observation of Students in Schools (BOSS), 242, 248
Behavioral skills, reintegration and special education exit, 241–242
Benchmarks:
  goals, setting, 141–142
  norms, data-based decision making, 86
  reintegration and special education exit, 230

screening, 58–59, 63–64
student performance, pre-established benchmarks, 81
Big Ideas in Beginning Reading, 40–41
BOSS. See Behavioral Observation of Students in Schools (BOSS)
Brief experimental analysis (BEA), 112–113

Case studies:
  data-based decision making, 92–93
  Drawbridge Elementary School, 92–93
  effective school programs, developing, 49–52
  eligibility determination, 193–196
  Lakeside Elementary School, 49–52, 72–73
  Macenaw Elementary School, 193
  monitoring progress, 151–152
  oral reading fluency, 244–245
  organizational change, RTI as, 267–275
  reintegration and special education exit, 243–251
  screening, 72–73
  traditional model, moving from, 22
  Woebegone Central School, 49–52
CBM. See Curriculum-Based Measurement (CBM)
CC. See Correct classifications (CC)
CEI. See Classroom Ecological Inventory (CEI)
Center on Instruction, 83, 279
Classroom data, decisions based on, 90–91
Classroom Ecological Inventory (CEI), 240
Classroom grouping, and screening, 65–67
Classroom performance and direct assessment, 168–169
Classroom teacher, building intervention capacity of, 102–104
Collection of data. See Data-based decision making; School-wide data collection

Comprehension, reading, 39–40
Construct validity, screening, 56–58
"A Consumer's Guide to Analyzing a Core Reading Program Grades K-3: A Critical Elements Analysis," 40–41, 44
Contemporary models of LD, 12–14
  general definition of RIT, 14–15
  history, 12–14
  large-scale implementations of RTI, first, 15–17
Correct classifications (CC), diagnostic accuracy and screening, 62
Cost, screening, 67–70
Criterion reference test, long-term goals, 212–213
Criterion-related validity, screening, 57–58
Criterion, SLA used to determine, 136
Critical Foundations of Algebra, 42–43
Curriculum-based assessment, 167–168
Curriculum-Based Measurement (CBM), 13
  and AYP, 91
  classroom data, decisions based on, 91
  and cut scores, 87–89
  direct assessment, 167
  Instructional Placement Standards, 134, 135
  long-term goals, monitoring, 210–212
  measurement of performance, frequency, 144
  oral reading fluency, 85, 123–124
  rates of progress expected, 138
  Reading-CBM data, 199
  reintegration and special education exit, case study, 245–246, 250–251
  student progress monitoring, 128–129, 133
  and successful performance, 134
  summative and formative evaluations, 160–171
  support, need for more decided, 175–176
  tasks, 69
Cut scores, 87–89
  pros and cons, 88–89
  use of data, 88

Data-based decision making, 75–94
  AIMSweb, 76
  classroom data, decisions based on, 90–91

collection of data, 75–76
cut scores, 87–89
DIBELS Monitor, 76–79
graphing student data, 76–80
kindergarten classroom, universal screening data by students, 78
management of data, 75–76
norms, 84–87
student performance criterion, establishing, 80–83
Data-based formative evaluation, reintegration and special education exit, 231–232
Data collection. See Data-based decision making; School-wide data collection
Data point analysis, 147
Decision-making criteria, screening, 58–65
  diagnostic accuracy, 60–65
  outcomes, 61–62
Decision making, data-based. See Data-based decision making
Decision rules, use of, 146–148
Decisions made after intervening, 153–178
  comparisons, making appropriate, 161–163
  direct assessment, 165–169
  fade, decision to, 169–174
  formative versus summative evaluations (see Formative evaluations; Summative evaluations)
  support, need for more, 174–177
Developing interventions for students at risk for failure, 97–125
  academic interventions, 116–118
  brief experimental analysis (BEA), 112–113
  district intervention resources, 121–122
  "floating RTI," 99
  group-level interventions, 99
  instructional hierarchy, 108–112, 117
  integrity of intervention plan, measuring, 119–120
  Intervention Bank, 121
  intervention capacity, expanding, 121–122
  "intervention footprint," 97
  intervention support, 102–108
  inventory building, 121–122
  key research-based building blocks, 116–118

models for planning interventions, 98–102

problem-solving model, 99–102

reading intervention, case example, 122–125

"scientific, research-based interventions," determination of, 114–116

shared intervention time, 99

standard-treatment protocol, 98–99, 106

Diagnosis, intelligence testing and, 11–12

Diagnostic accuracy and screening, 60–65

correct classifications (CC), 62

negative predictive power (NPP), 62

outcomes, 61–62

positive predictive power (PPP), 61–62

sample statistics, 64

sensitivity, 61–62

specificity, 62

DIBELS. *See also other headings beginning* DIBELS

benchmarks, 141–142

long-term goals, monitoring, 210

reintegration and special education exit, case study, 243–244

DIBELS Data System, 132–133

DIBELS Monitor, 76–79

benchmarks, 81–83, 86

classroom data, decisions based on, 91

first grade benchmark goals, 81–83

Grade 2 year-long comparison, 79

DIBELS Oral Reading Fluency (DORF), 58–59, 63–64

establishing student performance criterion, 83

Direct assessment, 165–169

classroom performance, 168–169

curriculum-based assessment, 167–168

Curriculum-Based Measurement (CBM), 167

student responses, 166–167

Discrepancy-based models, learning disability, 6–11

reliability, 6–9

validity, 9–11

Dissemination studies, 115

District intervention resources, 121–122

District RTI model, building capacity in, 264–267, 273–275

Diverse learners:

effective instruction for, 25, 29–33

explicit teaching, 30

opportunities to respond, 33–34

scaffolding, 30–31

systematic instruction, 34

DORF. *See* DIBELS Oral Reading Fluency (DORF)

Douglas, Ann, 22

Drawbridge Elementary School (case study), 92–93

Dynamic Indicators of Basic Early Literary Skills. *See entries beginning* DIBELS

EBIs. *See* Evidence-based interventions (EBIs)

Ecological palatability and screening, 67

Effective instruction, general elements of, 26–32

diverse learners, 25, 29–33

instructional approach, 28

Efficacy studies, 115

Efficiency, screening, 67–70

Eligibility determination, 181–196

case studies, 193–196

comprehensive evaluation, 190–193

and instructional need, 188–190

model for decision making, 182–190

and performance, 186–188

and progress, 183–186

Emotional skills, reintegration and special education exit, 241–242

Establishing student performance criterion, 80–83

benchmarks, pre-established, 81

data, use of, 81, 83

pros and cons, 83

Evaluations:

Evaluating Potential Screening Tools checklist, 70

formative versus summative, 155–157

summative, 155–161

Evidence-based interventions (EBIs), 115–116

Exit. *See* Reintegration and special education exit
Expectations, 46–47
    achievement, discrepancy-based models, 8
Expert judgment, successful performance, 133–134
Explicit teaching, diverse learners, 30

Fade, decision to, 169–174
    how to face, 172–174
    responsible fading, 224–225
    time to fade, 171–172
Failure, developing interventions for students at risk, 97–125
FCRR. *See* Florida Center for Reading Research (FCRR)
Federal RTI regulations, monitoring changes in, 266–267, 274–275
Feedback, 111–112, 118
    stakeholder understanding and support, promoting in RTI systems change, 257–262, 269–270
Fidelity:
    assessment of, 284
    of implementation (*see* Implementation fidelity)
"Floating RTI," 99
Florida Center for Reading Research (FCRR), 41, 279
Fluency, 37–38
    oral, 80, 84–85, 123–124, 244–245
    stage, instructional hierarchy, 111–112
Formative evaluations, 163–165
    data collection procedures, planning, 163–164
    factors to consider in planning for decision making, 165
    summative data used in, 169
    versus summative evaluations, 155–157
    use of, 160–162

General definition of RIT, 14–15
Generalization stage, instructional hierarchy, 112
Goals, development. *See* IEP goal development

Goals, setting, 127–152
    benchmarks, 141–142
    criterion, SLA used to determine, 136
    decision rules, use of, 146–148
    goal statement, 142–143
    graphing performance, 143–146
    implementation fidelity, 148–151
    individualized goals, developing, 129
    measurement materials, SLA used to determine, 135–136
    norms, SLA used to determine, 136–138
    rates of progress expected, 138–142
    and success, 131–133
    survey-level assessment, 129–131
    time frames, SLA used to determine, 134–135
Goal statement, 142–143
Good, Roland, 81
Graphing performance, 143–146
    "Chart Dog" application, 145–146
    constructing progress grafts, 144–146
    frequency of measurement, 144
    progress and eligibility determination, 183–184
Graphing student data, 76–80
Group-administered tasks, screening, 69
Group-level interventions, 99
Growth rates, 138–139
Heartland Agency, 15–18
Hendrick Hudson District Board of Education v. Rowley, 223
History of learning disabilities, 3–22
Hypothesis testing, reintegration and special education exit, 231–232

IBA. *See* Intervention Based Assessment (IBA)
IDEIA. *See* Individuals with Disabilities Education Improvement Act of 2004 (IDEA)
IEP evaluation, 134–135
IEP goal development, 197–219
    critical data for developing, 216–217
    examples, 215–216
    long-term goals, 205–213 (*see also* Long-term goals *for detailed treatment*)

reintegration and special education exit, 228
short-term goals, 199–204 (*see also*
Short-term goals *for detailed treatment*)
Implementation fidelity, monitoring, 148–151
increasing fidelity, strategies, 149–150
informing interventions, 150–151
teacher checklists, 149
24-hour check-in, 150
Implementation of RTI, 282–286
components for, 278–279
Indexing stakeholder opinions, reintegration
and special education exit, 242–243
Individual instructional planning and
screening, 66
Individualized goals, developing, 129
Individualized intervention plans, 106–107
Individual progress monitoring and screening,
66–67
Individuals with Disabilities Education
Improvement Act of 2004 (IDEIA), 97
eligibility determination, 191
federal regulations, 101–102
individualized goals, developing, 129
reintegration and special education exit, 222,
224, 229
Information, value of in screening, 65–67
Informing interventions, 150–151
Institute for Education Sciences, 41, 114
Instructional hierarchy, 108–112, 117
acquisition stage, 111
feedback, 111–112, 118
fluency stage, 111–112
generalization stage, 112
student learning stage, matching
intervention to, 109–111
Instructional match, 116–117
Instructional need and eligibility
determination, 188–190
Instructional Placement Standards, 134, 135
Instructional support system, reintegration
and special education exit, 230–231
Instructional Support Teams (ISTs), 15, 16
Integrity of intervention plan, measuring,
119–120
Intensive intervention, 107–108
Intervention Bank, 121

Intervention Based Assessment (IBA), 15, 17
Intervention capacity, expanding, 121–122
"Intervention footprint," 97
Intervention planning, 101
Intervention support, students at risk for
failure, 102–108
classroom teacher, building intervention
capacity of, 102–104
individualized intervention plans,
106–107
intensive intervention, 107–108
three-tier continuum, 102–108
Inventory building, 121–122
Inventory of existing resources, systems
change, 264, 272–273
Iowa:
Department of Special Education, 181–196
Heartland Agency, 15–18
IQ:
achievement discrepancy, 197, 280–282
studies of, 4
IQ tests. *see also specific test*
and diagnosis of learning disabilities,
11–12
reliability, 8–9
validity, 9–11
ISTs. *See* Instructional Support Teams (ISTs)

Kaufman, Nadeen, 192
Key research-based building blocks,
116–118
Kindergarten classroom, universal screening
data by students, 78
Kirk, Samuel, 3
Knowledge brokers, selection of, 266, 274

Lakeside Elementary School (case studies):
effective school programs, developing,
49–52
screening, 72–73
LD. *See* Learning disabilities
Leadership and RTI effectiveness, 284
Learning disabilities:
contemporary models, 12–14
definition, 3
diagnosis, intelligence testing and, 11–12

discrepancy-based models, 6–11
history of, 3–22
identification, 5, 20–21
research-based RTI models, 18–19
"specific learning disability," defined, 4–5
traditional model, moving from, 22
Limitations of RTI, 282–285
Long-term goals, 205–213
administration of tests, 206–207
CBM for monitoring, 210–212
considerations, 205–213
consistency of measures, 209–210
criterion reference test, 212–213
measures used for establishing, 205
monitoring, 206
reliability in monitoring, 206, 214
screening, universal screening data, 207–210, 213, 216
sensitivity of measures, 207
validity in monitoring, 206, 214

Macenaw Elementary School (case study), 193
Mainstream Assistance Team (MAT), 13
Mathematics programs, 41–44
Critical Foundations of Algebra, 42–43
curricular issues, 42–43
instructional issues, 44
Mather, Nancy, 192
Measurement:
materials, SLA used to determine, 135–136
performance, frequency of, 144
Minneapolis Public Schools Problem-Solving Model (MPSM), 15, 17
Minnesota Public Schools, 263
Models for planning interventions, 98–102
problem-solving model, 99–102
standard-treatment protocol, 98–99, 106
Monitoring:
long-term goals, 206, 210–212
progress (see Monitoring progress)
reintegration and special education exit, success, 232–243
short-term goals, 200–201, 204
Monitoring progress, 66–67, 127–152
case study, 151–152
criterion, SLA used to determine, 136

decision rules, use of, 146–148
and eligibility determination, 183–184
expert judgment, 133–134
graphing performance, 143–146
growth rates, 138–139
implementation fidelity, 148–151
measurement materials, SLA used to determine, 135–136
norms, SLA used to determine, 136–138
rates of progress expected, 138–142
responsibility for, 143–144
student progress monitoring, 128–142
and success, 131–133
time frames, SLA used to determine, 134–135
written expression, 246
Motivation, 117
MPSM. See Minneapolis Public School's Problem-Solving Model (MPSM)
Multi-year RTI implementation plan, 262–264, 271–272

National Center for Student Progress Monitoring, 129
National Center on Learning Disabilities, 279
National Center on Response to Intervention, 279
National Center on Student Progress Monitoring, 83
National High School Center of the American Institutes for Research, 279
National Mathematics Advisory Panel (NMAP), 42, 48
National Reading Panel (NRP), 38–40, 48
National Research Center on Learning Disabilities, 21, 83, 181
NCLB. See No Child Left Behind (NCLB)
Negative predictive power (NPP), 62
Networking, 267, 275
New York, School-Based Intervention Team (SBIT), 13–14
Next steps in RTI, 285–286
NMAP. See National Mathematics Advisory Panel (NMAP)
No Child Left Behind (NCLB), 87, 97, 283

Adequate Yearly Progress (AYP), 90–92
Nonresponders, defined, 283–284
Nonsense Word Fluency, 136
Norms. *See also* Norms, data-based decision
    making
    SLA used to determine, 136–138
    success, 131–133
Norms, data-based decision making, 84–87
    data, use of, 86
    oral reading fluency, norms, 84–85
    pros and cons, 86–87
NPP. *See* Negative predictive power (NPP)
NRP. *See* National Reading Panel (NRP)
Office of Special Education Programs, 13
Off-task behaviors, observation data, 247
Ohio, Intervention Based Assessment (IBA),
    15, 17
Open Court, 114–115
Opportunities to respond by students,
    33–34
Oral reading fluency, 80, 123–124
    norms, 84–85
    reintegration and special education exit,
        case study, 244–245
Oregon, University of, 40–41, 81, 141
Organizational change, RTI as (case study),
    267–275
Organizational reform, 282–283
Outcomes, graphing, 127–152

Peer-Assisted Learning Strategies (PALS), 123
Pennsylvania, Instructional Support Teams
    (ISTs), 15
Performance:
    data-based decision making, establishing
        student performance criterion, 80–83
    and direct assessment, 168–169
    and eligibility determination, 186–188
    graphing, 143–146
Phonemic awareness, 34–35
Phonics, 35–37
Plan evaluation, 101
Positive predictive power (PPP), 61–62
President's Commission on Excellence in
    Special Education Report, 11
Problem analysis, 100–101

Problem identification, 100
Problem-solving model:
    failure, students at risk for, 99–102, 106
    intervention planning, 101
    plan evaluation, 101
    problem analysis, 100–101
    problem identification, 100
    support, need for more decided, 177
Procedures, promise of, 277–282
Progress:
    and eligibility determination, 183–186
    monitoring (*see* Monitoring progress)
Promise of RTI procedures, 277–282
REACh. *See* Response Education for All
    Children (REACh)
Reading intervention, case example,
    122–125
Reading/literacy programs:
    alphabetic principle, 35–37
    comprehension, 39–40
    evaluating programs, 40–41
    fluency, 37–38
    generally, 33–34
    phonemic awareness, 34–35
    phonics, 35–37
    vocabulary, 38–39
    word recognition skills, 35–37
    written responses of students, 33–34
Regulations:
    Commission of Education, 7
    federal RTI regulations, monitoring changes
        in, 266–267, 274–275
REI. *See* Reintegration and special education
    exit
Reinforcement, time-based approach to, 111
Reintegration and special education exit,
    221–251
    academic skills, 240–241
    activities, 233–234
    behavioral skills, 241–242
    benchmarks, 230
    case study, 243–250
    continued supports, 228
    Curriculum-Based Measurement (CBM),
        245–246, 250–251
    data-based formative evaluation, 231–232

determining success, 238
ecological inventory, 239–240
emotional skills, 241–242
exit decisions, making, 232–243
fading of services, responsible, 224–225
goal or domain, exiting in, 239
growth of special education, 222–223
history, 221–223
hypothesis testing, 231–232
IEP goal development, 228
importance of, 222–223
indexing stakeholder opinions, 242–243
Individuals with Disabilities Education
    Improvement Act (IDEA), 222, 224, 229
instructional support system across tiers,
    230–231
legal support for, 223
monitoring success, 232–243
personnel responsible, 233–234
plans for reintegration, 236–237
progress-monitoring schedule, 236
questions to answer, 233–234
rationale, 221–223
receiving environment, assessment of,
    239–240
research support for, 250–251
responsible reintegration, 224–225
social skills, 241–242
stakeholder beliefs and concerns, 225–232,
    237, 248
student considered for exit, 232–2350
success, monitoring, 232–243
success, procedures for ensuring, 225–232
tools and considerations, 239–243
"trial out" period, 236
Reliability:
    discrepancy-based models, learning
        disability, 6–9
    long-term goals, monitoring, 206, 214
    screening, 55–56
Research-based RTI models, 18–19
Resistance by teachers to RTI, potential, 261
Response Education for All Children
    (REACh), 97
Responsible reintegration, 224–225

Rowley, Hendrick Hudson District Board of
    Education v., 223

SBIT. See School-Based Intervention Team
    (SBIT)
Scaffolding, 30–31
School-Based Intervention Team (SBIT),
    13–14
School readiness survey, 257
School-wide data collection, 53–73. See also
    Screening
    Tier 1, 53
"Scientific, research-based interventions,"
    determination of, 114–116
    dissemination studies, 115
    efficacy studies, 115
    evidence-based interventions (EBIs),
        115–116
    system evaluation studies, 115–116
    transportability studies, 115
Screening:
    benchmarks, 58–59, 63–64
    classroom grouping, 65–67
    construct validity, 56–58
    cost, 67–70
    criterion-related validity, 57–58
    decision-making criteria, 58–65
    diagnostic accuracy, 60–65
    ecological palatability, 67
    efficiency, 67–70
    Evaluating Potential Screening Tools checklist,
        70
    group-administered tasks, 69
    individual instructional planning, 66
    individual progress monitoring, 66–67
    information, value of, 65–67
    inter-rater/inter-scorer, 55
    kindergarten classroom, universal screening
        data by students, 78
    long-term goals, universal screening data,
        207–210, 213, 216
    outcomes, 61–62
    reliability, 55–56
    staff buy-in, 70–72
    teacher buy-in, 70–72
    test-retest, 55

validity for purposes of, 54–55
Self-assessment, teachers, 149
Self-monitoring, 120
Sensitivity, 61–62
Shared intervention time, 99
Short-term goals, 199–204
    data for developing, 202–203
    difficulties in evaluating, 201–202
    establishing, example of, 204
    monitoring, 200–201
    probes for monitoring, 204
    Reading-CBM data, 199
    subskills, impact of instruction on, 200
SLA. *See* Survey-level assessment
Slopes, creating, 148
Social skills, 241–242
Special education exit. *See* Reintegration and
    special education exit
Specificity, diagnostic accuracy and screening,
    62
"Specific learning disability," defined, 4–5
Staff buy-in, screening, 70–72
Staff feedback, 257–262, 269–270
Staff support, 259–262, 270–271
Stakeholder beliefs and concerns, reintegration
    and special education exit, 225–232,
    237, 248
Stakeholder understanding and support,
    promoting in RTI systems change,
    257–262, 269–271
    informing about RTI model, 258–259, 269
    resistance by teachers to RTI, potential, 261
    staff support, 259–262, 270–271
Standard deviation from the mean, 6–7
Standard regression analysis, 6–7
Standard score comparison, 6–7
Standard-treatment protocol, 98–99, 106
State University of New York at Oswego, 76
Steering group, 256–257, 266–269
Student Interaction in Specific Settings, 242
Student responses, direct assessment, 166–167
Subskills, impact of instruction on, 200
Success. *See also* Success, performance
    reintegration and special education exit,
    225–243
Success, performance, 131

expert judgment for defining, 133–134
norms, 131–133
Summative evaluations:
    critical uses of data, 162–163
    formative versus, 155–157
    at Tier 1, 157–161
    at Tier 2, 158–159, 161–162
    use of, 160–162
Support, need for more decided, 174–177
Survey-level assessment:
    criterion, determination, 136
    measurement materials, determination,
        135–136
    norms, determination, 136–138
    norms, use of, 132
    setting goals, 129–131
    and successful performance, 134
    time frames, determination, 134–135
Systematic instruction, 34
System evaluation studies, 115–116
Systems change, 255–275
    district RTI model, building capacity in, 264–
        267, 273–275
    federal RTI regulations, monitoring changes
        in, 266–267, 274–275
    inventory of existing resources, 264,
        272–273
    knowledge brokers, selection of, 266, 274
    multi-year RTI implementation plan,
        262–264, 271–272
    networking with other school districts, 267,
        275
    organizational change, RTI as, 267–275
    resistance by teachers to RTI, potential, 261
    school readiness survey, 257
    staff feedback, 258–259, 269–270
    staff support, plan to build, 259–262,
        270–271
    stakeholder understanding and support,
        promoting, 257–262, 269–270
    starting, steps, 256–267
    steering group, 256–257, 266–269

Targeted interventions:
    decisions made after intervening, 153–178

developing interventions for, 97–125
goals, setting, 127–152
monitoring progress, 127–152
outcomes, graphing, 127–152
Teacher Assistance Teams, 12
Teacher buy-in, screening, 70–72
Teacher checklists, 149
Teacher-led instruction, 133
Tier 1, 26
academic programs for all students, 25–52
and administrator support, 46
change in, influencing, 47–49
classroom teacher, building intervention
capacity of, 102–104
data-based decision making, 75–94
evaluating, 44–47
goals, articulation of, 47
and high expectations, 46–47
school-wide data collection, 53–73
summative evaluations, 157–161
Tier 2:
decisions made after intervening, 153–178
developing interventions for, 97–125
goals, setting, 127–152
individualized intervention plans, 106–107
monitoring progress, 127–152
outcomes, graphing, 127–152
summative evaluations, 158–159, 161–162
Tier 3:
eligibility determination, 181–196
IEP goal development, 197–219
intensive intervention, 107–108
reintegration and special education exit,
221–251
Time frames, SLA used to determine,
134–135
Transportability studies, 115

Trend line analysis, 147
slopes, creating, 148
"Trial out" period, reintegration, 236
24-hour check-in, 150
26th Annual Report to Congress, 222

United States Department of Education
(USDOE), 4, 266
Institute of Education Sciences, 114
Universal screening data. *See* Screening
USDOE. *See* United States Department of
Education (USDOE)

Validity:
discrepancy-based models, learning
disability, 9–11
long-term goals, monitoring, 206, 214
screening, 54–55
Vocabulary, 38–39

Wechsler Individual Achievement Test-
Second Edition (WIAT-II), 8
What Works Clearinghouse (WWC),
41, 44
Open Court, review of, 114–115
WIAT-II, 8
Will, Madeline, 221
Wisconsin, Response Education for All
Children (REACh), 97
Woebegone Central School (case study),
49–52
Word recognition skills, 35–37
Written expression progress monitoring,
246
Written responses of students, 33–34
WWC. *See* What Works Clearinghouse (WWC)

About the CD-ROM

INTRODUCTION

This appendix provides you with information on the contents of the CD that accompanies this book. For the latest information, please refer to the ReadMe file located at the root of the CD.

SYSTEM REQUIREMENTS

A computer with a processor running at 120 Mhz or faster

- At least 32 MB of total RAM installed on your computer; for best performance, we recommend at least 64 MB
- A CD-ROM drive

NOTE: Many popular word processing programs are capable of reading Microsoft Word files. However, users should be aware that a slight amount of formatting might be lost when using a program other than Microsoft Word.

USING THE CD WITH WINDOWS

To install the items from the CD to your hard drive, follow these steps:

1. Insert the CD into your computer's CD-ROM drive.
2. The CD-ROM interface will appear. The interface provides a simple point-and-click way to explore the contents of the CD.

If the opening screen of the CD-ROM does not appear automatically, follow these steps to access the CD:

1. Click the Start button on the left end of the taskbar and then choose Run from the menu that pops up.
2. In the dialog box that appears, type *d:* **start.exe**. (If your CD-ROM drive is not drive d, fill in the appropriate letter in place of *d*.) This brings up the CD Interface described in the preceding set of steps.

Using the CD with Macintosh

To install the items from the CD to your hard drive, follow these steps:

1. Insert the CD into your computer's CD-ROM drive.
2. The CD icon will appear on your desktop; double-click to open.
3. Double-click the Start button.
4. Read the license agreement and click the Accept button to use the CD.
5. The CD interface will appear. Here you can install the programs and run the demos.

WHAT'S ON THE CD

The following sections provide a summary of the materials you'll find on the CD.

The attached companion CD contains several documents (e.g., feedback forms, worksheets, flowcharts, checklists, surveys, and screening tools, as well as a list of resources for charting and monitoring individual and classroom progress) which educators and school district professionals can utilize in evaluating the need for and implementing an RTI program.

The following documents are included on the CD:

- **RTI Staff Feedback Form** (Form for gathering data on the benefits, concerns, and questions staff might have about implementing a RTI program in their school.)

- **RTI Implementation Planning Sheet** (A tool for school districts to use in developing a multi-year rollout of a comprehensive RTI plan.)
- **RTI School Readiness Survey** (An informal measure designed to help schools identify which elements of RTI they are already skilled in and which elements they should continue to develop.)
- **A Checklist for Evaluating Academic Programs** (A tool for evaluating student outcomes, school-wide indicators, and classroom indicators, and for summarizing a program's strengths and areas needing improvement, and for making specific recommendations/action steps.)
- **Special Education Decision-Making Flowchart** (A five-step flowchart for assessing a student's rate of progress, level of performance, current instructional need, and for making a referral for comprehensive evaluation and eligibility determination.)
- **Evaluating Potential Screening Tools: A Checklist of Essential Considerations** (A checklist for considering a tool's areas of validity, ecological palatability, and overall strengths and limitations.)
- **List of Resources for Managing and Graphing Tier 1 Data** (Annotated list of graphing and student progress monitoring resources.)
- **Tier 3 Worksheet: Are You Ready for Eligibility Determinations?** (Worksheet for school teams to assess their readiness in conducting Tier 3 activities.)

The following applications are on the CD:

Adobe Reader. Adobe Reader is a freeware application for viewing files in the Adobe Portable Document format.

OpenOffice.org. OpenOffice.org is a free multi-platform office productivity suite. It is similar to Microsoft Office or Lotus SmartSuite, but OpenOffice.org is absolutely free. It includes word processing, spreadsheet, presentation, and drawing applications that enable you to create professional documents, newsletters, reports, and presentations. It supports most file formats of other office software. You should be able to edit and view any files created with other office solutions. Certain features of Microsoft

Office documents may not work as expected from within Open Office.org.

Shareware programs are fully functional, trial versions of copyrighted programs. If you like particular programs, register with their authors for a nominal fee and receive licenses, enhanced versions, and technical support.

Freeware programs are copyrighted games, applications, and utilities that are free for personal use. Unlike shareware, these programs do not require a fee or provide technical support.

GNU software is governed by its own license, which is included inside the folder of the GNU product. See the GNU license for more details.

Trial, demo, or evaluation versions are usually limited either by time or functionality (such as being unable to save projects). Some trial versions are very sensitive to system date changes. If you alter your computer's date, the programs will "time out" and no longer be functional.

CUSTOMER CARE

If you have trouble with the CD-ROM, please call the Wiley Product Technical Support phone number at (800) 762-2974. Outside the United States, call 1(317) 572-3994. You can also contact Wiley Product Technical Support at http://support.wiley.com. John Wiley & Sons will provide technical support only for installation and other general quality control items. For technical support on the applications themselves, consult the program's vendor or author.

To place additional orders or to request information about other Wiley products, please call (877) 762-2974.